Utopias of Otherness

T0338063

Utopias of Otherness

Nationhood and Subjectivity in Portugal and Brazil

Fernando Arenas

University of Minnesota Press

Minneapolis

London

An earlier version of chapter 3 appeared as "Writing after Paradise and before a Possible Dream: Brazil's Caio Fernando Abreu," *Luso-Brazilian Review* 36 (1999): 13–21; reprinted by permission of the University of Wisconsin Press. Parts of chapter 3 also appeared in "Small Epiphanies in *The Night of the World:* The Writing of Caio Fernando Abreu," in *Lusosex: Gender and Sexuality in the Portuguese-Speaking World,* edited by Susan Canty Quinlan and Fernando Arenas (Minneapolis: University of Minnesota Press, 2002). An earlier version of chapter 4 appeared as "For Time That Passes: Subjectivity, Nation, and Utopias in the Fiction of Maria Isabel Barreno," *ellipsis* 1 (1999): 25–44; reprinted by permission of *ellipsis,* the journal of the American Portuguese Studies Association at the University of Illinois, Champaign/Urbana.

Lyrics by Caetano Veloso are reprinted here with permission of the artist.

Published by the University of Minnesota Press
111 Third Avenue South, Suite 290
Minneapolis, MN 55401-2520
http://www.upress.umn.edu

Library of Congress Cataloging-in-Publication Data

Arenas, Fernando, 1963–
    Utopias of otherness : nationhood and subjectivity in Portugal and Brazil / Fernando Arenas.
      p.   cm.
    Includes bibliographical references and index.
    ISBN 0-8166-3816-0 (HC : alk. paper) — ISBN 0-8166-3817-9 (alk. paper)
    1. Portugal—Civilization—21st century.   2. Brazil—Civilization—21st century.   3. Identity (Psychology).   4. Portuguese fiction—20th century—Criticism and interpretation.   5. Brazilian fiction—20th century—Criticism and interpretation.   6. Utopias in literature.   7. Literature and myth.   8. Difference (Psychology) in literature.   I. Title.
    DP681 .A74   2003
    869.3'4209353—dc21   2002014513

Printed in the United States of America on acid-free paper

The University of Minnesota is an equal-opportunity educator and employer.

12 11 10 09 08 07 06 05 04 03   10 9 8 7 6 5 4 3 2 1

To Greg, Maria João, Jorge, Beatriz, Juanpa, and Tico.

Family in the World

[eu quero] um colo ou um berço ou um braço quente em torno ao
meu pescoço... uma voz que canta baixo e parece querer fazer-me
chorar... o ruído de lume na lareira... um calor no inverno... um
extravio morno da minha consciência... e depois sem som, um
sonho calmo num espaço enorme, como a lua rodando entre estrelas

[I wish for] a lap or a cradle or a warm arm around my neck...
a softly singing voice that seems to want to make me cry... the
crackling of fire in the fireplace... heat in the winter... a listless
wandering of my consciousness... and then a calm soundless dream
in a huge space, like the moon turning among the stars
—*Livro do desassossego* (The book of disquietude), Fernando Pessoa

de onde nem tempo nem espaço
que a força mande coragem
pra gente te dar carinho
durante toda a viagem
que realizas no nada
através do qual carregas
o nome da tua carne

from where neither time nor space
may a force bring with it courage
so that we may give you love
throughout the journey
you undertake within nothingness
and through which you carry
the name of your flesh
—"Terra" (Earth), Caetano Veloso

Contents

Acknowledgments

This book is a tribute to Portuguese-speaking cultures, most particularly those of Portugal and Brazil. The passion I feel for these cultures has led me to devote a significant part of my life to academic endeavors related to them. So far, the experience has been quite fulfilling. *Utopias of Otherness* could obviously not have come to fruition if it were not for various key institutions and individuals, academic and nonacademic alike, that have supported and nurtured my passion throughout all these years. The University of Minnesota Graduate School and College of Liberal Arts were generous in providing me with a Faculty Summer Research Fellowship and a McKnight Summer Research Grant in 1996, a quarter's leave in 1997, and several faculty Research and Creative Activity grants between 1997 and 2000. The Department of Spanish and Portuguese Studies was generous in granting me a Summer Research Fellowship in 1995. In Portugal, the Fundação Luso-Americana para o Desenvolvimento (FLAD) and Instituto Camões were instrumental in allowing me to interview and conduct further research on Vergílio Ferreira in 1992. The continued support by FLAD, and especially the encouragement given to me by Luís dos Santos Ferro, has been an inspiration to continue the work of thinking, teaching, and writing about Portuguese culture.

The guidance, intelligence, and generosity of three colleagues and friends at the University of Minnesota have been essential to my growth as an academic, and I will always remain grateful to Connie Sullivan, Joanna O'Connell, and Amy Kaminsky. The wisdom of Carol Klee, Louise Mirrer, and Ron Akehurst has aided and reassured me during my early years as a junior faculty member. I am also thankful for the intellectual inspiration provided by John Mowitt. The new generation of scholars and colleagues fills me with joy and hope for the future, particularly Barbara Weissberger, Ofelia Ferrán, Alberto Egea, Tom Pepper, and Cesare Casarino. Rafael Tarragó, our Ibero-American librarian, is one of our greatest assets; his delightful conversation and earnest complicity with our work are always appreciated.

My development as a thinker and teacher would be impossible without the contribution of both graduate and undergraduate students. Not only do you continually challenge me from an intellectual standpoint, but you also make my days, even those cold Minnesota winter days! I'd like to express my special gratitude to Kátia Bezerra, Marcus Brasileiro, Susan Campbell, Elena Cueto, Wander Frota, Josh Gardner, Gerardo Garza, Shari Geistfeld, David George, Tom Haakenson, Mari Jordán, Kate Kane, Emily Knudson, Juli Kroll, Melissa Licht, Josh Lund, Julie Lynd, Paola Marín, Mónica Massei, Marilena Mattos, Malcolm McNee, Marissa Moorman, María Elvira Olaya, Yun Peng, Steve Rings, Tom Roach, Barbara St. Cyr, Blake Strawbridge, and Rebecca Ulland. The dedication and hard work of the technical and secretarial staff of the Department of Spanish and Portuguese Studies form the basis of our daily job existence. To Mark Ollenburger, Cindy Kovach, Elise Sorensen, Brooke Owen, Ulrika Speckman, Dijana Andic, and Dana Souther, thanks for your generous smiles and unwavering support.

Richard Morrison, humanities editor at the University of Minnesota Press, has been an enormous resource in the final and critical stages of this project. His insights and seemingly infinite patience are a gift to us all. Joe Blackmore's astonishing erudition and rigor as an outside reader of this project proved invaluable in the revision stages of the manuscript.

Deep feelings of appreciation go to my colleagues and friends in the field of Portuguese. Together we work arduously to promote knowledge and understanding of Portuguese-speaking cultures around the world, as well as passion for these cultures. I acknowledge Severino Albuquerque, Arthur Askins, José Carlos Barcellos, Ana Paula Ferreira, David W. Foster, Jaime Ginzburg, Jimmy Green, Russell Hamilton, Lúcia Helena, Randal Johnson, Anna Klobucka, Mário César Lugarinho, Inocência Mata, Laura Padilha, Phyllis Peres, Susan Canty Quinlan, João Camilo dos Santos, Ellen Sapega, Jorge Fernandes da Silveira, Ron Sousa, Nelson Vieira, and Richard Zenith.

I would also like to salute Erasmo Leiva, Pedro Lange, and Karen Bouwer, who made my brief passage through the University of San Francisco between 1993 and 1995 a gentler one.

The love and warmth of friends and family in various parts of the world are some of my most cherished belongings. May we all be less lonely throughout our journey. Greg Mullins, you have been the most consistent source of affection and intellectual inspiration since we crossed paths in graduate school. You will always occupy a special place in my heart. Maria João Pombo Lopes, Carlos Vargas, Maria Alexandra Pombo Lopes, Vítor Carneiro, and Ana Beatriz Carneiro, I can never thank you enough for your continued cultural, emotional, and logistical support in Lisbon and beyond. Jorge Fernandes da Silveira, you are my anchor in the Rio de Janeiro of the world. Fernanda Lima and Valéria Cardoso, *as minhas novas grandes amigas cariocas!* Francisco Caetano Lopes Jr., *sempre terei saudades tuas!* Beatriz Muñoz, Alberto "Tico" Arenas, and Juan Pablo Arenas, *¡los quiero cantidades!* Carlos Arenas, María Lucía Arenas-Uricoechea, Felipe Arenas-Uricoechea, and Alexandra Castro, *que Colombia sea un día un lugar de paz para todos.* Freddy and Neide Nieto, you were there at the beginning, throughout my undergraduate years, inspiring me to continue in academia and to pursue the study of Brazil as well as the Portuguese language. Ed Burke, Eduardo Cabrera, Alex Clapp, Paul Cunningham, Martine Fernandes, Neil Fischer, Rich Giambrone, Roger Harris, Jim Hoeft, Jerry Kramer, Kerry Mitchell, Stuart Menaker, Iliana Reyes, John Smith, Mary Lee Stauffer, and Mark Weiler, dear friends from the Twin Cities and the San Francisco Bay Area. Finally, those newly found friends and kind acquaintances with whom I cross paths on a regular basis in the cafés and streets and on the lakes of Minneapolis and at the downtown YMCA: your genuine curiosity and receptivity toward me as well as my work are a great encouragement in my daily life.

A todos, aquele abraço!

Minneapolis
July 2002

Introduction

Para o discurso cultural português, o Brasil existe superlativamente,
mesmo que essa existência seja quase sempre mítica, sobretudo
como suporte simbólico dos nossos antigos sonhos imperiais. Para o
discurso cultural brasileiro, Portugal existe pouco ou nada, mas, se
existe, é apreendido como o pai colonizador que o Brasil teve de
matar para existir.

Within Portuguese cultural discourse, Brazil exists superlatively,
even if such existence is almost always mythical, particularly as
the symbolic basis for our most ancient imperial dreams. Within
Brazilian cultural discourse, Portugal exists very little or not at all,
yet, if it does exist, it is seen as the colonizing father that Brazil had
to kill in order to exist.
> —Eduardo Lourenço, "Nós e o Brasil: Ressentimento e delírio"
> (Us and Brazil: Resentment and delirium)

The myth of the "country of the future," which has governed the modern Brazilian imaginary, has inevitably entailed the gradual erasure of
Portugal as a primary cultural point of reference. This myth is the result
of a complex historical and cultural metamorphosis that started with
the Christian utopian vision of the "earthly paradise" that was projected
onto Brazil from the moment of the Portuguese arrival in 1500. Both
mythical-utopian visions underscore the movement from a colonial to
a postcolonial era, as well as the peculiar relationship between a weak
(former) colonial power on the edge of Europe and the enormous potential of a (formerly) colonized giant in the New World. Thus, Brazil

has historically functioned as an imaginary compensatory mechanism for Portugal due to its smaller dimensions, as well as its economic and even ontological limitations. Brazil was in fact the "crown jewel" of the Portuguese colonial empire; hence its "superlative" place, according to Lourenço, within the Portuguese cultural discourse both before and after Brazilian independence. Yet in the earlier colonial period there was a convergence of interests between the white ruling classes of both the colony (i.e., the Luso-Brazilians) and the metropole, as they administered the territory and managed the trans-Atlantic slave trade. However, as the metropolitan rule increasingly became an obstacle to the political and economic aspirations of the white elites (now more decidedly Brazilian and far less Luso) in their quest for greater autonomy, independence became the only viable option. Conversely, in a subsequent postcolonial moment (which is ongoing), Portugal has become, from a Brazilian perspective, at once a distant historical echo, a suppressed memory, a distant parent, and a relatively important piece of a much larger cultural mosaic that is contemporary Brazil, as well as an "impoverished reality" in relationship to the vision of a country that sees itself as "forever modern" at the risk of obliterating its cultural memory.

The year 2000 marked the five hundredth anniversary of the Portuguese arrival at what would eventually become Brazil. In 1500 no one could possibly imagine what this new geographical space would become or what new human reality would emerge there, but in his "letter of discovery" Pêro Vaz de Caminha eloquently provided hints.[1] This "birth certificate" of Brazil revealed all the cultural underpinnings and ideological biases of Renaissance Europe, thus preparing the terrain for the colonial enterprise that would ultimately ensue. The utopian vision of paradise initially deployed inevitably gave way to the utilitarian task of catechization and submission of the infantilized natives, the extraction of raw materials, and the setting up of the necessary infrastructure for empire building. The Portuguese colonization of Brazil initiated in 1500, with all of its contradictions, excesses, abuses, and epic feats, constituted the basis for the emergence of a nation that eventually organized itself as the state that we know today.

Five centuries later, the festivities that were held in the region of Porto Seguro (in the southern part of the state of Bahia where the Portuguese first arrived) to mark the anniversary of the "discovery" or "founding" of Brazil were characterized by heightened tensions between the police

and scores of Pataxó Indians,[2] activists from the Brazilian landless peasant movement, labor union members, Afro-Brazilians, and opposition
groups who descended upon the region in order to stage a countercele-
bration. The Pataxó Indians, in particular, were violently repressed by
police forces as they attempted to reach Porto Seguro, where Portuguese
President Jorge Sampaio and Brazilian President Fernando Henrique
Cardoso were meeting. The quincentennial celebration and counter-
celebration provided a kaleidoscopic spectacle of conflicting words, gestures, and images underscoring the impossibility of uncritically com-
memorating historical events marked by colonialism (and its corollary,
slavery) and yet the need to commemorate the birth of a nation, however fraught with historical traumas and contemporary problems that
are to a great extent rooted in the experience of colonialism and slavery.

The festivities and counterfestivities surrounding the five hundredth
anniversary of Brazil's founding also underscored the fact that Brazil
and Portugal are in a vastly different historical situation now than they
were five hundred years ago, as well as the fact that there have been a
multiplicity of interpretations in both countries of the meaning of the
quincentennial. All of this is clearly reflected in the contrasting approaches
taken by the Portuguese and Brazilian presidents during the occasion:
the perspective advanced by Sampaio emphasized past Portuguese glo-
ries, paid tribute to the cultural richness of Brazil (to which Portugal
contributed), and politely acknowledged present and future socioeconomic challenges for Brazil, offering no apologies for the misdeeds
of colonial-era Portuguese. Meanwhile, the point of view offered by
Cardoso inevitably focused on present social ills that predictably
marred the five hundredth anniversary celebration. Though Cardoso
evoked the heroic deeds of past Brazilian leaders, he forcefully accentuated the huge socioeconomic gaps that continue to plague Brazil, stating that his country has "one of the world's most unfair societies."[3]

At the beginning of the twenty-first century, both Brazil and Portugal
are striving to become active players in the global economic, political,
and cultural arenas. Portugal is consolidating its (irrevocably peripheral)
place within one of the world's major power blocs (i.e., the European
Union) at the same time as it is endeavoring to give shape to a community of Portuguese-speaking nations that also encompasses Brazil,
Lusophone Africa, and East Timor. Meanwhile, Brazil has become a de
facto regional power in Latin America from an economic and political

point of view, although it struggles to attain socioeconomic stability and political democratization. Both nations nevertheless share a relatively peripheral condition in world affairs, a condition that one can argue is partly reflected in the scarce coverage throughout the world media of the five hundredth anniversary of Brazil's discovery compared to that of the quincentennial of Columbus's arrival on the American continent in 1492. This scant coverage can be attributed to the significant differences in the chronological moments commemorated (1492 vs. 1500) and the contrast between the notion of a European discovery of what would prove to be an entirely new continent versus the notion of a European discovery of what would be a new country, albeit of continental proportions. Different chronologies and proportions notwithstanding, there was a symbolic dimension to the limited world attention given to the five hundredth anniversary of Brazil that only reinforced the (semi)peripheral condition of both Portugal and Brazil in the world today—Portugal, on the edge of Europe, and Brazil, an island in an overwhelmingly English- and Spanish-speaking continent. Caetano Veloso summed up the condition of these nations when he evoked the image of fog surrounding the Portuguese language and the countries of the people who speak it, echoing Fernando Pessoa's vision of early twentieth-century Portugal as a nation on the margins of history, shrouded in fog, yet poised to renew itself through the power of the poetic word (see Pessoa's poem "Nevoeiro" [Fog] in *Mensagem* [Message], 1933). Decades later, Caetano translated Pessoa's vision into Brazilian music that has undoubtedly become the most obvious presence of the Portuguese language in the world today (Caetano Veloso, *Verdade tropical,* 13–19).

In the rest of this introduction, I deal succinctly with a vast array of images and ideas that have circulated in both Portugal and Brazil with respect to each other since 1500. Focusing primarily on literature and historiography, as well as on the popular and media cultures of both countries, I argue that Brazil and Portugal have profoundly influenced each other's sense of self, and that today this is particularly the case in Portugal with regard to Brazilian influence. Throughout the history of Luso-Brazilian relations, reciprocal ideas and images have contributed decisively to the formation and consolidation of a Brazilian postcolonial consciousness and the reconfiguration of a Portuguese national consciousness that must now face its limits as well as its potential within today's globalized environment without recourse to past colonial Brazilian utopias. In this book as a whole I focus on the emergence of the grand narratives of nationhood in Portugal and Brazil in the realm of intellectual thought and on their subsequent deconstruction in the contemporary literature produced in both countries, at the same time examining the shift from grand utopian visions to small utopian imaginings with regard to a possible better society, either nationally or transnationally. However, before venturing further into these major issues I invite the reader to explore this introduction, which provides a comparative framework in terms of Luso-Brazilian bilateral relations, reciprocal images, and ideas, in order to anticipate all ensuing discussions.

Luso-Brazilian Complicities

For several years now I have worked in the United States as a university professor and scholar in the rather small and highly specialized field of "Portuguese," which encompasses the study of the Portuguese language and the various aspects—literary, historical, social, political, and filmic, among others—of the cultures that speak it in Portugal, Brazil, Portuguese-speaking Africa (Angola, Cape Verde, Guinea-Bissau, Mozambique, and São Tomé and Príncipe), and East Timor.[4] In this book I argue for the continued importance of studying together Portugal and Brazil,[5] not only because of the obvious linguistic, cultural, and historical affinities between the two nations, but also because of the continued presence of Brazil and Portugal in each other's national life, the most powerful example of which is the large Brazilian presence in contemporary Portugal in the form of popular and media culture. Given the particularities of Brazil and Portugal, and their mutual relationship, a Luso-Brazilian intellectual project on national identity enriches debates concerning globalization, postmodernism, and postcolonialism. It also provides useful insights from a geopolitical standpoint, given the intermediate positions that both nations occupy in today's global system. Following the five hundredth anniversary of Vasco da Gama's arrival in India and the quincentennial of the Portuguese arrival in Brazil, it is time to reflect upon what has become of Portugal and Brazil at the dawn of the twenty-first century and how relations between both countries have evolved.

The main differences between Brazil and Portugal appear glaringly obvious when we observe statistical data referring to territorial size and population, as well as economic output. Brazil is also one of the largest multiracial and multiethnic countries in the world. This cultural reality is constitutive of its national identity. On the other hand, in spite of the relative racial and ethnic homogeneity of Portugal throughout history, Portuguese society is also rapidly becoming multicultural due to the decolonization of its former African colonies, as well as immigration from various parts of Africa and Brazil, and, in more recent years, from Eastern Europe.[6] This dynamic parallels contemporary demographic shifts throughout Western Europe, where in recent decades there has been a significant influx of immigrants from Africa, the Middle East, and Asia, and increasingly from Eastern Europe.

Portugal and Brazil share the particularity of being highly stable nation-states. Portugal defined its current borders in 1249 with the expulsion of the Moors, making it one of the oldest nation-states in Europe. Historically, there has been no internal threat to Portugal as a national, political, or geographical unit—since state and nation have coincided in conditions of cultural homogeneity (António Pinto 1)—in contrast to the situation in neighboring Spain. For its part, Brazil, in spite of significant regional differences and tremendous racial diversity, has retained a remarkable sense of cohesiveness that is reflected in its stable external borders. This has been partly the result of highly centralized colonial and postcolonial administrations as well as the widespread dissemination of Portuguese as a national language.

Brazil and Portugal today enjoy close diplomatic ties, and each country generally constitutes a priority within the foreign policy agenda of the other's government. Both governments have pledged continued and active support to the newly created Lusophone bloc, the Comunidade de Países de Língua Portuguesa (CPLP or Community of Portuguese-Speaking Countries), an attempt, similar to those represented by the British Commonwealth or the French Francophonie, to forge a bloc of nations united through a multipolar linguistic, cultural, and geopolitical set of interests. On the economic front, while Portugal and Brazil do not constitute each other's primary trading partners, they do invest a fair amount in each other's economies. In fact, most Portuguese foreign investment in the late 1990s targeted Brazil.[7] Brazil and Portugal today are active participants in world affairs and economic globalization. With the largest economy in Latin America, Brazil plays a pivotal role in Mercosul/Mercosur (comprised also of Argentina, Paraguay, and Uruguay), one of the key trading blocs of the Americas. Portugal—with its newly found prosperity, political stability, and international prestige as a member of the European Union—has begun forging new relationships of trade and cooperation with its former African colonies. In spite of their separate and relatively autonomous paths since 1822 (the year of Brazilian independence), Portugal and Brazil have remained present in each other's national lives in a multiplicity of forms and differing degrees of intensity from a symbolic, cultural, material, and affectional standpoint.[8]

The (post)colonial relationship between Brazil and Portugal is exceptional in ways that differ greatly even from those seen in special relationship between the United States and Great Britain. Already before its independence, Brazil's economic output and natural resource base was far greater than that of the metropole, creating a relationship characterized by the economic dependence of the mother country vis-à-vis the former colony. No other colonial power transferred its capital from the metropole to the colony as Portugal did between 1808 and 1821 due to the Napoleonic wars. This particular move led to the emergence of Rio de Janeiro as the center of the Portuguese empire. In fact, as Mota and Novais point out, during this era there was an inversion of the colonial pact between Portugal and Brazil whereby the metropole became a de facto appendix of the colony (as cited by Boaventura de Sousa Santos in *Pela mão de Alice* (By Alice's hand), 130–31). This is one of the most blatant examples of a Portuguese condition that Santos describes as intermediate and semiperipheral from a geopolitical point of view; simultaneously semicolonizers and semicolonized (this can be said in relationship to Brazil but also to England). Referring to Shakespeare's *Tempest*, he adds that the Portuguese colonizer was a hybrid who combined aspects of Prospero and Caliban: "If Prospero ever disguised himself as Caliban, it was through the mask of the Portuguese" ("Espírito de Timor Invade o Rio," 2).

In spite of the autonomy gained by Brazil in all spheres of its national life after 1822, the political framework that was established at first was that of a binational monarchy, whereby the same monarchical family ruled both countries (the father, João VI in Portugal, and the son, Pedro I in Brazil). Thus, the tight political links (as well as economic and cultural ones) between the two countries continued after independence (from a political standpoint, at least until the establishment of the Brazilian Republic in 1889). This reality was accompanied by the fact that heavy immigration from Portugal to Brazil did not stop in 1822 but in fact continued well into the twentieth century, subsiding only after the Portuguese Revolution of 1974.[9] The constant movement of the migratory wave from Portugal to Brazil was a manifestation of this peculiar (post)colonial dependence. It can be argued that emigration throughout the history of Portuguese colonialism in Brazil after 1500 (as well as in Angola and Mozambique, particularly after Salazar's ascent to power in 1933) served as an escape mechanism for millions of rural Portuguese in search of a better life, at the same time as it served as an economic strategy to rid the country of its poor while avoiding some of the pressing developmental problems that had plagued Portugal since the "epic navigators" set sail to India in the late fifteenth century. Still today, millions of Brazilians have grandparents or even parents who are Portuguese. On the other hand, Portuguese emigration to its traditional points of destination (Brazil, France, Canada, the United States, South Africa, Venezuela, etc.) has greatly diminished since Portugal entered the European Union in 1986. European integration has been to a large extent the catalyst for Portugal's rapid modernization and renewed economic prosperity, and has been the guarantor of its political stability. This situation has attracted tens of thousands of immigrants from Brazil during the Brazilian economic and political crisis of the 1980s and the early 1990s, and from Africa, primarily from the drought-prone Cape Verde Islands and war-torn Angola. In recent years, there has been a significant migratory wave from Eastern Europe, primarily Russia, Ukraine, Moldova, and Romania.

Cultural Influences and Reciprocal Images

It is a well-known fact that Brazilian popular and media culture exert an enormous influence on contemporary Portuguese culture (as well as on that of Lusophone Africa). This influence is reflected on a daily basis in the proliferation of Brazilian soap operas *(telenovelas)* on Portuguese public and private television channels, and now, with the advent of cable television, in the presence of several Brazilian channels (including Globo and Canal Brasil, which specializes in Brazilian cinema). The intense exposure to Brazilian culture in Portugal is surpassed only by the exposure to American (and to a lesser extent, British) pop and media culture (this is also reflected in popular music, where Anglo-American and Brazilian music have a large share of the Portuguese consumer market). Daily contact with Brazilian culture has produced significant changes in Portugal, particularly from a linguistic point of view.

If, on the other hand, elements of the British popular and elite cultures are clearly present in the daily life of the United States, the same cannot be said of the presence of Portuguese culture in Brazil; Portuguese popular culture (music, TV) has a minimal presence in everyday Brazilian life. At an experiential level, when in Brazil one is left with the impression that Portugal is "everywhere and yet no where," as Lourenço would describe it (Eduardo Lourenço, *A nau de Ícaro seguido de Imagem e miragem da lusofonia*, 157). In the realm of elite culture, some of the greatest writers of Portuguese literature, such as Camões or Eça de Queiroz, are indeed familiar to well-educated Brazilians through secondary or college education, while celebrated modernist poet Fernando Pessoa has achieved nearly cult status among well-read Brazilians. For his part, 1998 Nobel laureate José Saramago has constantly had books on Brazilian lists of bestsellers. Saramago's literary award was perceived in Brazil as being Brazilian as much as Portuguese. By the same token, the Nobel Prize has boosted the presence and prestige of Portuguese literature in Brazil, as well as throughout the world. However, even before this significant development, Portuguese literature was widely disseminated throughout the Brazilian university system, where there are M.A and Ph.D. programs in the field at most major Brazilian universities. Unfortunately, the same cannot be said about the institutionalization of Brazilian literature in the Portuguese university system, where there are few courses or degree programs in the field. In fact, Brazilian literature today is much less known in Portugal than is Portuguese literature in Brazil. This can be attributed to ethnocentric attitudes that have dominated the educational system in Portugal and therefore in literary studies curricula. Despite this contemporary literary chasm, Brazilian literature of the 1930s (that of Graciliano Ramos, Jorge Amado, and José Lins do Rego, among others) profoundly influenced Portuguese neo-realist writers (as well as emerging Cape Verdean writers of the time) and enjoyed wide readership. Meanwhile, the greatest Brazilian twentieth-century literary figures, such as poets Carlos Drummond de Andrade and João Cabral de Melo Neto, as well as prose writers João Guimarães Rosa and Clarice Lispector, remain well known within academic and intellectual circles in Portugal.[10]

In the realm of literature and other "high" cultural expressions, Brazil has a rather limited presence in Portugal. This can be partly explained by the obvious limitations experienced by cultural and artistic productions aimed at highly educated and specialized segments of the population, even in wealthier societies. Nonetheless, the dramatic increase in the number of cultural exchanges between Brazil and Portugal as a result of Brazil's quincentennial has led to a (re)discovery of Brazilian culture on the part of the Portuguese, particularly of Brazilian high cultural expressions such as the visual and performance arts, classical music, and cinema, with major retrospectives that have aimed at not only educating Portuguese audiences but also changing the perception of Brazil as a producer of exclusively pop cultural expressions such as novelas and MPB.

Yet, it remains de rigueur for Brazilian pop music artists to include in their European tours various Portuguese cities, where they have thousands of loyal fans. The intense exposure to the Portuguese language as it is spoken in Brazil has made the Portuguese population very familiar with its sounds and nuances to the point of decisively influencing the vocabulary and grammar used in Portugal, especially among youth. The opposite is not at all true; Brazilians, particularly less educated ones, experience great difficulty in comprehending Lusitanian Portuguese. Linguistically, European Portuguese today sounds exotic to many Brazilians and, more often than not, somewhat shocking, if not altogether jarring to their ears. In spite of the substantial growth, renewed vitality, and high quality of contemporary Portuguese pop music, Brazilian radio stations and audiences are rather reluctant to include it in their repertoire of sounds, either because of a perceived linguistic barrier or because of strictly marketing strategies that determine what musical products Brazilian listeners should consume. Still, Portuguese state-sponsored organizations and private enterprises sporadically organize large cultural events throughout Brazil that showcase contemporary visual and performance art, film, or classical, jazz, pop, or fado music produced in Portugal. These events have a limited scope and tend to reach primarily elite Brazilian audiences or Portuguese immigrants in large cities such as São Paulo, Rio de Janeiro, and others. Since Expo '98, which took place in Lisbon, and the five hundredth anniversary of Brazil, there has been an increase in the number of joint events, such as concerts featuring well-known Brazilian artists together with Portuguese in the hope of providing more visibility to Portuguese popular music in Brazil. Some of the most remarkable concerts at Ipanema Beach (in Rio) or Ibirapuera Park (in São Paulo) featured Caetano Veloso with Dulce Pontes and Angolan Waldemar Bastos, or Gilberto Gil with ethnic jazz singer Maria João. Beyond these highly specific instances, the presence of elements of contemporary Portuguese high or popular cultures in Brazil is quite limited.

Literary representations of Portugal and Brazil have been historically present in each other's national literature, especially during colonial times but also throughout the nineteenth century. (In terms of postmodern historiographical metafiction of the late twentieth century, Portuguese culture appears as the colonial presence within a Brazilian national space in the making. See Ana Miranda, Haroldo Maranhão, and João Ubaldo Ribeiro). Within the abundant literature of Portuguese navigations and "discoveries," Brazil is most definitely present as an object of description.[11] Throughout the colonial period, most literature produced in Brazil was inevitably linked to the metropole as much as to the colony itself; the most outstanding examples would be the literature of the great baroque figures of Luso-Brazilian letters, the Jesuit Father Antonio Vieira and poet Gregório de Matos. Within Brazilian colonial literature we find nascent signs of a distinct nationality that underwent an evolutionary process, much akin to what was seen in Angolan or Cape Verdean literatures between the nineteenth and twentieth centuries, which culminated in the works of the greatest Brazilian (and Latin American) writer of the nineteenth century, Machado de Assis. In Machado's fiction, Brazilian national identity was no longer a primary or explicit concern, while Portugal practically disappeared as an obvious cultural or historical point of reference or comparison.[12]

A large part of the fiction and poetry produced in Brazil after independence (1822) and before the modernist movement of 1922 was invested in the construction of a national literature intended to reveal— or propose—the contours of an independent and distinct nation. In this context, it is evident that Portugal necessarily appeared under a negative limning or as a point of contrast (i.e., that which is not Brazil). Here the figure of the Portuguese immigrant to Brazil played a major role. Nelson Vieira has offered the most exhaustive study of the representations of Portuguese and Brazilians in each other's literature (*Brasil e Portugal: A imagem recíproca* [Brazil and Portugal: The reciprocal image], 1991). In this study Vieira concludes that in spite of the degree of familiarity and affection that has existed between the nations throughout history, their dominant images of each other's peoples have generally been negative. The figure of the Portuguese immigrant to Brazil appears as the loaded signifier through which Brazilian authors (particularly of the nineteenth century) have expressed a lingering and complex colonial resentment, as well as a feeling of revenge vis-à-vis the former mother country, which has been viewed as an impoverished nation of rustic yet ambitious and arrogant immigrants. Vieira also argues that its negative relationship with Portugal underscores the insecurity of nineteenth-century Brazil, which was in the process of defining its identity and place in the world (122).

In nineteenth-century Portuguese literature, on the other hand, "Brazilian" figures were really the Portuguese who emigrated to Brazil but returned to Portugal. These "Brazilians" were also objects of satire and scorn on the part of Portuguese writers and were represented as unsophisticated and materialistic nouveaux riches.[13] This stereotype may indicate a classist as well as neocolonialist attitude on the part of Portuguese intellectuals. Interestingly, in neither case do we observe an attempt on the part of Brazilian or Portuguese writers to accurately represent the actual peoples living in the other country. In the literature of each nation, realistic and more accurate representations based on lived experiences in the other country have been rather rare, and unfortunately, the negative stereotypes of the immigrant/emigrant still largely prevail.[14]

The dominant notions that Brazil and Portugal have about each other in their collective imaginaries are doubtless manifold. When spending time in either country, one confronts the postcolonial paradox of a generalized contemporary indifference toward Portugal in today's Brazil and, on the other hand, the impossibility of ignoring Brazil in everyday Portuguese life. This paradox is also palpable at an interpersonal level when encountering Portuguese and Brazilians elsewhere in Europe or the Americas. There is a complex spectrum of feelings and perceptions that Brazilians and Portuguese have for each other (which Vieira amply describes in the realms of literature and oral folklore), which range from a sense of familiarity with each other's cultures, the discovery of uncanny similarities between them, a mutual feeling of "being at home" when Brazilians are in Portugal or vice versa, and sincere affection for each other to feelings of culture alienation, national chauvinism, active ignorance, paternalism, arrogance, or mutual mistrust. (Some of these traits are dramatically shown in a film by Brazilian director Walter Salles, *Terra Estrangeira* [Foreign land], 1995.) On the other hand, occasional tensions have also arisen in recent years on the diplomatic front due to the difficulties Portugal has encountered in adapting to the sizable immigration from Brazil and Lusophone Africa since the 1980s and the demand made by the European Union (EU) that countries such as Portugal that have special ties with former colonies curtail and control the migratory flow of non-EU citizens.[15] These diplomatic tensions have led at times to interpersonal tensions or to inflamed comments in the respective national media.

Brazil and Portugal continue to evoke images of the "exotic other" in their respective imaginaries. The "exoticism" they associate with each other may at times reach extremes of caricature or sardonic humor (see Vieira, *Brasil e Portugal*). For instance, Brazil (in the most extreme cases) may evoke in Portugal a whole repertoire of clichés associated with it in other countries as well, such as the images of a lush tropical beach paradise, sensuous mulattas, soccer players, or a country in a state of endless *carnaval*. In addition, Brazil may evoke images of poverty, violence, corruption, and vast socioeconomic injustices. In Brazil, Portugal may still appear in the popular imaginary of clichés as an archaic, poverty-stricken country, frozen in time, where black-clad, rustic peasant women sing an interminable litany of melancholic fados. These stereotypes reveal yet another and no less important facet of the highly complex world of Luso-Brazilian relations. These oversimplistic and distorted images of each other's countries will very likely be superseded in time by more balanced and accurate notions through increasing cultural and economic contacts (which are already occurring); through greater direct human contact, which continues to occur via immigration (a trend that is now directed more toward Portugal); or increasingly through tourism (in both directions), among other vectors.

Is it possible, as Eduardo Lourenço asks (in *A nau de Icaro*, 141), to overcome the historical-psychic-cultural complex of colonizer/colonized or father/son in the context of Luso-Brazilian relations? Or must current and future relations between the two countries be inexorably condemned to a dynamic of resentment, fascination, delirium, mythification, active ignorance, or indifference stemming from their colonial past?

The answer to both questions is inevitably "Yes and no." The (post)colonial link will always inform the cultural memories of both countries to one degree or another, yet such memories will be differently lived by Brazil than by Portugal. On the other hand, the evolution of binational relations will largely depend on the level and intensity of the economic, financial, political, cultural, interpersonal, academic, and media-based *exchanges* between Portugal and Brazil. Such exchanges will take place within a decidedly postcolonial framework and as part of a much wider global network of relations. In this context, both nations must defend their common interests and, together with the Portuguese-speaking nations of Africa, safeguard the place of the Portuguese language—while respecting cultural differences—in a world that is tending more and more toward linguistic and cultural homogenization. I hope that within the realm of intellectual-academic exchanges, this book will contribute to an updated, and perhaps more nuanced, view of national identities in Brazil and Portugal in an era of postmodern globalization, shedding new light into Luso-Brazilian intercultural connections while at the same time recognizing the fact that both countries are today inhabiting highly differentiated historical and cultural moments in relationship to each other.

Utopias of Otherness explores the changing definitions of nationhood, subjectivity, and utopias in late twentieth-century Portugal and Brazil. It departs from the premise that the histories of both nations were closely intertwined over several centuries of colonial experience and that they will remain key references for understanding the roots and early development of Brazil, on the one hand, and the history of Portuguese colonialism and the rise of modern Portugal, on the other. Today both countries are clearly inhabiting different moments in their respective national lives. Yet in relationship to the world at large, Brazil and Portugal are to varying degrees equally subject to the paradigmatic transition dictated by the economic, political, and cultural forces of postmodern globalization. At the same time, fiction writers in these countries have recognized important epistemological shifts that are taking place in intellectuals' definitions of nationhood and utopias that have an international scope and equally pertain to Portugal and Brazil.

This book is and is not, at the same time, a comparative study of contemporary Portuguese and Brazilian literatures and cultures. Although

Utopias of Otherness considers both nations under the same thematic aegis, not all chapters are organized in a comparative fashion. While I have attempted to refer to both cultures comparatively whenever pertinent, my ultimate desire is to provide a balanced portrait where differences and commonalities between Brazil and Portugal are given their due attention. Thus, I explore how Portuguese and Brazilian contemporary writers—Caio Fernando Abreu, Maria Isabel Barreno, Vergílio Ferreira, Clarice Lispector, Maria Gabriela Llansol, and José Saramago—have redefined the concept of nationhood for their respective countries. By the same token, these writers have invested themselves to varying degrees in utopian or emancipatory causes such as Marxist revolution, women's liberation, or sexual revolution, but, given major historical, cultural, and epidemiological changes throughout the world in the late twentieth century, they have shifted their attention to alternative modes of conceiving the ethical and political realms. It is at this point where nationhood, utopia, and subjectivity form a nexus of critical issues. Thus, in spite of the exhaustion or weakening of various twentieth-century utopias, certain manifestations of utopian thinking are still necessary. These authors, in different ways, posit "a utopia of the other" as reflected in new subjectivities and communities based on relationships of ethical responsibility and solidarity. They privilege one's relationship with the "other" as embodied in the form of a relationship with a family member, a loved one, a community, or the "reader." Ultimately, there is a clear shift from the earlier emphasis on national concerns to an emphasis on postnational concerns, where the destiny of "Western culture"—or, in some cases, that of "humanity" in the widest sense—occupies center stage. This postnational and humanistic reconfiguration has played a major role in the literary production of all the authors analyzed here; therefore, it is one of the main objects of study.

Utopias of Otherness presents a model of literary and cultural criticism that is significantly informed by the insights of history, geopolitics, critical theory, sociology, and philosophy. I have chosen to study a particularly diverse group of Portuguese and Brazilian authors who, in spite of their differences, are united by larger historical and philosophical issues where questions of gender, nationhood, and postcolonialism or sexuality, utopias, and globalization all intersect. Caio Fernando Abreu, Isabel Barreno, Vergílio Ferreira, Clarice Lispector, Maria Gabriela Llansol, and José Saramago are, implicitly and explicitly, interested in the destiny of their respective nations in today's globalized environment, as they are interested in the destiny of humankind at the turn of the new century, where there is profound skepticism in relationship to utopian ideologies of redemption, either religious or political. Yet they all believe in the ties of solidarity, love, and ethical commitment vis-à-vis the other, be it in the form of a lover, family member, community, or nation, or that of humanity at large. It is the strength that derives from these ties that allows them to live productively as writers, as citizens of their respective nation-states, and as participants in the contemporary global system.

This book provides English-speaking scholars one of very few Portuguese-Brazilian studies on nationhood available in any language, at the same time respecting national particularities; it explores how some of the current theoretical debates around nationhood, globalization, postmodernity, and foundationalist thought impact semiperipheral nations such as Brazil and Portugal; it critically studies various literary reformulations of utopian thought structures and hope in a purportedly postutopian era; it probes and expands queer and gender theories by broadening the cultural frameworks through which these theories can be considered; and it fosters a Portuguese-Brazilian critical dialogue that has been lacking in English-language academic circles.

Chapters 1 and 2 are primarily historical chapters. They trace the history of ideas that have defined Portugal and Brazil in the realm of intellectual thought and illustrate their transformations in the late twentieth century. Both chapters argue that the changes in the definitions of nationhood for both Portugal and Brazil, similarly and differently, are symptomatic of a multiplicity of developments associated with the postmodern, such as globalization and the rise of communication and information technologies, as well as global media and consumer cultures. At the same time, changing definitions of nationhood are connected to the shift from macrological ways of thinking about the construct of "nation," or of acting politically at the national level, to micrological modes of defining nationhood and the national political arena. Chapter 1 ("Portugal: Ideas of Empire and Nationhood"), more concretely, provides a historical framework in order to understand the formation of the Portuguese nation and the extent to which it has been shaped by the experience of empire. Furthermore, this chapter explores ideas of Portuguese nationhood within the realms of historiography, intellectual thought, and sociology, illustrating the epistemological shifts that have taken place since the Portuguese Revolution of 1974 and the subsequent decolonization of (former) Portuguese Africa and East Timor. Chapter 2 ("Brazilian National Identity: Intellectual Debates and Changing Cultural Realities"), on the other hand, maps out the dominant notions of Brazilian national identity in the twentieth century within the realms of anthropology, sociology, politics, literary and cultural criticism, and popular music. It highlights the transition from macrological approaches that have privileged constructs such as "racial democracy," social typologies such as "the cordial man," or geopolitical binaries such as the "national versus the foreign," to micrological perspectives that account for a fragmented nation where multiple and competing versions of nationhood, democracy, and modernization coexist.

Chapters 3 and 4 are dedicated to literary and cultural criticism. Chapter 3 ("Subjectivities and Homoerotic Desire in Contemporary Brazilian Fiction: The Nation of Caio Fernando Abreu") centers on Brazilian gay male fiction, especially on the work of Caio Fernando Abreu (when necessary, this chapter refers to other pertinent contemporary Brazilian writers who have been moved by problematics similar to Abreu's). It can be argued that Abreu's fiction is representative of the zeitgeist of Brazilian society of the last twenty years. Abreu traces the evolution of contemporary Brazil through the lives of those who belonged to the 1960s counterculture and who were greatly repressed by the military regime of the time. By the 1980s and 1990s, the survivors of this generation had experienced the excesses of political authoritarianism and the frustrated hopes of complete democratization for Brazil and, having indulged in the utopia of sexual liberation, they had to confront the ubiquitous threat of AIDS.

Chapter 4 ("Women's Difference in Contemporary Portuguese Fiction: The Case of Maria Isabel Barreno") focuses on contemporary Portuguese women's writing, in particular the work of Maria Isabel Barreno. This chapter explores how Barreno's fiction subverts the grand narratives of Portuguese nationhood by incorporating women's difference into the historical time of the nation while rejecting the seafaring/imperial paradigm that has governed the Portuguese collective imaginary for centuries. Barreno dramatizes the generalized contemporary crisis that derives from the weakening of utopias, myths, or redemptive ideologies that have predominated throughout the twentieth century in Portugal and beyond: Marxism, Christianity, fascism, colonialism, and nationalism. When necessary, this chapter refers to other pertinent contemporary Portuguese writers who focus on issues that are akin to those on which Barreno has focused.

Chapter 5 ("Worlds in Transition and Utopias of Otherness") brings together the analysis of literary texts, cultural issues, and philosophical concepts. It discusses an additional group of Portuguese and Brazilian writers other than Barreno and Abreu, namely Vergílio Ferreira, Clarice Lispector, Maria Gabriela Llansol, and José Saramago. Here the focus is on the ontological status of "utopia" in a contemporary world where various political and social utopias have been put severely into question. A utopia is understood here as a vision or imagining of a future better world. However, this chapter argues that there has been an important shift from grand utopian visions to smaller utopian imaginings of a better world. The authors studied here suggest that in spite of the exhaustion or weakening of various utopias that governed the human imaginary nationally and transnationally until the late twentieth century—those of Marxism, Christianity, women's liberation, or sexual revolution—certain strands of utopian thinking are still necessary for the survival of humanity. Thus, in a multiplicity of ways these authors posit new modes of human possibility embodied in communities and subjectivities based on an ethical commitment to and solidarity with "the other" in order to build a more "decent" and humane life. This chapter is organized into four subsections that discuss the conceptual uses of utopia, the dominant national utopias in modern Portugal and Brazil, the continued need for utopias in contemporary societies, and micro-utopian expressions in postmodern Portuguese and Brazilian fiction.

Finally, the conclusion presents a series of final comparative remarks regarding the status of the nation in all Brazilian and Portuguese authors contemplated throughout this study.

CHAPTER ONE

Portugal

Ideas of Empire and Nationhood

Chapters 1 and 2 situate the reader within the currents of history and intellectual thought that have influenced the ideas of national identity for both Portugal and Brazil. Although the two nations are treated separately in each chapter in order to highlight individual particularities, comparative allusions are made in order to illustrate the ways Brazil and Portugal impinge upon each other's respective national identity formation. Before embarking on the literary and philosophical discussions that will occupy all subsequent chapters (chapters 3 through 5), discussions that emphasize the notion of the weakening of the nation-state and its correlative myths or utopias in favor of "postnational" modes of conceiving identity and citizenship, it is crucial to define the dominant ideas that have shaped the modern Portuguese and Brazilian nations, at the same time illustrating their transformations in the late twentieth century.

The Portuguese Nation and Empire: A Brief History

The realities of both nation and empire have been closely intertwined in the last five centuries of Portuguese national existence, from the period of maritime expansion and "discoveries" in the late fifteenth century until the Portuguese Revolution and the decolonization of Africa and East Timor in the mid-1970s.[1] Modern debates on the questions of "national identity" and the "destiny" of the nation have been inseparable from the fate of the Portuguese empire, which in turn has been greatly dependent upon larger geopolitical forces at any given historical juncture.

Portugal established its political borders in the thirteenth century. Its political and geographical stability coupled with its linguistic and relative cultural homogeneity was instrumental in forging a sense of national cohesion. Historian José Mattoso believes that a sense of Portuguese nationhood was achieved only over time, between the Middle Ages and the era of navigations and "discoveries" in the fifteenth and sixteenth centuries. According to Mattoso, Portuguese nationhood was above all a political project rooted in the geopolitical configuration of Iberian kingdoms in the early Middle Ages. D. Afonso Henriques's successful declaration of independence for the small kingdom or *condado* of Portugal in 1128 was a gesture against any potential union with other Castillian-dominated kingdoms in the Iberian Peninsula. This first step did not necessarily automatically provide a sense of Portuguese nationhood to the peoples who inhabited the kingdom; such a sense was initially achieved through the hegemony exerted by the king among the nobility and the clergy, but eventually would spread to the rest of the population. The gradual expulsion of the Moors, which was completed in 1249, and later on the wars with Castille in the fourteenth century, contributed to the creation of a common bond that at first revolved around a Christian identity (in opposition to the Muslims), and eventually a Portuguese identity (in opposition to Castille).

In synthesis, a sense of early Portuguese nationhood was the product of the actual power exerted by the monarchy across social classes; the military successes that signified an expansion of national territory and eventually the consolidation of national borders; the creation and sedimentation of symbols and myths that helped legitimate the Portuguese monarchy and allowed it to become coextensive with the nation itself; and finally, the development of Portuguese as a national language. A "sense" of Portuguese nationality became further entrenched in the era of navigations and "discoveries" when the Portuguese circled the globe, encountering vastly different peoples and cultures, becoming aware of their "distinctiveness" as a people or as a culture. In this particular period, partly due to the profusion of literature thematizing the encounters of the Portuguese with peoples of different customs and belief systems, the notion of "Portugueseness" became inextricably linked to the notion of "being Christian." This process was literarily reinforced in the sixteenth century by the epic representation of the seafaring Portuguese nation in *Os Lusíadas* (The Lusiads, 1572). Ultimately, the gradual process

of Portuguese national consolidation illustrates Eric Hobsbawm's asser-
tion that "nations do not make states . . . but the other way round" (*Nations and Nationalisms,* 10).

Portugal, along with Spain, inaugurated the first major era of globalization in the late fifteenth century, which in truth signified the rise of
Westernization (Jan Nederveen Pieterse, "Globalization as Hybridization") and imperialism. This was a direct result of maritime and colonial expansion on a worldwide scale never experienced before the 1400s.
At this particular moment, one of the most salient aspects of modernity
came into being, radically altering in exhilarating as well as catastrophic
ways the lives of millions of people throughout the globe. The early stages
of globalization—understood here to be a corollary to modernity—
were to a large extent characterized by the rise of the nation-state and
the creation of world markets through the establishment of mercantilist
empires, of which the Portuguese and Spanish were the first examples.[2]

Portugal's hegemony as a world power, however, was short lived, in
part due to intense competition by other rising European imperial powers. The Portuguese collapse in the battle of El-Ksar-el-Kebir (Morocco)
in 1578, the ensuing annexation of Portugal to the Spanish crown between 1580 and 1640, and the increasing threats to Portuguese dominance over maritime routes in the Indian Ocean by Holland and England revealed Portugal's intrinsic fragility on a global scale. In the
sixteenth century Portugal was already "stretched out" to capacity, given
its small population and limited natural resources. The interior agricultural lands were being depopulated by emigration, and there was a significant decline in the male workforce. Moreover, the expulsion of the
Jews in 1496 (a product of Castilian pressure as both Portugal and Castille
negotiated an inter-royal marriage between members of the two courts)
played a major role in Portugal's decline, because it meant the loss of a
vital human and material component within the mercantile and financial sectors.[3] It has been widely argued that the Inquisition also played a
major role in Portugal's economic and cultural decline (Antero de
Quental, *Causas da decadência dos povos peninsulares*),[4] and that it was
largely responsible for stifling technological innovations and cultural
production (António José Saraiva, *A cultura em Portugal: Livro III*). In
short, Portugal exhausted its capacity to maintain and expand its colonial empire and was quickly displaced from the center of the sixteenth-
century European geopolitical structure to the periphery. Portugal would

eventually become a subsidiary colonial power to England with its much vaster imperial ambitions, military might, economic power, material efficiency, and cultural vitality.

The change in Portugal's geostrategic position in worldwide colonial affairs, aside from its direct economic and political consequences, also brought with it a heightened sense of "civilizational decline" among the Portuguese intelligentsia, which is clearly reflected in Camões's epic poem *Os Lusíadas*. The epic poem was not only a triumphant celebration of empire but also a melancholic requiem, signaling its demise. In fact, *Os Lusíadas* appears subtly ambiguous; underneath the heroic clamor one can also hear dissonant voices of those who question the nature of the epic enterprise. Meanwhile, there were also two other key literary works from the period that radically undermined the claims for Portuguese (or European or Christian) moral and cultural superiority over that of other world civilizations (Fernão Mendes Pinto's *Peregrinação* [Peregrination], 1614) or that reveal the precariously human dimensions of maritime expansion (Bernardo Gomes de Brito's *História Trágico-Marítima* *[The Tragic History of the Sea]*, published in Portuguese for the first time in 1735–36). Even as the epic poem has remained the Portuguese canonical text par excellence, being considered the fulfillment of an entire literary tradition, both *Peregrinação* and *História Trágico-Marítima* enjoy wide critical attention as paradigmatic counternarratives to the triumphalistic discourses of maritime and colonial expansion embedded in *Os Lusíadas* in spite of the simultaneously dissonant and marginalized voices that are also present in the epic poem.[5]

Regarding the rise and fall of sixteenth-century global maritime hegemony, Spain would suffer a similar fate to Portugal, except on an even grander scale, given the profusion of Spanish geostrategic interests throughout Europe in the sixteenth century. The fiasco in 1580 of the "invincible Armada" (in which Portugal was also actively involved, because both Spain and Portugal were under the same crown), coupled with the internal and external wars that drained and destabilized Phillipine Spain and the decline in silver reserves from the American colonies in the early seventeenth century, brought the beginning of the decline of the Spanish empire. The dominance of the Spanish crown over Portugal, which started in 1580 as a result of Portugal's failed attempt at conquering Morocco in 1578, ended by 1640.

The process of Portuguese maritime and colonial expansion and the construction of empire took place in essentially three distinct major historical and geopolitical stages: the sixteenth century (Asia and the Indian Ocean), seventeenth and eighteenth centuries (Brazil), and the nineteenth and twentieth centuries (Africa). With its dominance over maritime commercial routes to and around Asia in decline by the late sixteenth century, Portugal's sights swiftly focused on the actual colonization of Brazilian territory. This constituted the second phase of Portuguese colonialism.[6] Brazil, with its continental land mass and enormous economic potential, would subsequently function until its independence in 1822 as a real and imaginary "compensatory" mechanism in relationship to Portugal's limited economic resources and geographical size. Brazilian independence was thus experienced as a traumatic moment for Portugal. Nineteenth-century historian Oliveira Martins described the Portuguese reaction to Brazilian independence as tantamount to the death of Portugal when he wrote: "Dobram por Portugal os sinos de finados" (The bells of mourning are ringing for Portugal) (Saraiva, *A cultura em Portugal*, 337). Thus, the nineteenth century entailed a major rethinking of Portuguese geopolitical priorities that eventually led to a shift of interests from Brazil to the African colonies. The third and final phase of Portuguese colonialism centered on its territorial possessions on the African continent.[7] This dynamic coincided with the "scramble" for Africa embarked upon by competing European colonial powers that aimed at exerting control over territories, peoples, and natural resources throughout the continent.

Thus, Portugal initiated a campaign of "pacification" of the peoples of the hinterlands of its respective colonies (Mozambique, Portuguese Guinea, and Angola) with the objective of establishing control of the entire territories and inhabitants. Portugal's colonial African campaign also involved its greatest international humiliation at the hands of the British. In 1890, England issued what historians call the "British Ultimatum," which forced Portugal to remain within the confines of its colonial possessions in southern Africa—Angola and Mozambique—as opposed to pursuing its dream of establishing a united Portuguese colonial territory that would extend from coast to coast. Britain's imperial dreams included control over a much vaster territorial domain, from Cape Town to Cairo; hence the "modest" Portuguese colonial ambitions would be an intolerable obstacle. Portugal risked losing its African colonies altogether.[8] The 1890 Ultimatum proved to be a lasting blow to Portuguese national consciousness, because it revealed ever so clearly the subordinate position of Portugal among European colonial powers at the turn of the twentieth century.

Despite Portugal's position as a secondary imperialist power in the global geopolitical framework at the beginning of the twentieth century, the symbiotic relationship between nation and empire in the Portuguese collective unconscious and in the political praxis of the state went virtually unchanged. In fact, the British Ultimatum served as a powerful motivating force for Portugal to renew and reinforce its commitment to empire, particularly its African components, during the First Portuguese Republic (1910–1926) as well as during the period of dictatorship (1926–1974).[9] The empire would play a very important role in the ideological frameworks of both republicanism and fascism in Portugal. Indeed, Valentim Alexandre argues that both liberal and right-wing nationalisms were imperialistic ("The Colonial Empire," 59). This explains the degree of continuity observed in the commitment to empire on the part of the Republic and, later on, the Estado Novo ("New State"). The Portuguese Republic actively engaged in the campaigns of "pacification" in Angola, Mozambique, and Portuguese Guinea, which had started in the late nineteenth century. In 1921, Norton de Matos, high commissioner for Angola, spearheaded a plan to effectively occupy all Portuguese colonial territories in Africa and initiate the modernization of Angola. It is believed that the downfall of the First Portuguese Republic was the result of various crises that took place in Africa, threatening Portuguese sovereignty (47). With the advent of Salazar's Estado Novo in 1933, colonial laws were systematized to the point where the state apparatus was placed at the service of the construction of the colonial empire (48).

With the success of anticolonial struggles after World War II, the historical tide shifted in favor of the independence of European colonies throughout Africa, Asia, and the Middle East. At this historical juncture, Portuguese colonialism was deemed anachronistic. Portugal saw itself increasingly isolated in world affairs, which forced the Salazar regime to change the political and juridical structure of its own colonial empire. In 1952, the colonies were reclassified as "overseas provinces," making them extensions of metropolitan territory, or of the "national body" (Luís Madureira, "Tropical Sex Fantasies and the Ambassador's Other Death: The Difference in Portuguese Colonialism"). These changes ultimately reinforced Portugal's control over the colonies and enabled Portugal to redefine itself as an "Afro-European power." Moreover, Salazar sought academic legitimation of Portuguese colonialism through the work of internationally renowned Brazilian sociologist Gilberto Freyre, in particular his notion of *lusotropicalismo* (lusotropicalism). The roots of lusotropicalism are located in Freyre's groundbreaking study of the origins of Brazil, *Casa-grande e senzala* (The masters and the slaves, 1933). Here Freyre argued for the central importance of the African, as well as Portuguese and Amerindian, contributions to the formation of Brazil. During one of the most racist and xenophobic periods of modern world history, Freyre celebrated interracial mixing and cultural hybridity, which, according to the author, are key to understanding Brazilian national identity. Within this framework, the Portuguese were described as a quintessentially hybrid people, culturally and ethnically caught between Europe and Africa. This hybridity, according to Freyre, predisposed them to adapt more readily to the various tropical civilizations into which they came into contact, particularly in Brazil, but also in Africa and Asia, and to racially mix with "native others" (5).[10] Lusotropicalism entails projecting the Portuguese colonial experience in Brazil onto the whole empire. Thus, we observe the deployment of an anthropologically informed consciousness with strong sexual and racial components that had specific geopolitical consequences because it concluded that Portuguese colonialism was "unique" and "distinct" (read "better") in relationship to other colonialisms.

Cláudia Castelo points out that besides ideologically legitimizing the colonial interests of the Salazar regime, Freyre's theorization also helped perpetuate a mythical image of Portuguese national identity that migrated from his sociological writings to the political field, and eventually to the realm of mentalities with lasting effects still today (*O modo português de estar no mundo: O luso-tropicalismo e a ideologia colonial portuguesa*, 14). Madureira, for his part, believes that Freyre's lusotropicalist discourse invested Portuguese colonialism with overt sexual contours, symbolically providing it with a dynamic civilizational role at the same time as it "occluded" the counternarrative of Portuguese decline that had been so dominant in literary/intellectual discourses since the nineteenth century (154). But as Portuguese colonialism in the 1950s and 1960s was assailed by the historical currents of independence throughout Africa, Asia, and the Middle East, the ideological appropriation of part of Freyre's thinking (in spite of his own contradictory and discretely anticolonial stance) by the Salazar regime was a late attempt at intellectually and symbolically legitimizing an anachronistic empire that the anticolonial and liberation movements throughout "Portuguese" Africa would eventually help dismantle in the 1960s and 1970s.[11]

The Portuguese Revolution of 1974 was the immediate catalyst for the decolonization of Portuguese Africa and East Timor,[12] but it has been argued that the "colonial war" or "liberation wars" in the African colonies were the primary cause for the downfall of the ailing Salazar-Caetano regime.[13] From the perspective of the international community of nations, and on the heels of other successful anticolonial struggles in Africa and Asia throughout the 1950s and 1960s, the survival of Portuguese colonialism in the 1970s had become morally and ethically untenable. Portugal was diplomatically isolated; moreover, it was materially and economically exhausted. The Portuguese military was profoundly demoralized and disaffected from the national-colonial cause in Africa. The number of Portuguese casualties in the wars in Guinea, Mozambique, and Angola was high, and there was a general restlessness among Portuguese junior officers regarding salary payments and the possibility of being sent to a fruitless war in Africa. The coup that eventually toppled the Salazar-Caetano regime was appropriately staged by junior officers.

Since 1974 Portugal has been reduced to its original precolonial borders on the Iberian Peninsula, plus the Azores and the Madeira Islands, and it has had to rethink its place in the world, particularly its relationship with Europe, its immediate geopolitical sphere, as well as with Portuguese-speaking Africa, with which it continues to have historical, economic, cultural, and linguistic ties. Portugal is now a full-fledged member of the European Union, having entered the EU together with Spain in 1986, and has undergone a process of democratization and modernization. Portugal has now become virtually unrecognizable given the changes that have occurred in the last twenty-five years. Its entrance into the European Union has ultimately been of enormous benefit not only for Portugal's material development, particularly in the realm of infrastructures (transportation, telecommunications, ports, hospitals, schools, and universities), but also in the realm of mentalities and national self-esteem (Mário Soares, "Portugal depois do 'fim do império': Balanços e perspectivas para o Próximo Milénio," 171). In terms of foreign policy, Portugal has forged renewed trade, cooperation, and partnership ties with independent Angola, Cape Verde, Guinea-Bissau, Mozambique, and São Tomé and Príncipe.[14] Furthermore, Portugal has played an active diplomatic role on behalf of East Timor, which struggled to regain the independence it won from Portugal in 1975, lost through Indonesia's forced annexation soon after, and has recovered since 1999.[15]

As Portugal continues to renegotiate its geopolitical location in today's globalized environment, it is obvious that the legacy of its ties to the sea and of empire still plays a large role in the national collective imaginary. This is reflected, for instance, in the euphoria expressed in official discourses surrounding the celebrations of the five hundredth anniversary of the Portuguese arrival in Brazil, which reveals, in turn, the continued mythical and "superlative" existence of Brazil within the Portuguese cultural imaginary. Yet the festivities surrounding the quincentennial of Vasco da Gama's arrival in India, culminating with the 1998 World Exposition in Lisbon, constituted a veritable apotheosis for Portuguese culture and the dominant myths related to its maritime past. Expo '98, in fact, emerged as a major "spatialized event" (Appadurai) symbolizing Portugal's transformation into a modern nation, in close dialogue with the world and with one of its most pressing ecological problems, namely how to deal with the sea as the heritage and the future of humanity. At the same time, it represented a grand-scale "repackaging of Portugal's national imagery" (Wallis, 267; Kimberly Dacosta-Holton, "Dressing for Success: Lisbon as European Cultural Capital," 174); the multicultural festival evoked historical realities and myths of the past, together with projections toward the future. Expo '98 provided the opportunity for a massive, and now largely successful, urban transformation of the host city. It was also the culmination of a continuum of international events during the 1990s that have placed Portugal, at least temporarily, at the center of European and world cultural and political currents (in 1992 Portugal occupied the presidency of the European Union, Lisbon was declared the 1994 European Cultural Capital, and the city of Oporto was the European Cultural Capital in 2001, among other honors). In addition, Expo '98 showcased the richness and vitality of contemporary Portuguese culture, at the same time allowing for a unique and particularly intense cultural exchange between all Portuguese-speaking nations.

It is impossible not to be overtaken by the realization that Portuguese national identity continues to be intimately and irreversibly linked to the era of maritime expansion, "discoveries," and colonial empire, in spite of all the major historical, political, socioeconomic, and cultural changes that have taken place in Portugal over the last twenty-five years. This reality was most vividly demonstrated by the mass mobilization of Portuguese civil society in September of 1999 on behalf of East Timor in the aftermath of its vote to declare independence from Indonesia and the ensuing killings, forced evacuation, and material destruction carried out by pro-Indonesian militia forces against the East Timorese. Not since the April Revolution of 1974 had the Portuguese people so over-whelmingly been galvanized around a single national cause. This galva-nization could be attributed to a series of reasons related to humanitarian sensibility and the sheer horror at the turns of events; to cultural, reli-gious, and linguistic empathy; to the notion that since 1975 East Timor has constituted "unfinished business" for the Portuguese state and its society as a whole; to a sense of historical and moral indebtedness, responsibility, and guilt; and to a renewed sense of national self-confidence and citizenship, together with Portugal's significantly more mature relationship to its colonial past.[16]

National Identity in the Portuguese Intellectual Field

With the end of Portuguese colonialism and fascism, the isomorphic equation between Portuguese national identity and empire has changed. Readings of Portuguese identity that have relied on myths associated with the period of maritime and colonial expansion and that have sought to legitimate Portuguese national existence as part of a "messianic mani-fest destiny" have increasingly given way to interpretations based on contemporary political, socioeconomic, and cultural circumstances that are more in accord with Portugal's actual role in the world today. These interpretations do not deny the weight of the Portuguese imperial legacy in the national imaginary and culture, but they seek to redefine and re-assess its relevance to the nation in a postcolonial and globalized era where Portugal's impact is fairly limited. There are several key contem-porary thinkers who have contributed a great deal to current debates around the question of Portuguese national identity: Eduardo Lourenço and Boaventura de Sousa Santos, as well as José Mattoso and António José Saraiva, among others.

In spite of their divergent theoretical and disciplinary frameworks, Eduardo Lourenço and Boaventura de Sousa Santos ultimately arrive at similar conclusions regarding Portugal's geopolitical and geocultural location in the world. Lourenço centers on the ideological or mythical underpinnings of narratives of Portuguese nationhood throughout history. Santos, for his part, short-circuits the canonical narratives of nationhood, creating an alternative narrative that focuses on concrete sociological and geopolitical variables that inform and shape Portugal as a national reality today.

After closely reading both thinkers side by side, one is left with the contrasting effects of their work: Lourenço's reliance on the narratives of Portuguese "decline" that have proliferated within literature and historiography unavoidably results in a negative dialectic vis-à-vis the nation. The pessimistic aura that surrounds many of Lourenço's writings on Portugal—in relationship to itself or to Europe—stands in stark contrast to that surrounding Santos's sociological approach, which appears more "pragmatic" and "optimistic." Santos relies less on a pathology of the nation and more on a therapy regimen of what needs to be done to transcend the metanarrative of Portuguese "decline." However, even though Lourenço and Santos represent seemingly contrasting schools of thought with regard to Portuguese national identity, they are equally invested in the search for a vision of Portugal that is commensurate to its actual weight in the world today, at the same time as they relativize the weight of its "glorious" past.

Eduardo Lourenço, considered one of the most important and original intellectual figures in contemporary Portugal, has focused primarily on Portuguese literature (of all periods), but also on historiography and philosophy and, most recently, on contemporary media culture and globalization.[17] Lourenço's best-known work is entitled *O labirinto da saudade* (*The labyrinth of longing*, 1978), and in it he centers, among other things, on the question of national identity and on the complex of national self-images that have populated the realms of Portuguese literature, as well as historiography and philosophy, since the sixteenth century. In his classic study Lourenço assumes a critical consciousness that synthesizes and dissects a genealogy of voices from among the Portuguese intelligentsia that reveal an acute feeling of *ressentiment* regarding the nation's cultural, geopolitical, and economic decline since the era of navigations and "discoveries." Lourenço analyzes a multiplicity of narratives that have sought to explain Portugal's place in the world in different historical moments and through varying ideological prisms. In short, he deconstructs the equation of nation and empire that has dominated the intellectual horizon of Portuguese elites for centuries, and, at the same time, through the hegemony exerted by the elites—either culturally or politically—came to play a dominant role in the wider Portuguese collective imaginary.

Lourenço starts from the premise that there has been a considerable gap between the ideal representations of Portugal projected in historiographical accounts and its real circumstances in the world. This particular gap reflects the contradictions facing a small nation that for a brief time in history became a world power but went into decline soon after. Camões's epic poem *Os Lusíadas* dramatically reveals a deep-seated tension between the triumphant celebration of accomplished historical feats culminating with Vasco da Gama's arrival in India and the mourning over heroism lost and a nation that had lost its purpose. The historical fate of becoming an imperial(istic) nation radically shaped Portugal's self-image to the point where nation and empire became inextricably linked. Lourenço argues that once it became a widely acknowledged reality that the Portuguese empire, while continuing to exist, had seen itself relegated to secondary status in relationship to other European imperialist powers, the national reason for being was transformed into a "longing" *(saudade)* for what Portugal used to be.

The nineteenth century represents the epitome of this dynamic, where the idea (as well as the reality) of Portugal's decline as a nation became an obsession for its intelligentsia. In fact, for António José Saraiva the Portuguese imaginary has been historically dominated by the myth of the Crusades, which propelled the Portuguese expansion to the south in the Middle Ages, as the Moors were being expelled, and eventually guided the nation's maritime and colonial expansion between the fifteenth and sixteenth centuries. Saraiva also argues that the countermyth of "decline" superseded the myth of the Crusades in the nineteenth century. This countermyth became the driving force during this period for novelists, poets, and historians alike, and it essentially entailed the search for an explanation of Portugal and its place in the world, for an understanding of its national "ontology," and for the formulation of a diagnosis of its ills. Romantic authors such as Almeida Garrett and Alexandre Herculano inaugurated this national "self-analysis" in the early nineteenth century, and it reached its highest point with the Geração de 70 (Generation of 1870). This movement brought together some of the most prominent intellectual figures of late nineteenth-century Portugal: Antero de Quental (poet and spiritual leader), Oliveira Martins (historian), Teófilo Braga (literary critic), and Eça de Queiroz (novelist). In the main manifesto of the movement, entitled "Causas da decadência dos povos peninsulares" (The causes of Iberian decadence), Antero de Quental denounced the Inquisition as well as religious and monarchical absolutism as the primary causes of the decline of the Iberian Peninsula. This movement—heavily influenced by liberal-socialist ideas in circulation throughout Europe at the time—had an acute and painful awareness of the enormous cultural and technological gap that existed between modern Europe and Portugal (or the Iberian Penisula as a whole). The Geração de 70 caused great scandal at the time but was also aware of its limitations in terms of the degree of impact it had on the larger Portuguese society. Its efforts ultimately did not result in any lasting concrete political change.

Eduardo Lourenço is certainly an heir to this nineteenth-century intellectual tradition, as well as its analyst. In *O labirinto da saudade* Lourenço utilizes Freudian psychoanalysis in order to decipher Portugal's "pathology" as a nation so as to "uncover the masks" that have been confused with the "true" face of the national being (18). Thus, he identifies three traumatic moments in the formation of the Portuguese nation. The first traumatic moment was the birth of Portugal out of a family feud between mother and son. D. Afonso Henriques waged a battle against his mother, Countess D. Teresa in Guimarães (1128), whose love affair with Galician count Fernando Peres de Trava could have led to the absorption of the Condado Portucalense (a small kingdom that comprised today's northern regions of Portugal) into the kingdom of Galicia, which was itself subordinate to Castile. This founding moment marked Portugal's independence from any hypothetical pan-Iberian kingdom, which would have presupposed its subordination to Castile/Spain, as well as centuries of animosity and mistrust between Portugal and Spain. The second and third national traumas, according to Lourenço, were the Spanish occupation of Portugal (1580–1640) and the issuance of the British Ultimatum (1890). In both instances, Portugal's subaltern position within Europe was made evident. In both cases, the extent of Portugal's actual autonomy as nation-state was threatened, and in the former case, the viability of the Portuguese nation-state was called entirely into question.

Lourenço also brings to the fore the question of myths, more concretely the importance of narratives that explain the existence and fate of the nation. Lourenço recognizes that national "myths of origin" are inevitable—for instance, the myths of the miracle of Ourique, the return of King Sebastian, or the Fifth Empire—and that these have been profuse within Portuguese culture.[18] If these myths have indeed provided the intelligibility and legitimation necessary to forge a national "imagined community," they have also ultimately served, according to Lourenço, to hide (or repress) the fundamental fact that Portugal, as a national being, has constantly lived in a "state of intrinsic fragility" (*O labirinto da saudade,* 19). Moreover, Lourenço stresses the lasting strength of Brazil as that symbolic foundation of former Portuguese imperial dreams that continue to play an important role even after nearly two centuries of Brazilian independence (*A nau de Ícaro,* 150). Thus, the powerfully seductive myths of Portuguese nationhood have served as psychic compensatory mechanisms for a nation that is hyperaware of its limitations in the world.

Working within a different disciplinary framework from that of Eduardo Lourenço—sociology, jurisprudence, and geopolitics—Boaventura de Sousa Santos focuses on the social, political, and epistemological parameters of what he terms Portugal's "paradigmatic transition" to postmodernity.[19] One of his aims is to find alternative ways of thinking the political in a purportedly "post-Marxian" era—more concretely, the possibility of forging "emancipatory subjectivities" in an era otherwise depleted of emancipatory values. Santos is one of the most innovative thinkers in the realm of Portuguese social sciences, and in recent years he has garnered considerable respect internationally. His particularly global scope provides him with a unique perspective from which to analyze Portugal's location in the contemporary world system and to problematize historically dominant notions regarding Portuguese national identity.

Santos is critical of readings of Portuguese national reality—particularly within the areas of literature, literary and cultural criticism, historiography, and philosophy—that rely excessively on "myths"; more specifically, he examines myths that suggest a teleological reason for Portugal's being in the world of nations. Among the twentieth- and twenty-first-century critics Santos has in mind here—even more than Eduardo Lourenço—are figures such as Agostinho da Silva, Teixeira de Pascoaes, and António Quadros.[20] Literary and cultural critic Agostinho da Silva, for example, posits a redemptive belief in the Holy Spirit as a fundamental component of the primeval Portuguese mentality that would bring to the world an ecumenical "future kingdom of universal love" reminiscent of António Vieira's or Fernando Pessoa's notion of the Fifth Empire (for a definition see note 18 to this chapter). The Portuguese nation would be the result of a "permanent spiritual source" that would function as a cornerstone of European salvation, or even as the driving force for a divine plan of world purification or regeneration. After Agostinho da Silva had lived in exile in Brazil during part of the Salazar regime, his idea of Portugal eventually shifted to an idea of the Portuguese-speaking world as a "prefiguration" of the aforementioned kingdom. Poet and philosopher Teixeira de Pascoaes, on the other hand, developed a metaphysical thought expressed through poetry and based on the concept of *saudade* (longing) that he thought would encompass the "essence" of the Portuguese soul. *Saudade,* according to Pascoaes, was the primary differentiating ontological trait of the Portuguese nation in relationship to other nations in the world. It comprised cultural elements that were unique to Portugal, such as the messianic myth of King Sebastian, as well as notions of popular religious independence based on the medieval Portuguese church, among others. Pascoaes' glorification of the notion of *saudade* was also the result of an early twentieth-century republican desire to overcome the idea of Portuguese decline, thus endowing Portugal with a distinctive cultural aura in the world.

As a literary and cultural critic, António Quadros has been most invested in the spiritual, and even esoteric, dimensions of Portuguese nationhood and national identity, much in the line of Fernando Pessoa (one of his primary objects of study). For Quadros, the nation is a collective and "transtemporal" living being whose teleological project is manifested through its language, culture, and intellectual thought. According to Quadros, a nation cannot achieve its "plenitude of being" without what the ancient Greeks called a *païdeia,* which signifies a collective and synchronous value system, political organization, educational system, or complex of artistic and cultural expressions. Quadros is critical of the contemporary Portuguese *païdeia,* which he believes to be misguided in its pragmatism and utopian commitment to a greater European project. For Quadros, the Portuguese national essence lies in the mythic, symbolic, and prophetic richness found in the era of navigations and "discoveries." The basis for Portugal's future within the messianic or providential myths put forth by Quadros, Pascoaes, or Silva lies essentially in its irretrievable past, or, as Miguel Real has stated, in the "imaginary historical center" within Portuguese messianic thought that could be represented by an endless cycle where the future would be inextricably linked to a lost past (*Portugal: Ser e representação,* 57). Until recent years, this imaginary historical center has remained dominant within the Portuguese intellectual field and has had a profound resonance in the collective unconscious of the nation as well.

However, Boaventura de Sousa Santos argues that mythical or symbolic readings of the nation, such as those put forth by Agostinho da Silva, Teixeira de Pascoaes, and António Quadros, have been at odds with Portuguese socioeconomic, geopolitical, and cultural reality throughout history, and have consequently led to a feeling of chronic malaise on the part of intellectuals with regard to Portugal. José Mattoso, on the other hand, shares Santos's critical stance regarding mythical or essentialistic readings of Portuguese national identity. From a historical standpoint he argues that Portugal was initially a political-administrative entity before it became an "ethnic" or "cultural" entity. What created and sustained Portuguese identity in the Middle Ages was the State (*A identidade nacional,* 83). A sense of Portuguese national identity was the result of concrete historical and political processes; therefore Mattoso believes that the idea of a national "manifest destiny" is highly questionable. Both Boaventura de Sousa Santos and José Mattoso also point to the elitist character of the interpretations of the nation produced by the Portuguese intelligentsia; these interpretations have not been based on "empirical evidence" (i.e., political or socioeconomic facts); moreover, they have had little bearing upon the lives of the vast majority of Portuguese, and ultimately have not translated into concrete efforts to improve Portuguese society.

Santos, for his part, relies on sociological and geopolitical facts as raw material and uses the theoretical insights of various disciplines within the social sciences and humanities as his hermeneutical prism, paying close attention to sociohistorical dynamics that have shaped the

Portuguese national reality and that nation's place within the world system. Santos highlights the salient characteristics of the Portuguese nation-state within the context of globalization. These point to a "weakening" of the nation-state whereby the decolonization in the 1970s represented a process of "deterritorialization" and the entrance into the European Union in the 1980s entailed a process of "reterritorialization." Both processes signified a shifting of national borders, where the latter underscored a relative loss of national sovereignty in exchange for inclusion within a supranational structure. Moreover, both pivotal moments coincided with a heightened globalization of national economic and political affairs throughout the world.

According to Boaventura de Sousa Santos, Portugal is a semiperipheral nation in today's global system (a categorization partly based on Wallerstein's theory of world systems theory).[21] From a developmental standpoint, Portugal is located at an intermediate stage; social variables such as population growth rate, laws and institutions, and consumption patterns are more representative of core nations, while infrastructures, cultural policies, and types of industry are more representative of less-developed nations (Santos, *Pela mão de Alice*, 53). This simultaneity of varying stages of development, according to Santos, is more accurately descriptive of Portugal's material, socioeconomic, cultural, and political fabric as a nation-state. Moreover, Santos advances the metaphor-concept of "border" *(fronteira)* in order to describe not only Portugal's geopolitical location from a regional and global standpoint but also the effects of such location in terms of its cultural "way of being" throughout modern history.[22] More concretely, this ontological "border condition" is exemplified by the fact that Portugal is simultaneously European and "barbarian" (i.e., Prospero and Caliban), as well as colonizer and emigrant. Instead of seeing this hybrid condition as a disadvantage, Santos regards it as one of the Portuguese culture's most fluid and dynamic traits, enabling it to function historically as a bridge between the cultures of its center and the elites of its colonial peripheries. At the same time, according to this view that is reminiscent in some aspects of lusotropicalism, through a mimetic process the hybrid Portuguese colonizer incorporated and assimilated elements of the various cultures with which he came into contact.

Here, in a critically daring move, Santos goes so far as to appropriate Brazilian Oswald de Andrade's concept of "cultural anthropophagy," which Andrade defines as a constitutive cultural strategy of Brazil in terms of its geopolitical location in the world. Through this strategy Andrade affirmed a Brazilian postcolonial identity vis-à-vis metropolitan Europe in the early twentieth century and has had lasting effects that are still seen today, but through Santos's theorization Andrade's concept has undergone a paradoxical process of postcolonial inversion where the former colonizer has become the "cannibal." Here Santos claims for Portugal a late twentieth-century postmodern "border" identity based on a peculiarly hybrid and cannibalistic (former) colonial identity. Interestingly, in a recent interview Santos refined this position by stating that while at an individual level there were numerous cases of Portuguese colonists who in fact absorbed and became absorbed by the culture(s) of the colonized, Portugal—as a whole and as the center of its empire—was not as profoundly influenced by its multicultural peripheries as the other way around.[23] Thus, Santos's productive though polemic critical move "lusotropicalistically" reevaluates and transculturates what can be considered positive with regard to Portugal's colonial past and projects it to a desired (and more truly) multicultural future for Portugal in terms of its national identity, as a result of contemporary immigration from its former colonies. Here we observe a major break with the Portuguese metanarratives of decline or myths of "manifest destiny" described so far that have dominated the intellectual field, as well as an attempt to update defining notions of Portuguese culture.

In fact, Boaventura de Sousa Santos, along with José Mattoso, rejects the idea that Portugal is somehow a privileged nation with a mythical or messianic "manifest destiny" that somehow has not been lived to its fullest potential, or that after being lived briefly in the sixteenth century this destiny has somehow vanished but can one day be retrieved. Both, therefore, distance themselves from the discourses of "decline" and "decadence" that have historically dominated the intellectual exegesis of Portugal as a national reality. Santos, in fact, calls for a (national) "self-critical common sense" with regard to Portugal (*Toward a New Common Sense*, 57), more specifically, a balanced attitude that recognizes the relative strengths and weaknesses of Portugal from a social, political, economic, and cultural standpoint, at the same time acknowledging Portugal's potential as well as its distinctiveness as a nation. This attitude must contend with Portugal's semiperipherality on a global scale, as well as with the increasingly attenuated borders of its national being. National forces are now more than ever relativized by the force of contemporary global dynamics exemplified by the transnationalization of systems of production; the adoption of a single European currency; the increased interdependence of financial markets throughout the world; the massive and multi-directional population flow of tourists, migrants, or refugees; and the development of information and communication systems on a planetary scale. This intensification of global interactions reveals a shifting dialectic of deterritorialization/reterritorialization (54), where even the most powerful states no longer entirely master their own territory in all facets of national life.

We can conclude that Boaventura de Sousa Santos, Eduardo Lourenço, and José Mattoso believe that the metanarrative of the Portuguese nation linked to its maritime-colonial past has now weakened, and that, by virtue of its weakening, its corollary—the metanarrative of decline or the longing for a past that is irretrievable—has exhausted itself. Portugal (or its intellectuals and the nation-family as a whole) must come to terms with a modest yet privileged destiny in the concert of nations. Lourenço believes that now, at the dawn of the twenty-first century, Portugal must design, conceive, and invent a future for itself, without resorting to myths based on former colonial empires or overvalued utopias of European integration (*Nós Como Futuro*, 25). Santos believes that there is yet another important development for Portugal that is representative of what he terms "the paradigmatic transition" to postmodernity, which has been thoroughly discussed in the abundant literature that has theorized the postmodern and the nation for various parts of the world; more concretely, the integrity of the universal subject upon which the national metanarrative depends has been shattered (Pease 3). In fact, what is seen in contemporary Portugal is a surge of micronarratives of the nation, a multiplication of subjectivities that speak for their differing individual, group, or localized identities and interests. This at the same time as Portugal's borders have become relatively porous, and its sovereignty substantially attenuated. So the question remains, Who speaks for Portugal today? (to paraphrase Paulo de Medeiros, "Introdução: Em nome de Portugal," 21). We could say that the Portuguese national metanarrative linked to the sea and its imperial past, though weakened, has not altogether disappeared (witness the Expo 98 extravaganza). The "empire" has not been lost in terms of "memory" or "symbolic space," as Eduardo Lourenço asserts ("Espírito de Timor Invade o Rio," 2). Portuguese national identity has been, and will continue to be, linked to the memory and the symbolic space of empire.

However, for some time now, in the realm of literature—particularly within contemporary fiction and poetry—numerous voices have posited alternative ways of thinking Portuguese identity that are more inclusive of differences of gender, sexuality, and race; that subvert and reconceptualize dominant Portuguese metaphors of "the sea"; or that hypothesize new and different ways of "being" in the world as individuals or as a nation-family. Here I wish to highlight some of the novelists and poets who have most consistently and creatively explored the problematics of Portuguese nationhood and identity in the late twentieth century and the early twenty-first century: António Lobo Antunes, Maria Isabel Barreno, Al Berto, Fiama Hasse Pais Brandão, Maria Velho da Costa, Vergílio Ferreira, Lídia Jorge, Luiza Neto Jorge, Maria Gabriela Llansol, José Cardoso Pires, and José Saramago. In chapter 4 I focus specifically on Portuguese literary discourses, privileging the work of Maria Isabel Barreno, while in chapter 5 and the conclusion I offer comparative readings on the question of postnational utopias in Portuguese and Brazilian literatures, including writers Vergílio Ferreira, Maria Gabriela Llansol, and José Saramago.

Alternative narratives of nationhood are also seen in contemporary Portuguese film, for instance in the work of João Botelho, Pedro Costa, Joaquim Leitão, João César Monteiro, Manoel de Oliveira, and Teresa Villaverde as well as in popular music and modern dance (to name some of the most salient examples). In the realm of Portuguese pop music, there has been a virtual explosion of sounds and aesthetic projects in close dialogue with contemporary musical trends around the world, and many musicians have been creatively reworking Portuguese musical traditions, among them Pedro Abrunhosa, João Afonso, José Afonso (the pioneer), José Mário Branco, Clã, Fausto, Sérgio Godinho, Maria João, Rádio Macau, Madredeus, and Amélia Muge. One of the most fascinating developments in the realm of Portuguese popular music has been the emergence of new fado. Artists such as Mafalda Arnauth, Paulo Bragança, Cristina Branco, Camané, Mísia, Ala dos Namorados, and Dulce Pontes have modernized and revitalized the musical and aesthetic contours of traditional Portuguese fado by blending them with global musical currents such as hip-hop, new age, modern classical music, jazz, trip-hop, and Brazilian- and modern African–inflected pop sounds.[24] What was once utilized as an ideological vehicle to bring about collective acquiescence with regard to the fate of material poverty, emigration, or the political status quo under the patriarchal and authoritarian Salazar regime—here Amália Rodrigues probably became an accomplice in spite of herself—has now become an instrument of irony and subversion of gender roles, or in general of cultural clichés associated with traditional society, as well as a means of paying sincere homage to the richness and depth of Portuguese poetic and musical roots.

All of these projects—whether literary, cinematographic, musical, or choreographic—are vital expressions of new subjectivities and alternative ways of thinking the nation that must also be taken into consideration together with the empirical facts—socioeconomic and geopolitical—central to Boaventura de Sousa Santos's reading of Portugal when reflecting upon the significant shifts in Portuguese national identity that have occurred in the past twenty-five years.

CHAPTER TWO

Brazilian National Identity

Intellectual Debates and Changing Cultural Realities

In a vein similar to that of chapter 1, which focuses on macrological views of Portuguese nationhood and their eventual weakening or relativization in today's cultural landscape, this chapter traces the movement from the emergence of grand narratives of national identity since the 1930s in the Brazilian intellectual field to the upsurge of a multiplicity of smaller narratives of nationhood across various discursive fields, social arenas, and media in contemporary Brazil. Thus, we observe a shift from macrological approaches that have privileged constructs such as "racial democracy," social typologies such as "the cordial man," or geopolitical binaries such as the "national" and "foreign" to micrological perspectives—in some cases, ones developing outside the intellectual field—that account for a fragmented nation where there are multiple and competing versions of nationhood, democracy, and modernization.

Five hundred years after its inception, Brazil is consolidating its position as an important actor on the economic, political, and cultural fronts at the regional and global levels. At the same time, the project of modernity as it impinges upon the construction of Brazilian nationhood has achieved a number of its intended goals, such as industrialization, agricultural self-sufficiency, a sophisticated mass media, one of the world's most dynamic popular culture scenes, and a relative degree of democratization. By the same token, Brazil's modernization reveals significant gaps, contradictions, and disparities at the level of income and land distribution, cultural rights, and environmental protection, to name only a few key examples. Those attempting to define Brazilian national identity must bear in mind this profoundly heterogeneous array of factors.

Brazil, in spite of its racial and cultural heterogeneity as well as territorial vastness, presents itself as a highly unified nation-state. This stable national unity can be attributed to the rigidly centralized colonial administration; the level of economic integration achieved during colonial times, which was further consolidated after independence (Ribeiro, *O povo brasileiro*); and the enduring power of patriarchal family structures (Freyre, *Casa-grande e senzala*), together with a substantial degree of political coercion over time. All these factors combined have aided the widespread dominance of the Portuguese language as another determining factor for Brazilian national cohesion. Brazil is unquestionably one of the world's most racially and ethnically mixed nations, and this basic fact has played a large role in debates around Brazilian national identity, clearly becoming the most celebrated component during the quincentennial and yet the root of much contestation given Brazil's conflictive historical development. Hence, the roots, meanings, and consequences of this reality and its bearing upon the Brazilian nation have long been an object of reflection in literary, historiographical, anthropological, and sociological texts. Thus, a central point within any exegesis of Brazil is that the nation was forged out of a significantly complex and oftentimes painful colonial process, which resulted in an exceedingly rich, novel, and contradictory human reality. The primary ethnic, racial, and cultural matrices of colonial Brazil—Portuguese, African, and Amerindian—eventually absorbed and, by the same token, were transformed by various migratory waves that were encouraged by the "ideology of whitening" that led governments in the late nineteenth century and the early twentieth century to further Europeanize a Brazilian population where the African matrix already figured quite prominently.[1] As a result of this large-scale immigration, a multiplicity of other cultural, racial, and ethnic layers were added to the initial proto-Brazilian matrices: Italians, Spaniards, Germans, eastern Europeans (particularly Jews), Japanese, Arabs (from the former Ottoman Empire), and Chinese—aside from Portuguese, who continued to immigrate en masse to Brazil during this period. Brazil's multicultural character has been a source of tremendous cultural vitality, even as it has been a source of tension given the nation's history of slavery and racism. At the same time, this particular cultural reality, coupled with dramatic socioeconomic contrasts deriving from the fact that the country presents one of the largest pools of natural resources in the world, one of the ten largest economies, and yet one of the most unequal ratios of wealth and land distribution, has led cultural critics to consistently highlight the liminal and contradictory character of the Brazilian nation. Here the cultural and the socioeconomic inevitably impinge upon one another, given that poverty tends to be racially marked (as in the United States and other multiracial societies throughout the Americas, the poor tend to be of African or Amerindian descent in disproportionate numbers). These socioeconomic disparities and racial inequalities were at the heart of the countercelebrations of Brazil's five hundredth anniversary, described earlier, which marred the official festivities in Porto Seguro, Bahia.

Thus, Brazil's "kaleidoscopic" reality in socioeconomic, racial, and cultural terms has led critics to define it as a "hybrid society" long before this term became common in debates around a possible Latin American postmodern condition; as a "space in between" (Santiago, "O entre-lugar do discurso latino-americano"), emphasizing the fact that Brazilian culture (or Latin American culture in general) cannot be defined in terms of "unity" or "purity" because it is neither entirely European nor African nor Amerindian; or as the "borderlands of Western culture" (Hess and DaMatta, *The Brazilian Puzzle*). Silviano Santiago views Brazil as deviating from the Western norm because it has transfigured the European cultural element—and, I must add, the African and Amerindian elements as well ("O entre-lugar do discurso latino-americano," 18). For his part, Roberto DaMatta points out that in terms of language, high culture, and formal institutions, Brazil is clearly a Western nation, but that in terms of popular and material culture, as well as folklore, Western elements have mixed and mingled with those of non-Western cultures (David J. Hess and Roberto DaMatta, eds., *The Brazilian Puzzle*, 2).

Some of the defining notions of Brazilian national identity were substantially developed in the 1930s, when the Brazilian intellectual field was revolutionized by the work of thinkers such as Gilberto Freyre, Sérgio Buarque de Holanda, and Caio Prado, Jr. Building upon and departing from the seminal insights provided by earlier generations of pioneering intellectuals that included figures such as Phillip von Martius, Varnhagen, Capistrano de Abreu, and Paulo Prado, among others,[2] this generation inaugurated new ways of thinking about Brazil by providing innovative interdisciplinary frameworks that reflected changes in the social sciences and the humanities (primarily across the fields of anthropology, sociology, history, and economics) in the first half of the twentieth century.[3] Their projects coincided with the reigning nationalistic political context of Getúlio Vargas in the 1930s, which favored nationally driven intellectual and cultural projects.[4] The work of these thinkers was widely influential throughout most of the twentieth century in terms of intellectual currents focusing on Brazil. They have offered macrological perspectives on the nation that focus on questions such as race and slavery, the colonial economic structure, the management of geographical space and natural resources in the colonial period, and the cultural and sociological roots of "the Brazilian character." All three— Caio Prado, Jr., Sérgio Buarque de Holanda, and Gilberto Freyre—believed that the colonial epoch was a primary point of reference for those who wish to better understand modern Brazil. The works of Freyre and Buarque de Holanda, in particular, have been largely responsible for the intellectual legitimation of and further dissemination of powerful myths about the nation that are still alive today in the collective Brazilian imaginary if we think of notions such as "racial democracy" (in Freyre's case) or the "cordial man" (in the case of Buarque de Holanda). All three critics (as well as most others discussed here) coincided in the belief that from a cultural standpoint, an entirely new and original society was created in the tropics through the colonization of Brazil.[5] They were unanimous in stressing the importance of racial miscegenation in the formation of a (new) Brazilian macroethnicity.[6] Finally, all critics viewed Brazilian colonial society as essentially correlative to a patriarchal and slave-based monocultural economy.[7] However, more contemporary trends in Brazilian historiography call into question monolithic approaches to colonial society that predominated until the late twentieth century and in contrast present more heterogeneous views, for instance, of gender relations, local or regional socioeconomic structures, and cultural manifestations in the formative years of the Brazilian nation.[8]

Gilberto Freyre's intellectual contribution revolutionized debates concerning Brazilian national identity, because it was the first modern study that simultaneously focused on race, slavery, ethnicity, sexuality, gender, and colonialism as they pertain to Brazil.[9] *Casa-grande e senzala* (The masters and the slaves, 1933) constituted a break from the *Indianismo* tradition that was prevalent among Brazilian romantic writers, and later on among modernists, by emphasizing for the first time the fundamental role of the African slave in the formation of Brazilian culture. The Indianism of Brazilian romantics and modernists, however, must be differentiated. For the romantics, the Indian appears as a mythical figure who is most closely associated with the American roots of Brazil (in contrast to the Portuguese or the African). The Indian appears to be imbued with a profoundly epic and lyrical spirit, suggesting that he or she is representative of a "pure essence" of Brazilianness. Furthermore, Amerindian cultures are seen as the source of an ancient and uniquely Brazilian imaginary. Romantics such as José de Alencar have been criticized for (suspiciously) privileging a human and symbolic element of Brazilian culture that is already rather remote from the daily realities of the Brazilian Northeast (where Alencar originated) in the nineteenth century, in contrast to the African slave who was far more intimately associated with Alencar and his contemporaries (Roberto Reis, *The Pearl Necklace: Toward an Archaeology of Brazilian Transition Discourse*). For modernists, on the other hand, the Indian roots of Brazil are less mythified than in nineteenth-century romanticism, though no less problematically incorporated into a larger national literary-aesthetic project. These roots have been systematically studied in terms of their material culture and folk traditions by figures such as Mário de Andrade, and eventually have been incorporated into avant-garde literary production (and, in the case of M. de Andrade, into his ethnomusicological work) as well. The Indian element has been appropriated by the Brazilian literary avant-garde and given a key role in its linguistic and aesthetic revolution. Nevertheless, it has been cannibalistically appropriated—as have been European avant-garde tendencies—to the extent that it has contributed to a hybrid notion of Brazilian nationhood. Modernist or avant-garde texts (in particular, Mario de Andrade's novel *Macunaíma*) stress the idea of a nation that is profoundly hybrid (the result of the mixing and intermingling of multiple cultures), where the European component will no longer dominate, but neither will the indigenous nor the African.

Gilberto Freyre, on the other hand, argued that in spite of the degree of oppression to which African slaves were subjected, their cultural contributions lie at the core of the Brazilian nationality. By the same token, he privileged the role played by the Portuguese in colonial Brazil and portrayed them as "founding fathers" of the "greatest modern civilization of the tropics" (*Casa grande e senzala*, 190). Freyre, in fact, not only viewed the experience of Portuguese colonialism in Brazil as a "historic inevitability," but also deemed slavery a "necessity," given that it was the most efficient system of organizing and managing an otherwise chaotic and dangerous reality (244). On the other hand, the role and contributions of Amerindians to Brazilian culture occupied a relatively marginal space in Freyre's study (this would be radically reversed decades later with the work of anthropologist Darcy Ribeiro).[10] Freyre nevertheless suggested that the contradictions and antagonisms that are constitutive of Brazilian colonial society are somehow "historically resolved" through racial and cultural miscegenation (laying the basis for the concept-myth of "racial democracy," which most critics attribute to Freyre even if he did not explicitly coin the term per se), but here he was thinking primarily of the confluence of the African and European elements, because the Amerindian element progressively vanished from his analysis. As Gilberto Freyre minutely explored the "history of intimacy" within Brazilian slave society, the *casa grande e senzala* (the master's house and slave quarters) were posited as a "primal scene" of Brazilian nationality. Freyre's work, however, has also been strongly criticized for presenting what is viewed as a patriarchal and aristocratic perspective that seems to express nostalgia for the old northeastern society of masters and slaves. Furthermore, his totalizing gesture of having the intimate history of the northeastern slave experience (from the white master's perspective) metonymically stand for the experience of all of Brazil has been widely problematized. Freyre also managed to garner the profound antipathy of the intellectual left, particularly in the 1960s, due to his widely known association with conservative and authoritarian political forces in both Brazil and Portugal at the time. Yet with the increased attention devoted to (post)colonial studies in Brazilian(ist) intellectual quarters in recent years, there has also been a resurgence of interest in the cultural contribution of thinkers such as Gilberto Freyre, as well as Sérgio Buarque de Holanda and Caio Prado, Jr.[11] In a contemporary era that is less polarized ideologically, the intellectual contribution of polemic figures such as Gilberto Freyre is now being reassessed in a different light by scholars such as Eduardo Portella, Evaldo Cabral de Mello, Enrique Larreta (who is cowriting Freyre's first biography), Elide Rugai Bastos, Hermano Vianna, and Joshua Lund, among others.[12] Most critics converge in the notion that Freyre opened the path for new readings of Brazil that are more heterogeneous and that posit difference as a constitutive aspect of identity (Portella, "Gilberto Freyre, além do apenas moderno"),[13] thus laying the ideological basis (with all of its contradictions and ambivalences) for a multicultural reading of Brazilian national identity that has now more than ever been espoused by Brazilian society, as the celebrations surrounding the quincentennial attest. This multicultural reading regards Portugal as a key contributor alongside African, Amerindian, and other European and Asian contributors, who as a whole have forged Brazilian national identity over five hundred years. Clearly Portugal's contribution is no longer seen as more important than that of African and Amerindian cultures for the emergence and development of the nation.

Sérgio Buarque de Holanda, for his part, analyzed the sociopolitical and economic basis of colonial Brazil in order to understand how it shaped Brazilian society until the twentieth century in his seminal work *Raízes do Brasil* (Roots of Brazil, 1936).[14] Buarque de Hollanda posited a number of social typologies in terms of the human element that colonized Brazil, with the intent of explaining the cultural underpinnings of Brazil's sociopolitical and economic development. In his argument, the Portuguese constitute the cultural matrix of the Brazilian nationality, yet he pointed out how the Portuguese became progressively influenced by their interaction and intermixing with the Amerindian and African populations to ultimately form the cultural core of colonial Brazil. Buarque de Holanda—as Candido points out in his introductory essay— stressed the gradual dilution of the colonial (and mostly rural) Iberian roots of the Brazilian nationality as the country embarked, particularly in the twentieth century, on its course to modernization, and as it transformed itself into a more urban and cosmopolitan society.

Sérgio Buarque de Holanda argued that there are key character traits as well as institutions that dominated Brazilian colonial life that will continue and thrive long past independence and that will mark modern Brazilian society—for example, the importance of the cult of personality and of obedience to authority, which according to Buarque, have been inherited from Iberian cultures. The patriarchal basis of family life and the maintenance of a large property- and slave-based society (the latter of which lasted until 1888) will have lasting consequences in terms of political practices, race and gender relations, and land distribution, which still haunt Brazilian culture. Buarque de Holanda went on to argue that Brazil found elements of itself at odds with one another in the second half of the nineteenth century (during the Second Empire) in its quest for political modernization. More concretely, the attempt at incorporating liberal bourgeois ideals into Brazilian culture was incompatible with a slave-owning society. This particular aspect of Sérgio Buarque's analysis was the forerunner to Roberto Schwarz's concept of "misplaced ideas."[15] Still, Buarque maintained that in post-slavery Brazil liberal democratic ideals continue to be at odds with the actual socioeconomic and cultural realities of contemporary Brazilian society, given the levels of poverty and underdevelopment that are still prevalent.

Buarque de Holanda's best known and polemic cultural notion is that of "the cordial man." This notion figured prominently in his typology of a Brazilian national character. It referred to a heightened degree of hospitality and generosity among Brazilian people that, according to this critic, is still rooted in the experience of the landed patriarchal society. Cordiality is indicative of a spontaneous, informal, nonrational and nonritualistic individual/collective existence. The individual lives for the other. Yet this cultural characteristic, according to Richard M. Morse, does not necessarily translate into social solidarity beyond the individual's immediate circle ("Balancing Myth and Evidence: Freyre and Sérgio Buarque," 54). In fact, it works against the possibility of establishing a normative democratic framework. Buarque de Holanda believed this was one of the major political challenges in Brazil's path toward democratization. Anthropologist Roberto DaMatta helps clarify the notion of the "cordial man" when he contrasts it to the authoritarian ritual that is enacted by the utterance "Do you know to whom you're speaking?" (*Você sabe com quem está falando?*).[16] This ritual underscores the Brazilian dilemma between hierarchical, authoritarian, and at times violent traits present within the culture, and the desire for a harmonious and nonconflictive society expressed in the notion of cordiality.

A radically different approach to that of Gilberto Freyre and Sérgio Buarque de Holanda was presented by Caio Prado, Jr. His Marxist-inspired *Formação do Brasil contemporâneo* (The colonial background of modern Brazil, 1942) deeemphasized the racial, ethnic, cultural, and sociological considerations so prominent in the work of Freyre and Buarque de Holanda. In his pioneering work Prado meticulously studied the economic base or infrastructure of colonial Brazil, which he characterized as a "vast commercial enterprise" that was dependent upon large property ownership, slave labor, and single-product exports. Prado's work greatly influenced Brazilian intellectuals, especially in the 1960s due to his more detached and nonsentimental approach to colonialism. The legacy of his innovative analysis of Brazil's colonial economic base is palpable in Florestan Fernandes's study of race and class in Brazilian society, while the geopolitical dimension of his work has clearly informed dependency theory.

The Brazilian intellectual debates around the dialectic between the national and the foreign have their roots in the economically oriented work of Caio Prado, Jr. This dialectic has been a primary concern in Brazilian literature, especially modernist literature. This concern had been present in Brazilian literature even prior to Prado's work, though his contribution was to add an economically informed basis to the discussion. Geopolitical dynamics and their cultural repercussions have also been a central concern to literary and cultural critics, particularly in the work of Antonio Candido, Roberto Schwarz, and Silviano Santiago.[17] Antonio Candido, for example, has underlined the dominance of the dialectic between the local and the cosmopolitan in Brazilian cultural life in his *Literatura e sociedade* (Literature and society, 129). Candido's argument has two interconnected and fundamental propositions that are cultural and socioeconomic in nature. In both cases there is an underlying geopolitical dimension. More specifically, the anxiety deriving from the local/cosmopolitan dialectic among Brazilian intellectuals is a result of the experience of colonialism. Interestingly, the anxiety suffered by nineteenth-century Brazilian intellectuals regarding the dependent, imitative, or subordinate aspects of their culture in relationship to Portugal or France was similarly displayed by the Portuguese intellectuals of the *Geração de 70*, in an altogether different political configuration, with regard to central and northern Europe. The two cases are, nevertheless, closely interrelated, as they reflect a generalized economic, geopolitical, and cultural peripherality of the Portuguese-speaking world that is still felt in today's globalized environment albeit in an attenuated and rarified fashion.

The unequal relationship of dominance/subordination to which a colony is subjected undoubtedly has lasting sequels after independence, producing a sense of national anxiety. This dynamic is manifested in the realm of cultural production as well as within the economic sphere. The two impinge upon each other, creating a relationship of dependency of the former colony (Brazil) with regard to the former colonizer (Portugal) and, by extension, to European core countries, namely France (culturally) and England (economically). Brazil, and Latin America in general, suffers the added particularity of having been colonized by nations that became peripheral and dependent in relationship to core central and northern European countries. Furthermore, Candido argued that Brazil's quest for cultural (specifically, literary) self-affirmation has had two phases, the romantic and the modernist. The former attempted to overcome Portuguese influence, and the latter achieves a linguistic/literary rupture vis-à-vis Portugal. Heloísa Buarque de Holanda, in fact, argues that the modernist moment marked Brazil's cultural independence from Portugal (and, we could say, from Europe in general). Nevertheless, there are economic and geopolitical questions that remained unresolved throughout the twentieth century that are related to Brazil's economic underdevelopment. Among the Brazilian intelligentsia, there will be a shift from vivid concern regarding cultural dependency to concerns related to economic underdevelopment and its flip side, economic dependency. Candido pointed out that in the 1950s there was a change among intellectuals, from awareness of Brazil's great potential as a nation to an acute perception of its underdevelopment, poverty, and atrophy. Candido offered no particular solution to these major socioeconomic problems (this dilemma would later be taken up and further developed by Candido's disciple, Roberto Schwarz), but he nevertheless problematized the role of intellectuals and their degree of impact on the socioeconomic dilemmas facing the nation-state. One of Candido's key contributions has been to directly link literary criticism to social concerns.

Key questions posited by Antonio Candido are related to the continued relevance or lack of relevance of the dialectic between the local and the universal or between the national and the global. These are questions that Silviano Santiago and Roberto Schwarz have nuanced and updated through differing ideological lenses, offering insightful views in contemporary debates around national identity, globalization, postcolonialism, and postmodernism as they pertain to Brazil or Latin America.[18] According to Candido, Latin American intellectuals should recognize the "placental link" that unites them to Europe and accept the fact that the originality of Latin American cultural production is a rather recent phenomenon (see Becker's translation of his seminal work, *On Literature and Society*, p. 130). Antonio Candido has considered Brazil, or

Latin America as a whole, part of a broader cultural world where the products of their cultures would function as variants. Foreign cultural influences can be (and have been) assimilated creatively. Ultimately, Candido posited a dependency within independence. A question that remains, to which neither Candido, Santiago, nor Schwarz has offered any clear answers, given the timing of the essays under discussion here, is whether the notion of "dependency" is still relevant in the era of postmodern globalization. I shall return to this question shortly.

Although sharply aware of the economic and geopolitical dimensions underlying the dialectic of domination/subordination within the debate around Brazilian national identity, Silviano Santiago has been more interested in exploring its ideological and discursive implications.[19] Relying on French poststructuralist thought (e.g., that of Foucault and Derrida)— an ideological strategy of which Santiago himself is keenly aware—he deconstructs the hierarchy inherent in the binaries copy/original and cultural inferiority/superiority. These binaries have historically framed discussions about Brazilian (or Latin American) cultural production and its relationship to Europe (either the peripheral mother countries or core central or northern European countries). The concept of "cultural influence" is also suggested by this hierarchical framework. In essence, it presupposes for European culture an original and essential basis that is "pure" versus the derivative, imitative, and "impure" cultures (or, for that matter, races) of Latin America. Silviano Santiago argues that through the dynamic of *mestiçagem* (or miscegenation), notions of racial, ethnic, and cultural "purity" or "unity" have been systematically destroyed; therefore, the framework of the discussion about national identities in Latin America must be completely rethought. Invoking the quintessential Brazilian cultural metaphor of "anthropophagy" or "cannibalism," which had been developed earlier in the century in Oswald de Andrade's "Manifesto Antropófago" (Cannibalist manifesto, 1928),[20] Santiago adds that the "foreign cultural element" has long been appropriated, translated and transfigured by the "artistic hand" or intellectual mind of Latin Americans (23), and that this was the case even during the primordial moments of contact between Europeans and Amerindians in the sixteenth century. According to this argument, far from inadequately imitating European cultural gestures and practices, the Amerindians were transforming and adapting them to their own cultural frames of reference. Hence, from a cultural standpoint, Latin America as a whole occupies a "space in between," and this liminal or hybrid location, which supersedes highly problematic notions of cultural "purity" or "unity," is one of its primary contributions to the world. (This argument is fully shared by Roberto Schwarz and Darcy Ribeiro, in spite of their ideological or methodological differences.) Furthermore, this position is echoed by other Latin Americanist critics who have theorized the postmodern, although focusing primarily on the cultural realities of Spanish-speaking Latin America: Néstor García Canclini, Nelly Richard, Bernardo Subercaseaux, and George Yúdice.

Roberto Schwarz, for his part, displays cultural and geopolitical preoccupations similar to those of Silviano Santiago, but follows the ideological and methodological path laid out by Antonio Candido (see Schwarz's *Misplaced Ideas: Essays on Brazilian Culture*). In essence, Schwarz articulates a class-conscious reading of national identity that was already implicit in Antonio Candido's work. He is less interested in discursive formations and more keen on identifying the class dynamics that underlie any discussion of the supposedly artificial, inauthentic, or imitative character of Brazilian (or Latin American) cultural life. Schwarz distances himself from abstract philosophical critiques of nationhood or national identity (such as Santiago's) that deemphasize historical and socioeconomic factors. The "real" causes of Latin America's cultural peripherality, according to Schwarz, lie in its chronic socioeconomic inequalities. The painfulness of an imitative culture is produced by the socioeconomic structure of the nation-state, which is, by the same token, located in a hierarchical (and neocolonial) world system. Schwarz believes that the debate around whether the culture of Brazil or Latin America is a "copy" or an "original" has been erroneously posited. It has been essentially an intellectual debate engaged in by elites that primarily affects the elites. In spite of being an elite problem, the question of imitation, says Schwarz, is not a false problem; however, it must be treated at an aesthetic as well as at a political level. Brazil's socioeconomic backwardness cannot be seen in isolation from the progress of advanced countries. On the cultural front, Brazil has dynamic elements that display originality as well as a lack of originality.

As different as their ideological proclivities and methodological frameworks may be, Schwarz and Santiago focus mostly on similar cultural problematics and reach conclusions that are not far apart. Despite his critique of the adoption of foreign conceptual systems to analyze

Brazilian national reality, Schwarz's Marxist conceptual framework must not be less subject to this same critique than Santiago's poststructuralist framework. On the other hand, Schwarz's class-conscious reading of the cultural dialectic between the national and the foreign is indeed important, but it does not solve the dialectic itself. It analyzes the nature of this dialectic, pointing to a relationship of cause and effect that impacts Brazilian cultural production, between an internal socioeconomic dynamic within Brazil and an international geopolitical and economic context that has now become even more entrenched with the advent of postmodern globalization more than a decade after Schwarz's essay "Nationalism by Elimination" was first published.[21] This diagnosis further develops Antonio Candido's arguments on cultural dependency at the same time as it covers similar territory to that covered by Silviano Santiago in his own reading of cultural dependency. Santiago is interested in mapping the transmission of ideas from a European cultural core to a Latin American cultural periphery and the ways in which these ideas have been successfully appropriated and assimilated by Latin American intellectuals themselves (and his essay "O entre-lugar do discurso latino-americano" is in fact an actual example of the cultural process he describes). Schwarz, on the other hand, is interested in specifying the socioeconomic context in which Brazilian (or Latin American) intellectuals are operating and the place they occupy within this socioeconomic context, as well as within the movement of ideas and cultural trends between cores and peripheries.[22] The works of Silviano Santiago and Roberto Schwarz are remarkable examples of how (academic) Marxism and poststructuralism have been incorporated and assimilated into the Brazilian intellectual field in order to successfully diagnose a wide spectrum of nationally specific cultural problems. In spite of the sociopolitical awareness displayed in both schools of thought (Schwarz's position vis-à-vis poststructuralism notwithstanding), they do not solve the *aporia* raised by the constitutive gap between the work of intellectuals (and their association to elite classes and institutions) and that of the social field.

We may summarize the main coordinates of our discussion on Brazilian national identity thus far as follows: the Brazilian colonial experience is indispensable as a primary frame of reference in order to understand the core racial, ethnic, and cultural configuration of the Brazilian nation; authoritarian and nonegalitarian strands present in Brazilian cultural, sociopolitical, and economic practices and structures today are *in part* remnants of the experience of colonialism; Brazil's (neo)colonial condition of (semi)peripherality in the world system has had a decisive impact on its cultural production and the definitions of Brazilian national identity put forth by intellectuals as well as artists. This geopolitical reality lies at the basis of the dialectic between the national and the foreign that has preoccupied intellectuals throughout the history of modern Brazil.

There are other related debates that have captivated Brazilian(ist) intellectual thought since the 1960s: debates regarding the elite status of the Brazilian intelligentsia, its relationship to the state, and the definitions of nationhood put forth by the state, oftentimes in synchronicity with the intelligentsia. The latter debate points to the close connection that existed between Brazilian intellectuals and the power of the state, particularly under the populist and nationalistic regime of Getúlio Vargas between 1930 and 1945. In this particularly rich era in terms of cultural production, the nation became identified with the state and its elites, including its intellectual elites (Reis, *Pearl Necklace;* Randal Johnson, "The Dynamics of the Brazilian Literary Field"). Other critics, such as Marilena Chaui, add that the national question has been utilized by the Brazilian state, in varying historical moments and under differing ideological guises, as a strategy to build social cohesion in a nation where there are dramatic socioeconomic differences (*Seminário,* 20). Moreover, the national question in Brazil has also been closely linked to its process of modernization from 1930 until the last right-wing dictatorship, between 1964 and 1984. More specifically, it can be argued that through most of the twentieth century in Brazil—in spite of the oscillations between military dictatorships and democratic regimes—there was a lasting conflation between the project of nationhood, the state, and modernization (analogous to what we have seen in Portugal between nation and empire during the First Republic and the Salazar era).

In Brazil, modernization has become inseparable from the project of the nation, particularly since 1930. One of the key facts underlying this phenomenon is that both democratic and nondemocratic regimes have acted as modernizing agents and have embraced modernization as a top national priority. Before 1930, the agricultural sector (most specifically, the coffee industry) was the motor for industrialization and, concomitantly, urbanization. During the Vargas era, industrialization significantly accelerated with the establishment of the policy of import substitution. This led to greater economic diversification and self-sufficiency with regard to basic consumer goods. After the 1950s, the process of modernization vastly intensified with the rise of the automobile industry. The last major industrialization phase took place under the military dictatorship of the 1960s and 1970s, and it was largely financed by multinational capital. In this period, Brazil experienced a major economic boom in the industrial, commercial, and financial sectors. Thus, Brazil rapidly grew into one of the world's largest economies, radically changing its geoeconomic and sociocultural profiles.

Toward the end of the military dictatorship that lasted from 1964 to 1984, there was a gradual reestablishment of democratic institutions and practices in Brazil. The political transition toward a civilian regime and its progressive consolidation brought about significantly greater collective participation in the political process (one of its crowning examples would be the mass mobilization that led to the impeachment of former president Fernando Collor de Mello in 1992). The transition period between 1978 and 1984 (known in Portuguese as *abertura*, or opening) contributed to the significant growth of new social movements: movements on behalf of women, landless peasants, Afro-Brazilians, gays and lesbians, the environment, Brazilian Indians, street children, and so on. It is believed that the largest and most highly organized social movements in contemporary Latin America are in Brazil. In fact, the movement of landless peasants, or MST (Movimento dos Trabalhadores Rurais Sem Terra), is considered the most politically effective grassroots movement in Latin America.[23] The rise of social movements in Brazil has come in response to the lingering effects of patriarchalism, unfair land distribution, racism, violence, homophobia, and classism, among other socioeconomic ills. This important development in the 1980s and 1990s signals, on the one hand, that Brazilian nationhood is no longer exclusively defined by the state and, on the other hand, that it is the result of an unfinished and vastly unequal project of modernization. The significant flaws underlying the conflation of Brazilian nationhood with modernization have been profoundly problematized by the new social movements in the last two decades, but also by Brazilian film, literature, theater, and popular music prior to, but especially since, the 1960s, when we consider Cinema Novo and Tropicalism (to name the most outstanding cultural developments of that era).

In spite of boasting an economic output and an agroindustrial base comparable to or even larger than those of the core countries of Europe, North America, or Asia; one of the largest middle classes in the "Third World"; or one of the richest reserves of natural resources, Brazil still has one of the most unfair ratios of income distribution in the world. In fact, the Inter-American Development Bank's annual report on economic and social progress in Latin America for 1998 stressed the enormous income gaps throughout the region. Brazil and Guatemala present the greatest socioeconomic inequalities; there the wealthiest 10 percent absorb 50 percent of the national income and the poorest 50 percent absorb approximately 10 percent of this income. According to this report, the structural transformations of the 1990s, such as the end of inflation, an increase in productivity, and the opening of trade and financial markets, succeeded in redistributing income and wealth, but did not end its unfair concentration (Flávia Sekles, "Distribuição de renda piora").

In spite of its significant socioeconomic gaps, at the dawn of the twenty-first century Brazil has affirmed itself as a vast market of cultural goods, to the point where the nation is now identified with the notion of market (Renato Ortiz, *A moderna tradição brasileira,* 165). Brazil has become a net exporter of popular and media culture (primarily popular music and television). In fact, Renato Ortiz argues that Brazil's modernization has entailed a shift from defending the "national-popular" to exporting the "international-popular" (205). Today Brazil constitutes one of the world's largest advertising and mass-media markets, both as producer and as consumer (199). No longer is Brazil a peripheral nation in terms of cultural industries. The dialectic of the foreign and the national as traditionally conceived in the realm of culture no longer holds, especially if we bear in mind, for instance, the fact that most music consumed in Brazil today is domestic.

One of the most striking contemporary inversions of the center-periphery equation in the cultural sphere—as well as a postcolonial irony—is exemplified by the large presence and impact of Brazilian popular and media culture in Portugal (as well as in Lusophone African countries). Brazil maintains a presence on a daily basis in contemporary Portuguese life in the form of *telenovelas* (soap operas) and other TV programs, as well as Brazilian popular music (MPB); on the contrary, Portuguese popular culture is practically absent from Brazilian contemporary life. More than a dozen Brazilian *telenovelas* are broadcast each day on Portuguese television, alongside numerous other programs produced in Brazil. Following the advent of cable and satellite TV, there are now Brazilian channels, dramatically increasing the daily exposure of Portuguese audiences to Brazilian culture and Brazilian dialects of Portuguese. The accentuated cultural presence of Brazil has become an everyday reality in Portugal since the April Revolution of 1974 and has exerted a considerable amount of influence from a cultural and linguistic standpoint. One can draw parallels with the postcolonial irony of the United States' surpassing its former colonizer in terms of world economic, political, cultural, and linguistic dominance. Yet it could be argued that Great Britain, along with other English-speaking nations, benefits from the cultural hegemony of the United States and the preponderance of the English language in the world today in the realms of multinational pop music, film, the tourist industry, and information technology, to say nothing of the widespread use of English in the business world. In contrast, neither Brazil nor Portugal exerts any degree of cultural hegemony outside of their linguistic sphere, with the possible exception of Brazilian popular music. One cannot but agree with Brazilian pop star and intellectual Caetano Veloso when he suggests that if the Portuguese language is known at all around the world today (despite being among the ten most widely spoken languages) it is thanks to the force, richness, and vitality of Brazilian popular music (*Verdade tropical*, 17).

It is clear that the metanarratives of nationhood developed in the earlier part of the last century have weakened or been profoundly challenged, at the same time as a multiplicity of micronarratives of the nation have proliferated in the political arena (outside of the purview of the state or in direct opposition to it), as well as in the cultural realm (in either its popular or its more elite manifestations). The metanarratives of nationhood developed by intellectuals such as Gilberto Freyre, Sérgio Buarque de Holanda, and Caio Prado, Jr., were revolutionary for their time, at the same time providing productive conceptual frameworks through which to reflect upon questions of Brazilian national identity. However, the concept of "racial democracy," if not altogether discredited, has been problematized as disingenuously utopian and as a highly inaccurate account of the realities of race and ethnicity in Brazil, while the notion of the "cordial man" as a sociological or even a psychological type has been deemed largely inadequate to describe cultural nuances as well as internal differences in Brazilian society. Economicist models, on the other hand, even as they correctly privilege readings of class structure and world geopolitical hierarchies in interpreting Brazilian reality, do not take culture sufficiently into account.

Both Brazil and Portugal—though carefully guarding their differences—can be characterized today as semiperipheral nations or societies of intermediate development, that is, regions or nations that mix both core and peripheral forms of organization (C. Chase-Dunn and T. D. Hall, "Comparing World Systems: Concepts and Working Hypotheses," 865–66) and levels of development, where indicators such as population growth rate, collective infrastructures, consumption practices, industrial capacity, social stratification, and income distribution levels—to name a few key indicators—present a highly uneven scenario. By the same token, in terms of the size and the production levels of its mass media and popular music industries, as well as its export capacity in those areas, Brazil's position is more like that of a core nation. In view of contemporary Brazilian circumstances illustrated here, it is clear that "dependency" as an absolute hermeneutical concept pertaining to Brazil must be rethought. Even if globalization does not necessarily entail an equal flow of or access to cultural and other products from north to south and vice versa, Brazil plays a significant role from a cultural, economic, financial, and political standpoint in the contemporary globalized environment. The dialectic between the "national" and the "foreign" that has haunted intellectuals throughout the history of modern Brazil has also been questioned and reformulated by cultural currents such as Cinema Novo or the Tropicalism movement of the 1960s, whereby in a pragmatic and cosmopolitan gesture—though never losing sight of Brazilian local, regional, or national specificities and much in the vein of their "cannibalistic" Modernist forebears—contemporary creators and performers from the realms of popular music, film, and the arts have successfully absorbed and transformed international cultural currents and expressions, adapting them to Brazilian circumstances. The post-modern concepts of "transculturation" and "cultural reconversion" put forth by critics such as Néstor García Canclini to describe Latin American or, in this case, Brazilian cultural production are most adequate, because they suggest a more dynamic as well as pragmatic positioning on the part of Brazil vis-à-vis the historical dialectic of "national" and "foreign" than the concept of "dependency" would allow.

At the dawn of the twenty-first century and as it has celebrated its five hundred years of existence, Brazil has become an important global player. Its increased economic and political importance on the American continent, and beyond, has provided Brazil with an active role as a power broker. There have been repeated calls for Brazil to become a permanent member of the United Nations Security Council, alongside Nigeria and India. With the largest economy in Latin America, Brazil plays a pivotal role in Mercosul/Mercosur (which also comprises Argentina, Paraguay, and Uruguay), and it will certainly be one of the key players in a future Free Trade Zone of the Americas. Nevertheless, in spite of being at the center of one of the current free trade zones of the Americas, Brazil remains on the periphery of the major contemporary world centers of economic and political power (i.e., North America, the European Union, and Japan). Following the rise of financial markets in the late 1990s as a major economic force with significant political ramifications for nations across the globe, Brazil finds itself in a powerful intermediary, yet precarious, position as guarantor of financial stability for Latin America. At the same time, it remains economically vulnerable to the irrational fluctuations of the financial markets and dependent upon world financial institutions such as the International Monetary Fund.

Chapters 3 and 4 will highlight the contributions of Brazilian gay male writers and contemporary Portuguese women writers in redefining the parameters, respectively, of Brazilian and Portuguese nationhood in the realms of the political and the symbolic. These writers offer alternative perspectives to those advanced by the intellectuals studied in chapters 1 and 2, because they include in their writings key aspects of human subjectivity, such as sexuality and gender, that have been ignored or occluded by most of the thinkers introduced in the previous chapters in their macroanalysis of the nation. Through their attention to sexuality or gender concerns as they impinge upon individual and collective identities, gay writers and women writers question the universality of the construct of "the nation" at the same time as they posit alternative modes of collective solidarity or affectional attachment between members of national and globalized communities, even questioning and ultimately surpassing any sense of fixity that may be associated with the identity constructs of "gays" or "women."

CHAPTER THREE

Subjectivities and Homoerotic Desire in Contemporary Brazilian Fiction

The Nation of Caio Fernando Abreu

The late twentieth century was an era of tremendous upheaval for Brazil: a twenty-year dictatorship, a slow and lengthy transition toward democracy, periods of euphoria and despair, many unfulfilled promises but also remarkable achievements, painful betrayals and profound hope. This dramatic transition process has been amply recorded through a variety of cultural and artistic expressions such as cinema, popular music, and literature, to name some of the most outstanding. From the visceral and poetic films of Walter Salles, Sérgio Bianchi, and Sandra Werneck to the dazzling art-pop music and lyrics of Caetano Veloso, Gilberto Gil, Chico Buarque, Adriana Calcanhotto, Marisa Monte, Lenine, Zeca Baleiro, and Chico César to the remarkable fiction and poetry of Rubem Fonseca, Lygia Fagundes Telles, João Ubaldo Ribeiro, Nélida Piñon, Caio Fernando Abreu, Sérgio Sant'Anna, João Gilberto Noll, Sônia Coutinho, Arnaldo Antunes, and Waly Salomão, among many others, the changing Brazilian nation has been the object of critically passionate reflection and representation. While chapter 2 ("Brazilian National Identity: Intellectual Debates and Changing Cultural Realities") focused primarily on grand narratives of Brazilian nationhood as proposed by modern canonical intellectual thought, pointing to their relativization in a highly diversified contemporary cultural landscape, this chapter directs the reader's attention specifically toward the micronarratives of the nation put forth by contemporary Brazilian fiction, most particularly through the work of Caio Fernando Abreu, where there is a dynamic interaction between personal, national, and global concerns.

The literature of Caio Fernando Abreu speaks in the tones of an anguished subjectivity at the edge of life, painfully struggling to achieve a sense of inner balance at a time of faded individual and collective hopes. In Abreu's writing there is a sense of loss and profound solitude, as well as heightened skepticism about sexual and political utopias that nurtured the Brazilian (and, in general, Western) imaginary throughout the 1960s and 1970s. Abreu's narratives also speak powerfully of defiant yet fragile subjectivities on the margins of a semiperipheral nation at its own historical and civilizational crossroads, striving to become in a globalized environment where hardly any nation's destiny is within its own hands.

There is probably no other writer (male or female, poet or novelist) in either Brazil or Portugal who has focused on the confluence of nationhood, (homo)sexuality, and AIDS with the depth, richness, sensibility, and sophistication of Caio Fernando Abreu. He is considered by many critics (academic and nonacademic alike) one of the most important Brazilian writers of the last twenty years. Between the 1970s and 1996 (the year of his death) Abreu was a prolific author, having published approximately fifteen works, including short story collections, chronicles, plays, and novels.[1] Caio Fernando Abreu died of AIDS in February of 1996 in Porto Alegre, in his native state of Rio Grande do Sul.[2] He was also a well-known journalist for *Estado de São Paulo* and *Zero Hora*, among other print media, and some critics consider his chronicles written for *Estado* representative of the zeitgeist of Brazilian society in the 1980s and early 1990s. Abreu was one of the first Brazilian writers to thematize AIDS and was one of the most outspoken cultural figures with the disease. In spite of his critical stance with regard to monolithic categories such as "gay," "bisexual," or "heterosexual"; his antagonism toward the idea of being ghettoized as a "gay writer"; and his much stronger preference for a notion of fluid, plural, and interchangeable sexualities, Caio Fernando Abreu's cultural and political contributions are inevitably of great interest to queer communities inside and outside of Brazil. At the same time, the author and journalist brought out into the open, as few public figures have done in Brazil until recently, the issue of citizenship and human rights for nonheterosexuals.[3]

Since the mid-1970s and early 1980s, there has been in Brazil a sizable group of male prose writers who have dealt overtly with themes around homosexuality and bisexuality:[4] Caio Fernando Abreu, João Silvério

Trevisan, Silviano Santiago, Bernardo Carvalho, João Gilberto Noll, Herbert Daniel, and poet Valdo Motta, as well as Gasparino Damata, Darcy Penteado, Aguinaldo Silva, and Glauco Mattoso.[5] Of this group, Caio Fernando Abreu, João Gilberto Noll, and Silviano Santiago stand out as the better-known figures (Santiago is considered one of the most prominent contemporary intellectual figures of Brazil).[6] It is important to point out that the overt thematization of alternative sexualities in Brazilian literature is concurrent with the historical period known as the *abertura*, or opening (which lasted from the late 1970s until the early 1980s), when the military regime of the time, which lasted twenty years, gradually lifted its censorship of cultural production and political expression.

Caio Fernando Abreu belonged to the generation that believed or engaged in various utopian causes such as Marxist revolution, sexual liberation, and drug experimentation, which in many ways profoundly changed the prevalent values in contemporary culture but have nevertheless been severely questioned after major shifts in the global and national arenas: on the one hand, the exhaustion of the 1960s counter-culture, which, in the case of Brazil, had the particular distinction of being repressed by the authoritarian and ultra-nationalistic regime of the late 1960s and early 1970s[7] and, on the other hand, by the very contemporary and ubiquitous threat of AIDS, which has dramatically altered the world's relationship to sex for many years to come.[8] The result has been a generalized sense of loss, disorientation, and pessimism, acutely perceived by the author, which is the product not only of the contemporary global landscape, but also of a national historical trajectory that has seen many years of authoritarian rule (1964–1984), with all of its well-known political and economic consequences, and an ensuing decade of great insecurity and instability, wrought with frustrated collective dreams, persistently wide socioeconomic inequities, and unlikely saviors. This particular dynamic was vividly illustrated by the untimely death in 1985 of charismatic Tancredo Neves, the first democratically elected president after the dictatorship; years of economic stagnation, hyperinflation, and crippling foreign debt; the meteoric rise and fall of Fernando Collor de Mello between 1989 and 1992, when he was facing criminal prosecution on corruption charges[9]; impending ecological disaster in the Amazon (a problem that is not only Brazilian); a lingeringly wide socioeconomic gap between haves and have-nots; and a dramatic increase in urban violence, which is a direct consequence of the great social inequality. All of these elements, which have dominated the Brazilian landscape in past years (and continue to do so in varying degrees today), constitute the sociopolitical and cultural background of the fiction of Caio Fernando Abreu.

Abreu's fictional production establishes a rich and fluid dialogue with literature, music, and film from both Brazil and around the world. Abreu creates a complex intertextual web in which musical lyrics, rhythm, and melody, as well as scenes from films, inform fictional plots while poetry frames or occupies a prominent place within the geography of a given fictional text. Abreu's writings assume a culturally hybrid location for Brazil in today's globalized environment. The cultural referents of the Brazilian nation (MPB, Afro-Brazilian religion, and Brazilian literature, among others) interact with a multiplicity of referents from the outside (Hollywood, Portuguese and French literatures, Anglo-American as well as Hispanic literatures, and various musical styles, to cite just a few examples) through a dynamically synchronic process of cohabitation and appropriation where the cultural borders between what is considered "foreign" and what is considered "native" collapse. Various Latin American critics favor the notion of "appropriation"—among them, Chilean Bernardo Subercaseaux, who is quoted at length in George Yúdice's piece "Postmodernity and Transnational Capitalism" (8). Proponents of this model desire to go beyond Manichaean visions of native versus foreign, rejecting any notion of a "pure, uncontaminated" Latin American culture or the myths of cultural pluralism or essentialism with regard to Latin American identity. Appropriation entails an identity that is rather provisional, fluid, always in the process of becoming. In Caio Fernando Abreu's writings, Brazilian cultural identity is anything but a fixed, essential entity, unsullied by foreign contamination. The author unabashedly assumes for Brazil a position of liminality as it "negotiates its cultural capital" (Yúdice, "Postmodernity and Transnational Capitalism in Latin America," 18) with(in) today's globalized system.

Furthermore, Abreu was an integral part of a specifically "gay" or "queer" global culture that is reflected in the literature, film, and music of various parts of Europe, Latin America, and especially North America, which today constitute common points of reference for "gay" or "queer" subjects transnationally. The liminal position that Abreu claimed for Brazil within the spectrum of nations of contemporary globalized culture is analogous to the liminal position that the individual subject (i.e., the author or his various individual narrators) occupies[10] as part of an international "gay" culture that cuts across national borders through a variety of mass-media and massive population movements via tourism and immigration and that has been informing and transforming, at an accelerated pace, identity categories and lifestyles, particularly among the middle and upper classes. This transnational "gay" or "queer" culture is yet another alternative imaginary "landscape" comprising the contemporary global configuration; it cuts across Arjun Appadurai's five dimensions of disjunctive "cultural flows" (ethnoscapes, mediascapes, technoscapes, finanscapes, and ideoscapes),[11] forming its own fluid and dynamic network, or "queerscape."

Caio Fernando Abreu's introspective and profoundly lyrical prose is certainly heir to Clarice Lispector's resplendent writing. The attention paid to epiphanic moments of coming to awareness of being in the world reveals an important kinship between the two authors. There is a clear philosophical dimension to Abreu's work, where existential concerns occupy a prominent space alongside the author's reflections on sexuality (here, though, Abreu most remarkably departs from Lispector's primary concerns). In fact, there are examples within Abreu's fiction where frustrated erotic desire or the elusive emotional fulfillment achieved through the other appear as metaphoric expressions of a profound existential anguish. Furthermore, there is often an implicit or explicit reflection on the human condition in the late twentieth century. The reflection may present a national, individual, generational, or class specificity, or it may project itself toward the world in general. There is a deep sense of individual and collective pessimism and disillusionment that is partly the result of the crashing of utopias of various kinds in the past few decades, be they political, sexual, emotional, or even professional. The author saw AIDS as one of the most vivid and tragic embodiments of the crashing of the utopia of sexual revolution.

AIDS, according to Caio Fernando Abreu, is one of the major facets of contemporary life's insanity, a tragically vivid metaphor of the reality of a contaminated planet. In his last interview published in *O Estado de São Paulo* (12 September 1995), he reflected about AIDS in ecological terms, articulating what American critic Gabriel Rotello developed in an exhaustive manner in his controversial work *Sexual Ecology* (1997). Abreu believed that the crisis in the human immunological system is analogous to the crisis in the contemporary global ecological system.

The author, furthermore, did not glorify the fact of his being a person with AIDS, nor did he consider it a heroic or divine experience. He did not hide the sense of tragedy and misfortune that accompanies the disease. Ultimately, he believed that in the face of the disease, the human condition is innocent.

Together with Brazilian pop star Cazuza and writer and political activist Herbert Daniel, Caio Fernando Abreu was one of the earliest and most outspoken cultural figures to address the general public in Brazil concerning the AIDS experience. Through interviews and especially through his poignant and quite personal chronicles, collected in *Pequenas epifanias* (Small epiphanies, 1996), Abreu traced the emotional and physiological stages of the disease as they affected him personally. In fact, the experience of AIDS became conflated with Abreu's own life and writing due to the large amount of "pre-posthumous" attention lavished upon him by the media during his final years.[12] Caio Fernando Abreu became one of the most powerful and eloquent purveyors of news of the signs of the times of the countless known and unknown Brazilians and others who have come and gone through the merciless onslaught of the epidemic. However, contrary to the morbid writings of Hervé Guibert, the frenetic urgency of Cyril Collard's, or Reinaldo Arenas's desperate cry of victimhood, Abreu's writings, even those about AIDS, reveal a mildly optimistic spirit, despite the endless pain of witnessing the very limits of his own being and that of humanity in general. Most of the time, his writings on AIDS end inconclusively, pointing to an uncertain future as well as emphasizing the importance of living (in) the present with passion and hope.[13]

Caio Fernando Abreu's fictional and nonfictional production (between 1988 and 1995)—directly and indirectly—mirrors the various stages the author went through in coping with AIDS, as it affected him personally as well as the world around him. Given what is known about the progression of the disease within the body, HIV/AIDS has been characterized in terms of stages since the beginning of the epidemic (Susan Sontag, *AIDS and Its Metaphors*). In Abreu's fiction we witness at first the marks of the disease on the body's surface, then the fear of the unknown, as well as the setting in of a sense of life's ineluctable uncertainty. Later on, we sense the hovering presence of death and yet an unwavering commitment to living. In fact, from *Os dragões não conhecem o paraíso* (1988) on and throughout his later works, there is a hyperawareness of the limits of life. *Os dragões,* in particular, is built on an axis of negation or death. Almost all of the stories of this particular collection reflect upon death: "Linda, uma história horrível" (Beauty),[14] "O destino desfolhou" (The leaves of fate have fallen), "Os sapatinhos vermelhos" (The little red shoes), and "Dama da noite" (Queen of the night). However, this collection ends with an affirmation of life: the Chinese ideogram "Chi'en" (which represents the origin of all things) and an ironic quote on happiness from Ana Cristina César[15] that reads: "Chamem os bombeiros, gritou Zelda. Alegria! Algoz inesperado." (Call the firemen, shouted Zelda. Happiness! Unexpected hangman.) In spite of the profound melancholy that envelops most of Caio Fernando Abreu's narratives, they often end with a lingering expression of hope.

Along the rich spectrum of Caio Fernando Abreu's fictional writings that thematize AIDS, we find "Linda, uma história horrível." This short story from the collection *Os dragões não conhecem o paraíso* (1988), published in the United Kingdom in 1990 under the title *Dragons,* was probably one of the first fictionalized accounts of the AIDS crisis to appear in Brazilian literature. It was one of very few Latin American (and the only Portuguese-language) short stories featured in *The Penguin Book of International Gay Writing,* edited by Mark Mitchell (1995). This short story was a symbolic opening to the anthology *Os dragões.* It tells the story of a homecoming, a return to the place of one's origin. The narrator visits his mother, and upon arrival he faces a house in decline. In fact, the house is a mirror image of the narrator, a man in his forties who has AIDS, and his mother, more than twenty-five years older than he. They both display traces of illness, of time. Their habitual tense silences, signaling more than a communication gap, elliptically suggest the deep closeness of mother and son in their different, yet similar, existential states. There is an evident generational and sexual gap between mother and son, which both tacitly acknowledge and yet are mutually supportive of one another. Terminal illness in youth (in the case of the narrator) and impending death in old age (in the case of the mother) indelibly unite them. Their family ties are formed of more than blood; they are forged of human solidarity, of a shared solitude.

Passo da Guanxuma, the locale to which the narrator returns, constitutes an antimythical place of origin, an allegorical representation of contemporary Brazil. Despite the impeachment of Fernando Collor de Mello for corruption in 1992, the initial euphoria surrounding the implementation of a neoliberal monetary plan *(plano real),* and the presidency of Fernando Henrique Cardoso (now vastly unpopular), the Brazil that ails has not withered away. The headline "País mergulha no caos, na doença, na miséria" ("Country sinks into chaos, disease, and poverty") (*Os dragões,* 15; *Dragons,* 3), so prominent in this short story and so urgent in the Brazil of the 1980s, still echoes on the horizon.

In "Linda, uma história horrível," mother, son, pet dog, house, and country are all subsumed in decadence. The Kaposi's sarcoma lesions on the protagonist's chest mirror the vanishing purple of the living room carpet and the spots of the nearly blind and aging dog. But despite the horizon of ruins, of abjection, there remains a touch of hope, a touch of love that survives out of the links of solidarity between beings—in this case, family members. There lies the touch of beauty in an otherwise "horrible" story:

> Um por um, foi abrindo os botões. Acendeu a luz do abajur, para que a sala ficasse mais clara quando, sem camisa, começou a acariciar as manchas púrpura, da cor antiga do tapete na escada—agora, que cor?—, espalhadas embaixo dos pelos do peito. Na ponta dos dedos, tocou o pescoço. Do lado direito, inclinando a cabeça, como se apalpasse uma semente no escuro. Depois foi abrindo os joelhos até o chão. Deus, pensou, antes de estender a outra mão para tocar no pêlo da cadela quase cega, cheia de manchas rosadas. Iguais às do tapete gasto da escada, iguais às da pele do seu peito, embaixo dos pêlos. Crespos, escuros, macios.—Linda—sussurrou.—Linda, você é tão linda, Linda. (*Os Dragões,* 22)

> (One by one, he undid the buttons. He turned on the lamp, so that the room would be lighter and, with his shirt off, began to stroke the purple marks, the same colour as the stair carpet had once been—what colour was it now?—that spread beneath the hairs on his chest. With his fingertips he touched the right-hand of his neck, tilting his head as if feeling for a seed in the dark. Then he slumped to his knees. God, he thought, and stretched out his other hand to touch the near-blind dog, its coat dappled with pink patches. The same as those on the skin of his chest, beneath the hair. Curly, dark, soft: "Beauty," he whispered. "Beauty, you're such a beauty, Beauty.") (*Dragons,* 10–11)

After the publication of *Os dragões,* AIDS reappeared in the novel *Onde andará Dulce Veiga?* (1990), translated as *Whatever Happened to Dulce Veiga?* (2000). Set against the backdrop of an apocalyptic São Paulo, the novel is set in a city that is falling to pieces, terminally ill. Some of the characters themselves, including the protagonist, have AIDS. In fact, the idea of contamination permeates the narrative as a whole, as much as it comes to symbolize the state of the nation—that is, Brazil in the late 1980s—a nation undergoing one of the worst socioeconomic and political crises of its modern history. In this novel, the reality of the body that is HIV positive or that has AIDS is transferred to a metaphor of the contaminated nation.[16]

Onde andará Dulce Veiga? is centered around the figure of a mythical Brazilian singer, Dulce Veiga, who achieves cult status in the late 1960s, and one day, at the height of her career, mysteriously vanishes.[17] The protagonist, an anonymous male reporter for one of São Paulo's dailies, is assigned the task of researching her past and possibly tracing her steps. The reporter, a man in his forties whose name is never known, must meet with Dulce Veiga's daughter Márcia, a rock singer, who is the only one who may know of Dulce's whereabouts. In his search for Dulce Veiga, the reporter circulates swiftly through Rio and the Amazon region, but his nomadic meanderings take place mainly in the city of São Paulo, the Brazilian megalopolis, which functions in the narrative as a microcosm of the nation. This is the urban site where the vast array of cultural, socioeconomic, and political differences that make up the Brazilian nation converge and collide most dramatically. Some relevant examples that stand out in the novel are the large numbers of *nordestinos,* or Brazilian northeasterners—the result of massive internal migration—who now constitute the subaltern economic reserve for the megalopolis; Japanese Brazilians, one example of the many diasporic populations that are now an indissociable part of São Paulo; and gays, lesbians, and bisexuals, who clearly defy geographical, racial, ethnic, or class identity borderlines.

When the protagonist of Caio Fernando Abreu's novel finally meets the daughter of the long-lost cult figure, he ventures into an alternative world, à la *Almodóvar,* of multicultural, postpunk, junkie, lesbian-feminist rock singers. This world is a strident example of transnational cultural dissemination (Homi K. Bhabha, "DissemiNation: Time, Narrative, and the Margins of the Modern Nation," 170), a world of apocalyptic sounds where Carmen Miranda meets MTV, where the 1960s counterculture meets its own pastiche. Here once again, Abreu stages the meeting of the two generations that generally populate his narratives in the persons of the "exiled" character from the 1960s (in this case, the forty-something reporter) and the exhuberant twenty-something rock singers. The "Vaginas Dentatas," all-female rock band, not only stands in for the young middle-class generations of contemporary São Paulo, but for the Brazil that is dramatized in Abreu's fictional world. This is a Brazil located at an ebullient cultural semiperiphery[18] and, at the same time, inevitably absorbed by an English-speaking, corporate-dominated cultural multicenter that radiates to the four corners of the globe. But whatever happened to Dulce Veiga? Dulce Veiga's disappearance occurs when she is about to become a major star, at the same time that Brazil's dictatorial regime is becoming particularly brutal (1968, the year in which the Ato Institucional n° 5 was put into law, severely limiting constitutional rights). Dulce Veiga leaves behind her child, as well as her lover, a leftist activist, who in fact suffers the psychological and physical consequences of right-wing repression. Dulce "exiles" herself in the Amazonian hinterland and embarks on a life with a new age community that she eventually abandons. She remains for two decades out of sight of the Brazilian public, yet very present in the minds and hearts of all those who followed her in the late sixties. Her songs, her allure incarnate those values so dear to the 1960s generation that has now been left ideologically orphaned.

The reporter wanders through the labyrinthine decadence of São Paulo and the sun-bathed, violence-ridden madness of Rio, then on to Brazil's final frontier, Amazonia, where he finally meets Dulce Veiga, at least in a sense. This encounter shatters the mythical façade that has been projected upon her for years—a façade that has become tragically real in the person of Dulce's lover, who is now insane and addicted to heroin after having been severely beaten down during the repressive years of Brazil's dictatorship and having been totally abandoned by Dulce Veiga. He now lives in a perpetual state of delirium, dressed in Dulce Veiga drag, in a pathetic impersonation of her being as portrayed in her songs and her now faded allure. When the reporter encounters this grotesque impersonation of Dulce, he sees his own self reflected in the absolute other. It is the reflection of his own solitude and fears, his unfulfilled dreams—emotional, ideological, professional—and those of his whole generation.

There are two other contemporary Brazilian novels of this era that share many of the concerns found in Caio Fernando's *Onde andará Dulce Veiga?*, *Harmada* by João Gilberto Noll (1993), and *Estorvo* (Turbulence) by Chico Buarque (1991). All three narratives were written by authors of the same generation who came into adulthood in the sixties (Chico Buarque in fact played a pivotal role in the Brazilian counterculture as an immensely popular singer and composer). All three authors were deeply committed to Brazil's destiny as a society, but revealed an acute disenchantment vis-à-vis Brazil's intractable socioeconomic problems, as well as a shared feeling of loss of the utopian dimension, so fertile and strong in the 1960s.

The three novels in question are all nomadic in that both the structure and the subjectivity of their protagonists are in constant movement, searching for definition in a world of profound instability and crisis. These novels also dramatize in differing ways a search for origins at a time of great dispersal and disillusionment. João Gilberto Noll's *Harmada* is dominated by an unresolved tension between errancy and the search for roots that fully involves the narrator-protagonist. This unresolved tension is heightened by a sense of indefiniteness and provisionality regarding truths, actions, and facts that prevails throughout the novel. This is also the dominant note in Chico Buarque's *Estorvo*, in which the protagonist and the novel itself spin in circles that offer no exit from the existential drama of the narrator-protagonist or from the socioeconomic quagmire in which Brazil finds itself. In contrast to these two novels, *Onde andará Dulce Veiga?* displays Caio Fernando Abreu's greater degree of faith in the possibility of arriving at a lasting truth as illustrated by the novel's detectivesque structure, which unavoidably sets in motion an epistemological operation that is ultimately aimed at finding a truth or a place of origin. In this novel, this truth or place of origin is metonymically located within the figure of Dulce Veiga herself.

The "real" Dulce Veiga lives in a remote village in the idealized Amazon region. It is significant that Dulce should be inhabiting the Amazon, at the margins of Brazil's own marginality, the antithesis of the urban decomposition so oppressively evident in Caio Fernando Abreu's novel and the centerpiece of today's fragile global ecological puzzle. The Amazon encompasses here, as it has for many others in the past, an ultimate frontier, a repository of ever-so-elusive utopias, a possible new paradigm of development for being of self and of nation. In the Amazon Dulce Veiga is happy, removed from the world, close to her song, perhaps in search of still one more thing. The reporter learns from her the possibility of peace and a sense of purpose within his own horizons of incompleteness and finitude. However, the reporter is not to remain in this improbable promised land; his search will take him back to the urban hell that inescapably awaits him: his destiny, his truth are within him.

The continued belief in the possibility of finding utopia amid an apocalyptic reality is expressed years later in "Zona contaminada," a hallucinated multimedia spectacle from Abreu's collection of plays, published posthumously under the title *Teatro completo* (1997). Here we witness a dramatic synthesis of contemporary culture's gallery of all-encompassing horrors (the Nazi Holocaust, AIDS, the threat of nuclear war, and the threat of ecological disaster). The author's preoccupation with the state of the Brazilian nation shifts to the global stage, where the well-being of humanity as a whole has been severely compromised as never before in its history. Abreu's play resonates with Tony Kushner's monumental *Angels in America* (1992), where the approach to the new millennium is characterized by a nearly apocalyptic scenario of which the tragedy of AIDS is one of the primary symptoms. This symptom is compounded by a deep suspicion of organized religion (as well as the collapse of the utopia of socialism) and yet the utmost need for the redemption of an orphaned and battered humanity. Both Kushner and Abreu echo Susan Sontag, who in the early stages of the AIDS epidemic pointed out something that remains relevant today, that AIDS is one of the central elements of a series of unfolding disasters of contemporary society on a global scale; in fact, it is "one of the dystopian harbingers of the global village, that future which is already here" (*AIDS and Its Metaphors*, 93). Both Abreu's "Zona contaminada" and Kushner's *Angels in America*, anchored in their respective national realities but projecting themselves toward a globalized horizon, present multilayered symbolic structures where an apocalyptic view of humanity's fate in the late twentieth century is counterbalanced by an unwavering faith in the illusion of utopia. In both cases utopia involves one's forming a relationship of solidarity with the other. According to Mr. Nostálgio, one of the characters in Abreu's play, the illusion of utopia is a necessity in order to continue to humanly exist: "Ilusão, eu já dizia cá com os meus botões, ilusão é tudo que o humano—esse escombro patético—necessita para continuar existindo" (Illusion, as I was saying to myself, illusion is everything that human beings—such pathetic debris—need in order to continue to exist) (*Teatro completo,* 88; unless another source is quoted, all translations are mine).[19]

Fear and paranoia have also been an integral part of the AIDS experience from its onset. In Abreu's fiction, the anguish caused by the overwhelming fear and paranoia related to AIDS is surpassed by that caused by one's absolute desire and need for the other. The novella "Pela Noite," from the collection *Estranhos estrangeiros* (Strange foreigners, 1996) published originally in *Triângulo das águas* (Water Triangle, 1983)—possibly the first literary work in Brazil to thematize AIDS (Marcelo Secron Bessa, *Histórias positivas,* 51)—portrays a seemingly endless night of two prospective male lovers in the 1980s in the heart of the anonymous South American megalopolis of São Paulo.[20] Both men struggle to navigate the turbulent waters of the accumulated fears of contemporary life, in which solitude and AIDS figure prominently, in order to discover the possibility of love.

The possibility of desiring, finding, and loving the other, despite the history of abjection surrounding AIDS,[21] as well as the physiological and psychic limits imposed by it, is key to the short story "Depois de agosto" (After August), probably one of the last pieces written by Caio Fernando Abreu before his untimely death. According to Marcelo Secron Bessa, this particular short story stemmed from the author's own personal experience with AIDS (*Histórias positivas,* 98). In fact, Secron Bessa stresses the autobiographical thrust that permeates most of Abreu's fiction. "Depois de agosto" appears in the anthology *Ovelhas negras* (Black sheep, 1995), a collection of short stories representing different periods of Abreu's writing career that remained unpublished at his death. This story recounts the various stages that the protagonist (who has AIDS) must traverse toward his "undeath," that is, from the profound emotional and psychological impact of considering the seemingly irreversible course of the disease, which leads the protagonist to feel that "it is all too late," to a turning point in his existence where life, love, and hope are rediscovered:[22] "Talvez tudo, talvez nada. Porque era cedo demais e nunca tarde. Era recém no início da não-morte dos dois" (Maybe everything, maybe nothing. Because it was too early and never too late. It was just the beginning of their "undeath") (257). In one of the most poetic fictional renderings of the experience of AIDS, this short story features a man who comes to revalorize his life through his own inner strength and the promise of the other's love. The certainties of death and life are relativized in this narrative, at the same time as the layer of abjection that has historically enveloped the disease and those who must endure it becomes transvalued. The protagonist realizes that in the face of love's promise and the other's embrace, even in the most dire of life circumstances, it is always early and never too late to live and to love. Even when facing the most tenuous of horizons within an individual life cycle, the seasons of love can continue:

> Desde então, mesmo quando chove ou o céu tem nuvens, sabem sempre quando a lua é cheia. E quando mingua e some, sabem que se renova e cresce e torna a ser cheia outra vez e assim por todos os séculos e séculos porque é assim que é e sempre foi e será, se Deus quiser e os anjos disserem Amém. (257–58)

> (Since then, even when it rains or when it's cloudy, they always know when the moon is full. And when it is new or when it disappears, they know it will renew itself again and will turn full forever and ever, because such is the way that it has always been and will always be, God willing and if the angels say Amen.)

Sexuality and gender identity categories appear as highly unstable sites of signification in Caio Fernando Abreu's fictional world, where fixed notions of heterosexuality, bisexuality, or homosexuality are constantly called into question.[23] Abreu's textual space is populated by subjectivities representing a wide and fluid spectrum of genders and sexualities that escape facile containment within dominant ideological frameworks. The author attacks any ideological system that may marginalize or exclude difference or that may preclude the subject from realizing himself emotionally, sexually, and ontologically with whomever he chooses. Abreu also makes a case for rethinking the "sexual" borders of the nation-state. In a variety of forms and registers, the subjectivities that inhabit Abreu's fiction underscore the idea of the nation (in this case, the Brazilian nation) as a liminal signifying space marked by a heterogeneity of discourses and tense areas of cultural differences. As Homi Bhabha asserts, the nation "becomes a question of otherness of the people-as-one" ("DissemiNation," 150), where the difference outside, against which the nation defines its subjectivity, becomes a difference within. This constitutive internal difference marks the nation's finitude as a homogenizing entity. In Abreu's fictional and nonfictional production, nonhege-monic sexual identities play a key role in destabilizing, renegotiating, and demarcating the borders of the nation-state.

Abreu's best-known short story collection, *Morangos mofados* (Moldy strawberries, 1982) was his first work of fiction to bring to the fore questions around sexuality, most particularly homosexuality. In *Morangos mofados* there are narratives that feature characters who present a relatively clear sexual orientation, heterosexual or homosexual, though always problematized ("O dia que Jupiter encontrou Saturno," "Terça-Feira Gorda," "Sargento Garcia" (Sergeant Garcia);[24] beings who reveal an unclear correlation between sexual desire and identity, where there are even destabilizing agents such as alcohol that prevent the subject from defining himself sexually or ontologically ("Além do ponto"); or subjects who cannot be located in a binary (heterosexual/homosexual or male/female) given that identities are highly fluid and ambiguous, where even the borders between two beings remain tenuous, suggesting an implosion between the subject and the other ("Os sobreviventes").[25]

On a different register, in *Os dragões* we find the short story "Pequeno monstro" ("Little monster"), which features an adolescent's initiation into sex. It is the dramatization of a loss of innocence, but at the same time the discovery of self; a powerful moment of freedom and happiness at youth, one of the few encountered in the writings of Caio Fernando Abreu. The young protagonist of this story is spending summer with his family at a beach home. The adolescent boy is in the middle of his rebellious stage, feeling misunderstood and marginalized within his family. He also displays a self-hatred (hence, the nickname "little monster" that he is given) that starts to dissipate as soon as cousin Alex appears. Alex, interestingly one of the few characters with a name in the whole anthology, is a handsome college student who joins the family for vacations. His presence unleashes an erotic charge in the young boy that eventually leads to his first sexual experience.

This initiation to sex, and possibly to love, is overtly and unapologetically assumed to be gay. The adolescent protagonist lives a moment of intense self-valorization that escapes any moral constraints. He feels empowered for the first time after assuming the sexual dimension of his young being. By the same token, the author highly valorizes this event where the subject, in spite of his innocence, or perhaps because of his innocence, can experience a moment of authenticity—a freedom of which he will be inevitably robbed. Nevertheless, as ephemeral as this moment may be, it opens up the possibility of a life assumed in earnest and lived to its fullest potential.

On the opposite end of the wide spectrum of narratives featured in the collection *Os dragões* we find one of Abreu's most powerful short stories: "Dama da noite" (Queen of the night). Here the identity of the protagonist (a "dama" or "queen") is mired in uncertainty. This particular narrative is the product of an era besieged by panic over the body, fear of sex and AIDS. It is an Almodovaresque monologue in very colloquial speech performed by a forty-year-old woman—or perhaps a drag queen—who lives as a vampire in and for the underworld of the big-city nights.[26] The camp sensibility exhibited in the monologue performed by the actual *dama da noite* creates gender ambiguity, which is heightened even further by the word choice in the English translation, *queen.* The stage production by Gilberto Gawronski reinforces the gender ambiguity by presenting a completely androgynous character. The monologue, as a performative act, relativizes gender categories and points to their constructedness. The character speaking may as well be a female prostitute, a male transvestite and prostitute, or a woman posing as a male transvestite and prostitute. It is a question of packaging, a mask or a figure of simulation—as the character "herself" asserts at the end of the story. But, regardless of the "real" content of the package, the *dama* is a nocturnal being, living precariously at the margins of bourgeois society.

In "Dama da noite" the protagonist addresses an assumed male interlocutor who is twenty years younger. The crossgenerational axis upon which this particular narrative and various others by Abreu are constructed (the stories "Linda, uma história horrível" and "O rapaz mais triste do mundo" [The saddest boy in the world] in the collection *Os dragões* and the novel *Onde andará Dulce Veiga?*) is of utmost importance since it deploys a number of key thematic concerns of Caio Fernando Abreu that oscillate between the individual and the collective, the political and the ontological. This interfacing of generations brings together those who came into adulthood in the late 1960s and those who did so in the late 1980s. The former generation believed in the possibility of major political and cultural transformations and had—in the specific case of Brazil in the late 1960s—a clearly delineated enemy to fight against. On the other hand, the generation of the 1980s came into adulthood with AIDS as an inescapable and constantly menacing horizon. Furthermore, this generation not only saw the global crashing of the utopias for which the 1960s counterculture had lived, but, in the particular case of Brazil, it found itself submerged in political and socioeconomic despair. These cultural, political, and epidemiological circumstances were compounded by the fear of aging, together with the idea of growing old in absolute solitude.

"Dama da noite" represents a passionate affirmation of individual values that stand in opposition to hegemonic cultural structures; the protagonist encompasses those beings (drug users, transvestites, prostitutes, beings of all sexualities, vampire inhabitants of the night—all in all, "dragon-queers") that rebel against the notion of a homogeneous and monolithic culture. Dragons constitute the metaphor-synthesis of Abreu's anthology bearing the same name. Dragons are those subjects who inhabit the margins of social space, beings who contest the hegemonic values of a society steeped in falsehood and artificiality. They include adolescents, drag queens, and a wide spectrum of (pluri)sexual beings who escape containment within dominant frameworks of sexuality. The term *dragon,* which is used in Abreu's fiction for the purpose of designating alternative subjectivities along a wide and fluid spectrum of genders and sexualities, has certain parallels with the term *queer,* which has been adopted by gay, lesbian, bisexual. and transgender political activists in the United States for some years now.

The term *queer* has undergone a process of reappropriation and resignification—Judith Butler pointed out in her classic article "Critically Queer" (in *Bodies That Matter,* 1993)—having become (at least provisionally) vacated of its pejorative connotations in English. In a totalizing yet politically pragmatic gesture, the use of *queer* incorporates (however problematically) distinct groups such as lesbians, gay males, bisexuals, transgendered people, transvestites, and even heterosexual sympathizers whose political positions align them with the defiant marginality of the previously mentioned groups. The political parallels between "dragons" and "queers" are quite obvious, but "dragons" also evokes a poetic-philosophical dimension within the signifying economy of Abreu's fiction. Dragons belong to the realm of the mythological, as the creatures that at the time of the European navigators and explorers were believed to inhabit the unknown interiors of the barely "discovered" lands. These imaginary creatures promised *eldorados* as much as they inspired the deepest fears. Caio Fernando Abreu saw "dragons" indeed as a source of fear in contemporary bourgeois society, but they certainly do not belong (as the title of his anthology implies) to the paradise offered by conventional bourgeois life. Rather, they are archetypal projections of where human beings aspire to be, beyond a society dominated by false values. Their fire possesses a purifying force through which the subject can struggle for the possibility of forging authentic values and living them openly and constructively. Dragons not only populate the writings of Caio Fernando Abreu, but they also constitute Abreu's fictional attempt at affirming a decentered and tense cultural space that, by virtue of its location, is not only defiant but inevitably vulnerable and fragile, at the mercy of political, economical, juridical, and epidemiological forces over which one has little control.

The protagonist of "Dama da noite" defies in a paradoxical way the highly problematic stability of traditional heterosexual society, as she sets in motion the cultural anxieties that derive from historically dominant discourses around sex and sexuality, which today more than ever, in the age of AIDS, are conflated with discourses of disease. The *dama da noite* and all that she symbolizes is threatened as much as she is a threat:

> Eu sou a dama da noite que vai te contaminar com seu perfume venenoso e mortal. Eu sou a flor carnívora e noturna que vai te entontecer e te arrastar para o fundo do seu jardim pestilento. Eu sou a dama maldita que, sem nenhuma piedade, vai te poluir com todos os líquidos, contaminar teu sangue com todos os vírus. Cuidado comigo, eu sou a dama que mata, boy. (*Os dragões*, 95)

> (I'm the queen of the night who's going to contaminate you with her poisonous deadly perfume. I'm the carnivorous nocturnal flower who's going to make you dizzy and drag you to the bottom of her putrid garden. I'm the cursed queen who's mercilessly going to pollute you and infect your blood with every kind of virus. Beware of me—I'm the deadly queen.) (*Dragons*, 84)

"Dama da noite," on the other hand, is not only about rebellion; it is also about searching. If the utopias of various ideological forms and colors that were so prominent in the cultural landscape of the 1960s and 1970s have faded, there is one utopia that stubbornly remains, albeit tenuously: love. In fact, for Caio Fernando Abreu, the utopias of love and God are inevitable, lest the human subject submerge itself in a horrendous pit of absolute solitude. As much as Abreu is aware of the weakening of foundationalist thought in contemporary society, he also recognize that certain of its expressions—as contingent and provisional as they may be—are still a strategic necessity for our survival as human beings. And so through the nihilistic haze that looms in the short story "Dama da noite," as throughout most of Abreu's fiction, there is a faint glimmer of hope: the hope of collecting fresh and juicy strawberries in the contemporary civilizational dump, to evoke the central metaphor of *Morangos mofados.* The strawberries represent the dreams, the utopias of love—all in all, hope. This hope, though, is never unaccompanied by fear, a fear that "queen of the night" experiences as a vulnerable child who is left alone and abandoned:

> Fora da roda, montada na minha loucura. Parada pateta ridícula porra-louca solitária venenosa. Pós-tudo, sabe como? Darkérrima, modernésima, puro simulacro. Dá minha jaqueta, boy, que faz um puta frio lá fora e quando chega essa hora da noite eu me desencanto. Viro outra vez aquilo que sou todo dia, fechada sozinha perdida no meu quarto, longe da roda e de tudo: uma criança assustada. (*Os dragões,* 98)

> (Outside of the wheel, riding on my craziness. Sitting there stupid, ridiculous, couldn't give a shit, solitary, poisonous. Post-everything, you know what I mean? Ultra-gothic, ultra-modern, pure sham. Hand me my jacket, boy, it's bloody freezing out there and when it gets to this hour of the night my spell wears off. I turn back into what I am every day, shut in alone and lost in my room, far from the wheel and everything: a frightened kid.) (*Dragons,* 88)

Caio Fernando Abreu's fictional and cultural enterprise, and in particular *Os dragões,* is built upon an axis of negation from which the author desired to open up the possibility of a Zenlike return to origins so that the subject (that is, the subject predicated in Abeu's fiction) can engage in a transvaluation of values. Despite the cultural landscape of nihilistic desolation that prevails in postmodernity (to which Brazil is no exception) and that is so central to Abreu's fictional world, there is a nostalgic desire for the whole that is embodied in the idea of a return to origins. This is a clear example of the postmodern paradox that, on the one hand, describes a contemporary cultural moment beyond foundationalist thought and, on the other hand, verifies an endless need to retain certain of its expressions so that life can be more endurable and death more acceptable.

Toward the last years of Abreu's life there was a heightened sense of urgency in his fictional production that was a consequence of his being a person with AIDS. This sense of urgency enhanced his search for the "whole" as embodied in the figure of the "other." Prior to the advent of AIDS, the feelings that emanated from his fiction were those of disillusionment, disorientation, and solitude. These feelings stemmed from individual as well as national and global circumstances. By the early 1980s, at a national level, Brazil was just leaving behind a lengthy and relatively harsh dictatorship that had shattered the dreams of social revolution and democratization. On the other hand, on a global scale, the thriving and liberatory 1960s counterculture, which survived into the 1970s, was displaced by a wave of political, moral, and cultural conformism and conventionality in the 1980s. The AIDS epidemic would eventually become a posteriori, one of the ideal rationalizations behind this particular wave. In addition, in this earlier period Abreu's fiction dramatized, at an individual level, a profound ontological disjuncture within the subject, expressed in a variety of situations and forms, that in turn informed the social and erotic relationship of the subject with the other, as well as the act of literary representation itself (this is most vividly portrayed in *Morangos mofados*). The national and global circumstances alluded to partially explain the ontological anguish felt by the subject. After the possibility of social communion and political emancipation had been foregone, the subject was left orphaned of the utopias that had given sense to an era and to a generation. Furthemore, from a philosophical standpoint, the author is acutely aware of the impossibility of a unitary and self-identified subject. Such awareness brings about in Abreu's earlier fiction a host of solitary and fragmented characters that are located in the heart of contemporary anonymous urban life. Another factor that compounds the sense of ontological anguish that is profoundly felt by numerous characters in Abreu's narratives is internalized homophobia, itself a product of societal repression of homosexuality. This anguish is rendered in several short narratives of *Morangos mofados* ("Além do ponto," "Terça-feira gorda," and "Aqueles dois").[27] Homophobia appears as yet another formidable obstacle to the self-realization of the desiring subject and to erotic communion with the loved other.

Caio Fernando Abreu stands in contrast to most other Portuguese and Brazilian writers considered in this study due to the particular attention he gave to the erotic dimension of human existence—not just the homoerotic—and the degree to which he saw the (homo)erotic as affecting the self-realization of the subject or his ability to enter into a relationship with the other. Another Brazilian writer who reveals a degree of kinship with Abreu regarding the connection between (homo)erotic desire, subjectivity, and one's relationship with the other is João Gilberto Noll (mentioned earlier in this chapter). In his novel *Rastros de verão* (1986) one observes an attempt at forging an ethics of solidarity with the other (either male or female) predicated upon the bond of mutual emotional and erotic need between the I and the other. Yet, as in other works by Noll, the (male) subject (as well as the narrative itself) remains ontologically undefined and sexually ambivalent (particularly toward other men). There is an oscillation between the need for the other and the sense of burden and obligation that the other imposes. In Abreu's fictional universe, the ties of solidarity with the other based on emotional and erotic need are as strong as in Noll's; however, in Abreu's later narratives, most particularly those where AIDS emerges as a tangible reality, there is none of the ontological or sexual tenuousness that transpires in Noll's writing.

With the advent of AIDS, the need and desire for the other as expressed in Caio Fernando Abreu's fiction became greatly intensified. The utopia of the other took on a central role, and literature became one of its privileged sites. In this respect, Abreu revealed affinities with writers such as Clarice Lispector and Vergílio Ferreira. The later texts of both of these writers, as well as those of Caio Fernando Abreu, exemplify the ways in which the existential as much as the physiological circumstances of the author became more transparent in the creative process. Literary texts are written with a sense of urgency at the edge of life. They constitute concerted attempts at overcoming life's contingency while making the final stretch of life more livable. The existence of the literary work itself becomes synchronous with the existence of the writer, the former the reason for being of the latter. This symbiotic relationship is further enhanced by a heightened awareness of death as an inescapable horizon. This is clearly palpable in the works of writers such as Clarice Lispector and Vergílio Ferreira. In the case of Caio Fernando Abreu, one can sense the deep pain associated with the knowledge that he was living the last years of his life due to AIDS. To a writer in circumstances such as these, the search for the other through writing becomes paramount in overcoming pain and an overwhelming sense of solitude. This search becomes the remaining impulse that may make life more endurable, and death perhaps more acceptable. The relationship with the other and its absolute necessity constituted for Abreu an ultimate existential horizon for the constitution of the self and society in an era of shattered dreams, accentuated solitudes, and seemingly incurable life-threatening diseases.

There is a fundamental ethical dimension at work in the fiction of Caio Fernando Abreu that is inseparable from an emotional component that is at the same time deeply intertwined with the subject's relationship with the other (in the form of a lover, family member, or community). There is a profound creative investment on the part of the author (as well as that of his characters) in the "micrological" or more intimate levels of being. This particular dynamic is akin to what is found in the work of Portuguese writer Maria Isabel Barreno, who will be discussed in chapter 4 and will be at the center of the discussion in chapter 5. Thus, the investment in the other that is key in the fiction of Abreu (and in that of other writers discussed in this study) is implicated with the "philosophical anthropology" of Bakhtin, which comprises Bakhtin's notions about the self and the other, as well as on being and alterity.[28] As is widely known in the realms of literary and cultural studies, Bakhtin believes the subject cannot be in isolation, and it cannot achieve a degree of self-awareness in the world outside of its relationship with the other. In Bakhtinian thought, communication through dialogue is a fundamental aspect of existence. As Tzvetan Todorov states in *Mikhail Bakhtin: The Dialogical Principle* (1984), "It is the human being that exists only in dialogue; within being one finds the other" (xi). Furthermore, as Todorov says, quoting directly from Bakhtin, "To be means to be for the other, and through him, for oneself. . . . I cannot do without the other; I must find myself in the other" (96). Bakhtin arrived at his new interpretation of culture primarily through the analysis of language and the novel. By the same token, his reflections on language and the novel became a philosophical and even an anthropological basis, as Todorov would have it, from which Bakhtin posited his conceptions of being and dialogism.

There is also a confluence of interests between Caio Fernando Abreu, Bakhtin, and the philosophical thought of Emmanuel Levinas with regard to the question of alterity. The late French philosopher[29] posited the subject as "coming into being" or into an awareness of its being in the world through a complex of existential layers, for example, its insertion into the world, its solitude, and its mortality. This complex of layers ultimately leads toward alterity, or to the other person. Levinas plots a phenomenological itinerary of the subject in which alterity represents the highest plane. In Levinas's writings alterity appears boundless, and its most absolute expression would be God. There is a fundamental ethical dimension that is related to alterity whereby by entering into a relationship with the other, either through a commitment or through responsibility vis-à-vis social life or through an erotic encounter, the subject would enter into a "sacred" history. According to Levinas, God manifests itself through the relationship of the subject with the other.

In the fiction of Caio Fernando Abreu, the Bakhtinian notion of the impossibility of being without the other is a fundamental reality, but historical, ontological, and even physiological layers are added to this reality that are connected to a sense of urgency due to the reality of the author's impending death. Meanwhile, in the literary works of Bernardo Carvalho (*Aberração*, 1993, and *Os bêbados e os sonâmbulos,* 1996) and Silviano Santiago (*Keith Jarrett no Blue Note* [Keith Jarrett at the Blue Note], 1996)—two kindred writers to Caio Fernando Abreu—the "communion" with the other that is deeply longed for and ever so ephemerally attained in Abreu's fiction remains quite elusive; the feeling that prevails is that of resigned solitude in Santiago's narratives and that of diffuse stoicism in Carvalho's fiction, each of which is magnified by AIDS. Santiago posits in the subject an existential condition of foreignness both at "home" and "abroad," which is as cultural as it is intrinsically ontological, while Carvalho presents a highly globalized environment where characters of many nationalities and cultural backgrounds constantly cross borders at the same time as they cross each other's paths, ultimately remaining as disconnected and lonely as ever.

In contrast to the scenarios presented by both Santiago and Carvalho, in Abreu's fictional world, with its loss of hope in the possibility of global change or revolution (of various kinds) or with its loss of faith in totalizing narratives (religious, political, etc.), the other becomes a necessary utopia. This utopian dimension that Abreu attaches to alterity is to a large extent only implicitly conveyed in the writings of both Bakhtin and Levinas but practically absent from the fiction of Carvalho and Santiago. At the same time, while a relationship with a Judeo-

Christian God is central to the philosophical thought of Emmanuel Levinas as a sacred expression of alterity, in the writings of Abreu we detect a spiritual dimension that is oftentimes expressed through allusions to Afro-Brazilian religious beliefs and astrology. There is also in Abreu's writings a memory of and nostalgia for the presence of or faith in God, as well as the paradoxical realization of its necessity as a structuring myth for human existence. Yet the relationship with the other is posited in Abreu's writings as a primarily secular instance, though one still imbued with a sacred aura. Throughout Abreu's fiction, belief in the other is manifested ultimately with great pain and overwhelming solitude. Yet it is the remaining impulse that may make life more endurable, and death perhaps more acceptable:

> Atrás das janelas, retomo esse momento de mel e sangue que Deus colocou tão rápido, e com tanta delicadeza, frente aos meus olhos há tanto tempo incapazes de ver: uma possibilidade de amor. Curvo a cabeça, agradecido. E se estendo a mão, no meio da poeira de dentro de mim, posso tocar também em outra coisa. Essa pequena epifania. Com corpo e face. Que reponho devagar, traço a traço, quando estou só e tenho medo. Sorrio, então. E quase paro de sentir fome. (*Pequenas epifanias,* 14–15)

> (Behind the windows, I seize again that moment of honey and blood that God so delicate and swift, placed in my hands, in front of my eyes, so little used to seeing as of late: the possibility of love. I bow down thankfully and extend my hand, in the middle of the dust within me and I can yet touch something else. It's a small epiphany. With body and face. I can always redraw it in my mind trace by trace when I am alone and fearful. I smile and my hunger is almost placated.)

CHAPTER FOUR

Women's Difference in Contemporary Portuguese Fiction

The Case of Maria Isabel Barreno

The late twentieth century was a period of major historical transformations for Portugal. The single most important event was the April Revolution of 1974, which toppled the forty-year-old authoritarian Salazar/Caetano regime at the same time as it brought about the end of approximately five hundred years of Portuguese colonialism in Africa and Asia. Certainly, the end of Portuguese colonialism was the result of a historical dialectic between events in Portugal and the successful campaign of national liberation movements throughout Portuguese-speaking Africa and East Timor. Nonetheless, after a brief period of political turmoil, the April Revolution opened the path for the democratization of Portuguese society and the entrance into the European Union in 1986, which became the vital force for Portugal's rapid modernization. These significant events and the ensuing changes in Portuguese everyday life have been the object of profound reflection in the realm of literature, particularly in the work of writers such as António Lobo Antunes, Maria Isabel Barreno, Maria Velho da Costa, Almeida Faria, Lídia Jorge, José Cardoso Pires, and José Saramago. One of the most significant trends in late twentieth-century Portuguese literature was the emergence of women writers in significant numbers to the extent that by the late 1980s there were at least as many women as men publishing books.[1]

This major development allowed for a diversification of literary projects, topics, narrative strategies, styles, and perspectives within Portuguese literature. It also meant significant redefinitions of the concepts of nationhood and national identity, which have been key thematic concerns throughout the history of Portuguese literature. Gender or women's concerns were to a large extent merely implicit in or altogether absent from male-dominated canonical literature before the twentieth century, as well as from the realms of intellectual thought and historiography that have concerned themselves with defining Portuguese national identity as discussed in chapter 1 ("Portugal: Ideas of Empire and Nationhood"). The emphasis on issues of gender and female subjectivity among women prose writers and poets since the 1970s has led to a short-circuit of the metanarratives of decline that have dominated the Portuguese intellectual tradition, at the same time as it has critically undermined the cultural paradigms of the seafaring empire. Thus, the present chapter reflects a shift from the macrological perspectives that predominate in chapter 1 to micrological perspectives on Portuguese nationhood as posited by contemporary women writers, most particularly Maria Isabel Barreno.

Barreno shares with Portuguese women writers such as Lídia Jorge, Maria Velho da Costa, and Maria Gabriela Llansol—to name some of the most renowned—a special preoccupation with the ontological problematic of the subject as woman, as well as that of the collectivity as nation. Critic Isabel Allegro de Magalhães considers the latter especially common within Portuguese contemporary fiction written by women given the impact of the 1974 April Revolution as a watershed historical event (*O sexo dos textos*, 48–49). We might add that aside from the real and symbolic turn that 25 April signified for the Portuguese nation, women writers were also encouraged by the momentum stemming from the women's liberation movement of the late 1960s and early 1970s. The April Revolution, according to Darlene Sadlier (*The Question of How*, 1989) provided women an ideal opportunity to become politically active on a large scale. Significant constitutional gains were also made by women with the advent of democracy in Portugal after 1974.

Barreno has had a prolific career, publishing approximately fifteen works of fiction (novels and short story collections), together with several works of nonfiction. She is recognized by critics as one of the most important late twentieth-century Portuguese writers (who continues to be active today). In spite of this recognition, relatively scant critical attention has been devoted to Barreno. This study intends to change this situation by exposing her together with Caio Fernando Abreu, Vergílio

Ferreira, and Maria Gabriela Llansol (the latter two of whom are discussed in chapter 5) to an English-speaking audience. One of the primary reasons for privileging Maria Isabel Barreno is the fact that she deals in some of the most explicit, sophisticated, and compelling ways with the issues that are central to this book, that is, the changing ideas of Portuguese nationhood in the twentieth century, the place of female subjectivities within this evolving cultural landscape, and the reformulation or weakening of utopian thought structures related to Marxism, fascism, colonialism, and women's liberation. Most criticism focusing on Barreno has so far privileged the gender-related aspects of her works (which I still believe to be crucial for a full understanding of her literary production); however, I add a "postfeminist" dimension in my readings. This particular dimension can be described as a shift from macrological political projects to an emphasis on the micrological instances of daily life where there is an ethical commitment to the other in the form of a loved one, family member, co-worker, or community. We may describe this dynamic as a shift from global to more localized concerns that nevertheless have global resonances and implications.

Maria Isabel Barreno's fiction challenges the grand narratives of Portuguese nationhood by incorporating women's difference into the historical time of the nation while rejecting the maritime-imperial paradigm that has governed the Portuguese collective imaginary for centuries. In the collectively written and world-renowned *Novas cartas portuguesas* (New Portuguese letters, 1973), for instance, the grand narratives of nationhood are seen as inextricably linked to patriarchal ideology and its oppressive effects on women (as well as men) throughout history. Aside from being a devastating critique of patriarchal ideology, this groundbreaking work also became a powerful rallying cry for those advocating women's rights and solidarity among women in the early 1970s, both nationally and internationally. By the same token, the circumstances surrounding the production of *Novas cartas portuguesas,* more specifically the significant ideological differences between the three authors (Maria Isabel Barreno, Maria Velho da Costa, and Maria Teresa Horta), brought to bear the limits of collective political projects and the perils of conceiving a monolithic feminist agenda. Thus, Barreno's subsequent literary production reveals a relative skepticism with regard to macrological political projects at the same time as it dramatizes the generalized contemporary crisis that arose due to the weakening of various utopias, myths, or grand narratives that predominated throughout the twentieth century in Portugal and beyond: Marxism, Christianity, fascism, colonialism, nationalism, and women's liberation, among others. Simultaneously, we witness on the part of both the female and male subjects represented in Barreno's fiction a shift from an investment in grand utopian schemes to an emphasis on an ethical commitment in the micrological instances of daily life. This ethical commitment or solidarity entails confronting the difference within the self, as well as in the world at large. While Barreno does not abandon her engagement to feminist politics, there is a clear reformulation of its gender-specific parameters in favor of a more widely defined "humanistic" framework. The following is a cultural reading that charts Maria Isabel Barreno's recent literary trajectory and her changing frameworks with regard to subjectivity, nation, and utopia. Here I focus on most of her fictional production of the 1990s, with special attention devoted to *Crónica do tempo* (The chronicle of time, 1990), *O mundo sobre o outro desbotado* (The world over the other unleashed, [written in 1986, first published in 1995]), and *O chão salgado* (1992).

The novel *Crónica do tempo* is part of a vast and rich body of literary and filmic texts produced in Portugal for the last few decades that are deeply concerned with the destiny of the nation and its historical transformations. This novel presents various configurations of the evolution of the Portuguese nation throughout the twentieth century: the Salazar dictatorship, the Portuguese African empire, the April Revolution of 1974, decolonization, and eventually Portugal's entrance into the European Union. In *Crónica do tempo* Barreno not only focuses on the ideological shifts underlying these (and other) key historical moments within the national and global contexts, but also focuses on their effects within private lives, particularly within the life of the family as well as within the lives of the women protagonists. Barreno reflects upon the destiny of the Portuguese nation in today's globalized environment and, by implication, upon the destiny of the Western world at the end of the century, where there was profound skepticism toward religious and political ideologies of redemption. However, Barreno does not abandon her belief in the imperfect relationships of love and solidarity with the other, in the form of a lover, a family member, or the community at large. The strength that derives from the dialogical relationship of the subject with the other would allow for a fruitful existence and possibly a less painful acceptance of life's inexorable end.

In *Crónica do tempo* there is a profound interaction between individual, collective, national, and global realities. Several generations of the same family passionately live out the grand historical events of recent times: the repressive Salazar regime, World War II, the Portuguese Colonial War in Africa, the April Revolution, and the entrance into the European Union. Simultaneously, we witness the small dramas in the whirlwind of collective existence, the "micro-stories" in the private lives of the protagonists (marriage, disillusion, struggle, triumph, and failure— all in all, the cycles of life and death).[2] This novel clearly reflects that "curiously hybrid realm," in the words of Hannah Arendt, when describing national society: the realm where private and public interests flow unceasingly and uncertainly into each other "like waves in the never-ending stream of the life-process itself" (*The Human Condition,* 33–35).

As the title of Maria Isabel Barreno's *Crónica do tempo* indicates, time is one of the central characters of the novel—the time that inexorably propels individual and plural destinies, nations, and cities. Lisbon is transformed into (an)other city at the pace of sociohistorical transformations. With the flow of years, the city is the object of a profound reterritorialization that can be verified in the reconfiguration of urban spaces, the growing social mobility, the changes in interpersonal relations, and the ways of conceiving subjectivity, as well as gender and sexual identities.[3] The city reveals itself as the landscape where life's perplexity is more acutely felt. The subject inevitably suffers a gradual and sometimes dramatic ontological disorientation as he or she confronts the exhaustion of the myths, habits, and common symbolic referents within the collective imaginary that gave sense to a specific time and space.[4] The habits or myths that molded a given generation do not necessarily resonate with the same intensity in the next generation, thus creating a sometimes insurmountable gap between members of the same family or the nation. This gap is made especially acute by major historical ruptures such as coups d'états, wars, or revolutions. Diogo, one of the sons of the family that is portrayed in *Crónica do tempo,* belongs to the generation that grew up under the Salazar regime and had already reached adulthood when the April Revolution took place. He summarizes quite movingly the deep melancholy and impotence experienced by his generation when confronting the overwhelming force of time:

> Agora o que recordo é o tempo em que fui feito. O tempo que me fez, tal como sou. Por isso se diz "no meu tempo." Melhor do que ninguém, eu sei que o espaço nos faz. Quando choramos uma cidade antiga, choramos tudo o que a gerava. Tudo está ligado. Fui feito na ditadura. Choro o meu bairro, morto à noite. Lisboa morta. (151)

> (Now what I remember is the time that created me. The time that molded me into who I am. That's why we say, "in my time." More than anything, I know that spaces create us. When we lament the old city, we lament everything that made it unique. Everything is interconnected. I was made during the dictatorship. I long for my neighborhood, dead at night. Dead Lisbon.)

Jorge, the patriarch of the family portrayed in *Crónica do tempo,* is the axis of the novel: his life story opens the novel, and his funeral signals its ending. Jorge's life story, revealed in the form of an interview, serves as the catalyst for what follows: the story of three generations of a bourgeois Lisbon family in the course of the twentieth century. Jorge is the living example of the man of meager resources who became rich in Africa in the middle of the century given the freedom and privilege afforded him as a white male colonist. Jorge also benefits from his entrepreneurial talents and the favors of his wealthy lover, Arminda, nicknamed Dona Mimi. Eventually, Jorge marries Manuela, a young woman from a wealthy family, which allows him to gain legitimacy in the eyes of the conservative Lisbon society of the time. The marriage between Jorge and Manuela is a painful one due to the affectional imbalance between them, as well as Jorge's prolonged absences in Angola and the continued tension due to their divergent existential territorialities, manifested on the one hand by their vastly different temperaments and on the other by the profoundly contrasting roles and possibilities offered to them by patriarchal society as a man and a woman. However, Manuela possesses ample knowledge of Jorge's erotic domains (for example, his extramarital affairs) and exerts complete control over the private sphere of their home.[5] Manuela passionately follows the changes over the years in her neighborhood and her city. She is a prototype of the women who, for the greater part of this century, were unable to exert control over their life options given the severe inequality between the sexes. In spite of her limitations, Manuela achieves a great degree of autonomy in the private sphere, though not without pain and frustration.

Then come the children: Carlota, Diogo, and Rosa. Their generation will go through a painful time due to the harsh transition between varyingly difficult political scenarios (the fascist dictatorship, the colonial wars in Africa, and the revolution), as well as the significant shifts in values and myths that are central to their identities (the exhaustion of ideological utopias of the Left and the failure of the utopia of the "perfect marriage"). The third and last generation featured in Isabel Barreno's novel belongs to a postrevolutionary Portugal, a "generation X" that distances itself from the passions and disillusions of both parents and grandparents. We witness in this generation what Boaventura de Sousa Santos defines as an "archipelago of subjectivities," in contrast to the "group collectivism" that was so prevalent in their parents' generation (*Pela mão de Alice*, 96–97). Generation X is characterized by a heightened individualism in a globalized political and geocultural context where the weight of the nation and its historical burden are relativized. *Crónica do tempo* ends in the late 1980s with Jorge's funeral; it is the closing of a cycle, the meeting of generations, the inventory of passions and affections, the unraveling of time's threads.

Maria Isabel Barreno's novel features a very fluid narrative structure where the narrator assumes a multiplicity of individual and collective perspectives. This structure allows the author ample mobility in order to assume various political positions regarding a given character or the opinions uttered by that character. There is also a rich profusion of dialogues focusing on a multiplicity of historical and sociopolitical topics such as the relationships between Portugal and Spain and between Portugal and Brazil, the Inquisition, the expulsion of the Jews from Portugal, the torturously felt Portuguese geopolitical subalternity, and so on. The narrator converges with the speech or thought of a given character to the point where agency becomes ambiguous. At the same time, there is a simultaneity of temporal planes where voices from the past converge with voices of the present, creating a juxtaposition of histories and generations. Ultimately, the narrative structure of *Crónica do tempo* reflects a polyphonous horizon of voices and perspectives in a constant agonic relationship. Thus we witness the "liminal figure of the nation-space,"[6] internally marked by cultural differences in perpetual tension.

Maria Isabel Barreno doubtlessly desires to emphasize the parallels between narration and nation in their heterogeneous, decentered, fluid, and transitional forms. The dominant truths of a certain period, even those imposed by authoritarian regimes, are inevitably subjected to a process of dialogization in the everyday life of national society, as well as within the work of art.

Rosa, the youngest child of Jorge and Manuela, insistently questions the hegemonic truths of her time. Her point of view dominates the novel until its last third, and we could venture to add that many of her opinions are close to those held by Maria Isabel Barreno. Rosa is the main promoter of women's liberation as well as sexual liberation among her peers, both female and male. In the 1960s she emigrates to the United States and travels from coast to coast experiencing the political and cultural euphoria of the time. Rosa then hastily returns to Portugal in order to take part in the festivities of 25 April, "her generation's festivities" (*Crónica do tempo*, 182). Yet Rosa presents the most diverging positions within the ideological debates prior to and after the April Revolution, given her antidogmatic stances at a time when dogmas from both the Left and the Right proliferated. She stresses the importance of cultural and sexual rights that were not contemplated in the Marxist analysis of class relations and the capitalist system of production (this is a critique that is quite brilliantly developed by Isabel Barreno in her poetic essay entitled *A morte da mãe* (first published in 1972). In a more intimate domain, Rosa criticizes the so-called progressive heterosexual men of the time, who desired sexually liberated women but experienced great difficulty in accepting women who openly and actively assumed control of their sexuality. Rosa, along with her female counterparts, posits an "internal revolution" that may reach the most intimate dimensions of being, such as desire, marriage, gender identity, and sexuality. Before the 1960s these areas were traditionally ignored or repressed by right- and left-wing ideologies.

Through Rosa and the women of her generation who stood with her ideologically, Barreno puts forth a counterdiscourse that revindicates the Portuguese nation as a feminine and postcolonial erotic space in opposition to the Portuguese paradigmatic identity of the phallic and patriarchal navigator, as well as in opposition to the fascistic construct of women under the Salazar regime, where "women" were conflated with the ideas of government of home, Salazar, and the Portuguese "nation-family."[7] This discourse is a symbolic transcodification of the Portuguese nation and its colonial (and fascistic) past. This particular paradigm shift is reminiscent of the culturally defiant gestures in *Novas cartas portuguesas,* where the social spaces to which women have been historically confined (the convent, marriage, the patriarchal family) are vehemently rejected. Through Rosa and her generation in *Crónica do tempo,* the female subject enters into the linear or historical time of the nation, but she simultaneously refuses the ontological limitations imposed by the nation's "historical time."[8] The female subject enacts a rhetorical and symbolic short-circuit in order to incorporate her difference in the liminal figure of the nation, at the same time subverting the paradigms of Portuguese national identity, colonial and fascist alike.

Along with the themes of nation and subjectivity, *Crónica do tempo* explores the status of myths or utopias in the late twentieth century.[9] There is an acute awareness of, as well as a sense of vacuousness and melancholy on the part of the characters with regard to, the weakening, or the collapse, of the myths or beliefs that had guided the imaginary and the destiny not only of Portuguese culture, but of Western culture in general. Rosa synthesizes perfectly well the sentiment of the time: "Morreu o passado que nos amarrava. . . . Repara: colónias, convencionalismos, tiranias, foi tudo por água abaixo ao mesmo tempo. Ideologias políticas, religião católica, tudo se afundou" (282–83). (The past that used to tie us together is now dead. Look: colonialism, conventionalisms, tyrannies, everything went down the drain at the same time. Political ideologies, the Catholic Church, everything has collapsed.)

Jorge's generation saw the collapse of the Portuguese African utopia. This generation was made up of people, on the Left and on the Right, who had come of age in the earlier part of the century under Salazar's hegemony and who, for personal or financial reasons, actively engaged in the Portuguese colonial project in Africa. This generation witnessed the vanishing of the last Portuguese colonial dream, which itself signaled the expiration of five hundred years of empire. On the other hand, Diogo, Jorge's son, lives through the difficult experience of being neither one of the "saviors" of the April Revolution nor one of those who were "saved" by it. Diogo escapes from serving in the military in Africa, and he also does not involve himself directly with the Revolution. Even so, Diogo believes very passionately in the April Revolution. In fact, he embodies the contradictions and disillusionments of the Left, which become more acute as he eventually realizes that the freedom of some is obtained at the expense of others, even in the political systems that define themselves as democratic: "Diogo ouvia-o, queria acreditar. Queria a certeza do bem e do mal. Da sociedade justa, sem classes. Quando cantavam de braço dado, nas festas e excursões de estudantes, o *Canta, camarada canta*, era um prenúncio da sociedade ideal, todos sorrindo, a fraternidade implantada" (132). (Diogo listened and wanted to believe. He wanted the certainties of good and evil. A classless and fair society. When they used to sing together arm in arm in parties and school excursions, "Sing, comrade sing," it was the preamble to the ideal society, all smiles, the seeds of brotherhood.)

Carlota, the conservative daughter, insists on celebrating the fiftieth anniversary of her parents' marriage, in spite of everyone else's skepticism. Carlota holds firm to her belief in the "perfect marriage" until her own marriage collapses under the weight of its conflicts, disillusionments, and imperfections. However, the crisis of traditional values, the myth of the perfect marriage, and eternal love is not verbalized by Carlota, but rather experienced in the form of silent grief. Paradoxically, Rosa and her companions, who struggled for women's liberation and who questioned the institution of traditional marriage, are not substantially less unhappy. Says Rosa: "Dizem que foi uma geração infeliz, a nossa, porque começamos a pôr o casamento em causa. Mas de uma infelicidade mais limpa do que a da geração anterior" (187). (They say ours was an unhappy generation because we started questioning the virtues of marriage. Yet I believe that ours was a cleaner unhappiness than the one experienced by the previous generation.)

Rosa shares with her siblings' and parents' generations the same ontological perplexity caused by the radical shifts in ideological and historical paradigms at the end of the twentieth century, though Rosa assumes a pragmatic position in facing these shifts. Her attitude derives from the relative weight she ascribes to the grand narratives and historical movements and their effects on everyday life, as well as her skepticism vis-à-vis totalizing ideologies:

> Nenhuma sociedade é perfeita, nem os países comunistas se disseram perfeitos, no auge das suas crenças. Em todo o lado há mineiros e engenheiros, vidas desgraçadas e vidas cómodas. E muita frustração pessoal. Na América, que ainda se proclama o país das oportunidades, onde quiseres. Sonhávamos com uma revolução utópica; adolescente;

e foram felizes para sempre. Isso não existe. E quando queremos que uma sociedade siga os nossos sonhos, temos mentalidade de tiranos. (260)

(No society is perfect, not even the communist countries that called themselves perfect at the height of their beliefs. Everywhere there are miners and engineers, painful and comfortable lives. And lots of personal frustration. Even in America, which still proclaims itself the land of opportunities. Wherever. We dreamed of a utopian revolution, adolescentlike: "and they were happy forever after." That doesn't exist. When we want a society to follow our dreams, we become tyrants.)

Despite the skeptical relativism expressed by Rosa, she does not abandon certain ethical values, such as her solidarity with the other, which is exemplified by her commitment to family, to women's rights, and to community in general. This position reveals the inevitable need for some form of foundationalist narratives to give sense to life, to the space and time that we inhabit. Nevertheless, Rosa (and, by extension, the author herself) reduces the status of utopia to a truthful and precariously human dimension.[10]

In synthesis, what is the destiny of the Portuguese nation and the myths of its collective imaginary according to Maria Isabel Barreno? If we take *Crónica do tempo* as a point of departure and Rosa as a privileged subject of the authorial point of view, we verify an arduous struggle to overcome the "narcissistic neurosis" of Portuguese national discourse, centered on its colonial past.[11] At the same time, we witness a strong impulse that questions the sense of individual and collective guilt caused by national historical facts and, at another level, the sense of failure in the realm of family relations in the lives of the characters of *Crónica do tempo*. Barreno is interested in recognizing the "true" national dimensions of Portugal and rejecting the "imperial vocation" that has historically formed the nucleus of the Portuguese self-image. Eduardo Lourenço defines this nucleus as the "fusion of two images, the national and imperial" (*O labirinto da saudade,* 40–41). The utopian dimension of the Portuguese nation and the messianic character of its national discourse that have been historically dominant must accommodate themselves to the real proportions of the national being, according to Barreno's privileged character, Rosa: "D. Sebastião voltará, ressuscitará quando desistirmos de nos considerar excepcionais. Quando pusermos no chão o fardo de uma responsabilidade, de uma culpa, enormes, inventadas.

Todos os povos têm auges e decadências. Tudo é relativo. Tudo passa"
(263). (King Sebastian will return, he will come back to life the day when
we stop considering ourselves exceptional. When we let go of our burden of enormous and invented guilt and responsibility. All nations have
periods of glory and decline. Everything is relative. Everything passes.)
This view leads us to the sociological insights of Sousa Santos, whereby
on a geopolitical level, according to Boaventura de Sousa Santos ("Onze
teses por ocasião de mais una descobeta de Portugal," 110–11), Portugal
must renegotiate its position in today's global system on a new basis,
without triumphant or self-deprecating discourses, analyzing risks and
opportunities, bearing in mind Portugal's realistic potential within today's particularly dynamic transnational framework. Sousa Santos adds
that it is necessary to adopt a "cordial" attitude with regard to Portugal,
along with well-proportioned arguments focusing on the present, with
a view of the material and human circumstances of the nation that is
neither idealized nor nostalgic.[12]

The novel *Crónica do tempo,* as well as *O senhor das ilhas* (1994), represents a strand in Isabel Barreno's fictional production that focuses on
the historical development of the nation as a collectivity—Portugal in
the former case and Cape Verde in the latter—at the same time as it recounts the stories of the private lives of individuals and families and
how the larger historical events of the nation affect them. Barreno gives
special attention to women's subjectivity and the place of women in the
history of the nation, as well as within the family. In *Crónica do tempo,*
which takes place throughout the twentieth century—an era of increased
disenchantment and mistrust with regard to foundationalist political
and religious ideologies—the idea of solidarity with and ethical responsibility to the other acquires great relevance, to the point of supplanting
the passionate historical investment of human beings in failed revolutions and exhausted grand utopias. In *O senhor das ilhas,* on the other
hand, historical facts are created, fictionalized, or reconstructed and the
ontological status of history as a conclusive, totalizing, and teleological
process is destabilized. Furthermore, the epistemological operation that
establishes historical accounts as a locus of absolute and objective truth
is deeply questioned. In *O senhor das ilhas* the history of the Cape Verde
Islands or, more specifically, the experience of Portuguese colonialism
in the Cape Verdean archipelago during the eighteenth and nineteenth
centuries, is evoked. The novel centers on several generations of the

family of Portuguese patriarch Manuel António Martins. Martins was a real historical figure who, through his entrepreneurial skills, vision, and ambition, helped modernize the islands of Boavista and Sal. Martins was also a despot. The story of his family is emblematic of the roots of Cape Verdean culture: the traumatic encounter and miscegenation of European colonists and African slaves.

In her most recent fictional works, Barreno has continued to devote a considerable amount of time to outlining the ethical relationship of the subject to the other, but with a noticeable shift in which the national is deemphasized in favor of an emphasis on the micrological dimension of human lives, that is, the individual and private realms. This is also the case in Lídia Jorge's remarkable novel *O vale da paixão* (The soldier's blanket [translated from the French title, *La couverture du soldat*], 1998), where intimate family dramas become the privileged scenario for the dismantling of patriarchal ideology at the same time as the Portuguese nation-family becomes dispersed (and in some cases, liberated) through the experience of emigration. Portuguese emigration emerges here as the reverse side of the mirror of colonialism, both intimately connected throughout history and both paradoxically signifying Portugal's gradual disappearance into the wider world as the fragments of the nation are absorbed and assimilated into a multitude of other cultures.[13]

Another prolific contemporary Portuguese writer, António Lobo Antunes, is deeply interested in portraying the interaction between individual lives and larger cultural forces. While implicitly alluding to the macroforces of history and the undercurrents of ideology and myth, many of Lobo Antunes' novels center on individual lives, how these lives intersect, and how they are shaped by these larger forces and undercurrents over which individuals (both men and women) have little or no control. By focusing on the intimate realms of everyday life, the author draws attention to the fragility and precariousness of human existence, though there is no guarantee of an ethics of solidarity for collective survival (on this point Lobo Antunes detracts from all authors under consideration in this study, not just Barreno or Jorge). In fact, what predominates in novels such as *O manual dos inquisidores* (1996), *O esplendor de Portugal* (1997), and *Exortação aos crocodilos* (1999) is a profound melancholy and a disenchantment with history, national myths, and life in general, accompanied by a sense of what Maria Alzira Seixo has called a "tender cynicism," without the promise of redemption through the other that we generally observe in the writings of Maria Isabel Barreno.

Barreno's novel *O mundo sobre o outro desbotado* presents an entirely postnational scenario in which people in an undisclosed modern city undergo unusual sensorial experiences, such as perceiving, seeing, and hearing differently from most other people in the world. Medical and psychiatric authorities announce a visual and auditory hallucinatory epidemic. The hallucinating subjects become anguished because they are unable to comprehend their existential situation in the world. At the same time, they become outcasts because they are misunderstood by society, and in particular by those engaging in institutional discourses of power, represented by the medical and psychiatric establishment. Meanwhile, psychiatrists and medical doctors are fearful that they themselves may become contaminated by the mysterious hallucinations. Eventually, most people do become contaminated by the epidemic, which involves hearing voices, seeing the auras of objects, fearing tactile contact with objects, and having visions. Through an intriguing twist of science fiction (rare in Portuguese literature), it is revealed halfway through the short novel that the hallucinatory bout is a product of the contact being established between "aliens" and humans.

In an allegorical fashion, this novel posits a scenario in which human beings must confront the most alien being that is exterior to them. The encounter with the alterity of the alien represents a moment of revelation in that the borders between subjects collapse, disclosing an endless horizon that exceeds the individual subject, and yet it is there that the subject becomes most individuated. This is best exemplified by the actual moment of encounter between the protagonists of *O mundo sobre o outro desbotado* and the aliens:

E a revelação foi essa, a ausência de limites, entre tudo e todos, entre pessoa e pessoa, entre físico e psíquico. Aproximam-se então vertiginosamente do fim, e sentiram um aperto de estômago. A seguir entraram numa luz forte, sentindo eles próprios seres de claridade, transparentes no meio ambiente. Nada havia de assustador nessa ausência de limites que, julgavam até aí, definiam a individualidade. A definição desta era conseguida pela partilha, pelo entrelaçado, pelo tecido: fios e fios daquela mesma luminosa fibra se entrecruzando. (67)

(And such was the revelation, the absence of limits between everything and everyone, between being and being, between the physical and the psychic. They quickly approached the end and felt queasiness in their stomachs. Soon after, they walked into a powerful light, feeling as if they themselves were beings of clarity and transparence in the atmosphere. There was nothing to fear in that absence of limits which, they believed, defined their individuality. Its definition was ultimately the result of sharing, through the fabric, through the interweaving threads of that same luminous fiber.)

Here Maria Isabel Barreno enters into dialogue with the philosophical thought of Emmanuel Levinas.[14] For the late French philosopher believed that the subject "comes into being," or comes into an awareness of its being in the world, through a complex of existential layers (for example, its insertion into the world, its solitude, its mortality) that ultimately lead toward alterity or the other person. Alterity in Levinas's thought appears boundless; its most absolute expression would be God. Facing the radical heterogeneity of the other entails coming to know the other and entering into an intersubjective relationship with it or them, which would ultimately lead to an ethical commitment or a social obligation and responsibility on the part of the self in relationship to the other.

There are other outstanding examples in contemporary Portuguese as well as Brazilian fiction (see chapter 3 on Caio Fernando Abreu) that posit the encounter with the other as an ultimate ontological horizon for the subject (this dynamic will also be discussed in greater detail in the following chapter and the conclusion). José Saramago's *Ensaio sobre a cegueira* (Blindness, 1995), for instance, presents a disturbing narrative in which the world is suddenly overtaken by an epidemic of blindness. Everyone in the novel is mysteriously "contaminated" to the point at which human society collapses emotionally, institutionally, and materially. In view of the extreme circumstances, the protagonists become the most absolute other of themselves. This leads them either to self-destruction or to a radical transformation in which they must forge ties of profound solidarity with their fellow humans in order to survive. Displaying similar philosophical preoccupations, though with an entirely different approach and thematic emphasis, Vergílio Ferreira's novel *Na tua face* (Beauty at the surface of love's face, 1993) confronts the philosophical and aesthetic question of beauty and its consequences with regard to difference and alterity in the world. Ferreira's novel pushes the limits of canonical aesthetic, philosophical, and religious discourses around beauty by valuing the horrible, privileging the scatological, and fully incorporating the fragments of the incomplete, deformed, and battered body. We witness an aging protagonist who identifies with other-abledness, as exemplified by his relationship with the disabled characters featured in the novel. He is able to discover beauty in the "imperfect" body and to be overtaken by the joy of living expressed in the beings that inhabit those bodies. The protagonist's identification with physical difference in the other helps him accept his own difference as an aging man, echoing Vergílio Ferreira's own life circumstances in his later years.

In Maria Isabel Barreno's short novel *O mundo sobre o outro desbotado*, the human characters who initially find themselves isolated and marginalized due to their "other-worldly" hallucinatory experiences not only eventually meet each other and form a heterogeneous community of sorts, but also meet with the alien beings. The discovery of the other "within" as well as "without" and the coming together with the other through a shared sense of alterity not only provides them with a heightened awareness and necessary understanding of difference in the world or of the distinct ways of perceiving it and being in it, but also provides a communal strength that is necessary for survival. In this work the human world becomes clearer, wiser, and limitless in a realm in which (an)other world has literally "unleashed itself" upon it.

In Barreno's novel *O chão salgado*, the question of the subject's ethical commitment to the other—in this case, to family and loved ones in general—is greatly emphasized from a thematic and philosophical standpoint. Though this novel is not framed within a vaguely science-fictional setting such as that of *O mundo sobre o outro desbotado*, part of the plot in *O chão salgado* verges on the mysterious and fantastic, thus informing the everyday real that is represented in the novel. Conversely, national concerns reappear but in a rather diffuse manner and are only indirectly thematized. The Portuguese cultural and historical specificities that are so central to *Crónica do tempo* give way to a narrative in which circumstances of the nation and the national culture appear contingent and almost unimportant. Nonetheless, the traces of Portugal are still detectable through a tenuous outline that is delineated in the novel.

In *O chão salgado* Maria Isabel Barreno shifts the focus from the generational framework that structures her "historical" novels *Crónica do tempo* and *O senhor das ilhas,* which span several decades or even centuries to a narrative structure that is centered on the present and based upon a dual fictional plane. The first fictional plane features the life of Graça, a writer, her husband, Vítor, and their son, Tiago, who suffers from epilepsy. The second fictional place focuses on the story that Graça is writing. In *O chão salgado* we witness the dramatization of Graça's life as a writer, her relationship with her immediate family, the question of maternity, and the everyday interaction between wife and husband. Tiago's epileptic seizures, in fact, serve as a catalysts for Graça's writing. Graça is seen struggling to cope with her son's illness and the possibility that he may not survive over the long term. She must come to terms with her impotence in changing the course of Tiago's ailment. Thus, writing becomes the narrator's own internal pilgrimage in an attempt to find transcendental answers about her life circumstances, in which Tiago's illness plays a large part. Graça also reflects upon her own views regarding motherhood, which she sees more as an ethical commitment to humanity than as a contingent, though unquestionable, social obligation to kin. Graça ponders her most intimate domain as an individual within a family structure where she must relinquish a great deal of autonomy, together with the relationship with her husband, with whom there are significant communication gaps and not infrequent misunderstandings. Her sense of commitment to her family ultimately stems from a sense of solidarity with the other that surpasses the expectations of rigid family structures.

The question of the subject's ethical commitment to the other (the family, the community, loved ones, co-workers, etc.) is undoubtedly a constant within Maria Isabel Barreno's fiction and throughout most of the novels explored here. Such commitment appears as a shared goal, a necessary strategy for human survival, and an unavoidable utopia. However, in her collection of short sories entitled *Os sensos incomuns* (The uncommon senses, 1993), Barreno emphasizes the generalized incompatibility and incommunicability among people. Highly problematized here are solidarity with and ethical commitment to the other—for example, the idea of an automatic solidarity among women (an issue that was already at the core of the drama surrounding the collective production of *Novas cartas portuguesas*). In *Os sensos incomuns,* the space between the subject and the other is filled with ambiguity and misunderstanding. There is a constant risk of misinterpreting the being and actions of the other. Perception is an inadequate means to apprehend reality. There is not a "common sense" through which to judge the real. What predominates in human relations according to most stories in *Os sensos incomuns* is a constitutive "differend," that is, an unresolvable conflict or unbridgeable gap between beings. Partially sharing Jean-François Lyotard's position in *The Differend* (1988), Barreno suggests that the modern and universal "we" is inevitably compromised and that fragmentation and competing interests between individuals and groups is the common postmodern condition. We could ultimately locate Barreno between a Lyotardian skepticism vis-à-vis universal projects and an urgent need to find a common social bond among individuals and groups for the survival of humanity.

Meanwhile, in the novel *O chão salgado* the second fictional plane centers on the story that Graça is writing about. This story features Gracinda and Valentim, who escape the city on a journey to the Portuguese interior after Valentim suddenly collapses after being blinded by a dark shadow. The journey, which at first seems aimless, becomes a pilgrimage as Gracinda and Valentim encounter various significant people who will point them to special places where there are sources of secrets and possible truths. In fact, the search for secrets and truths becomes the force that propels the story of Gracinda and Valentim that Graça is imagining and creating, as well as Graça's own desire as a writer, mother, wife, and member of a larger human community.

New characters with important symbolic meanings meet with Gracinda and Valentim along their path of pilgrimage.[15] There is Gabriela, a strong and independent woman in her fifties who lives contentedly alone in a sunbathed village, who one day dreams of Valentim. In her village Gabriela befriends Vicente, a journalist in his late thirties. Together they engage in long conversations on a variety of issues that echo throughout the whole novel, following the intratextual play that has been established in the novel. For instance, they discuss the status of political utopias, since Vicente has expressed the desire to found a political party based on an anticorruption platform, guided by honesty and clarity, where the politician must be accountable. Gabriela deems the conjugation of politics and honesty a utopian impossibility. We observe here an accentuated, almost tireless, commitment to utopias by male figures—which is corroborated later when Vicente meets Valentim—and a distinct suspicion with regard to redemptive ideological schemes displayed by various women characters (this dynamic is reminiscent of the role played by Rosa in *Crónica do tempo*).[16] Throughout the pilgrimage, all four characters—Vicente, Gabriela, Valentim, and Gracinda—repeatedly meet, separate, and encounter other individuals. The encounter between Valentim and Vicente, for example, represents a coming together of similarly strong utopian impulses: Vicente is conducting a survey about the distance between problems in people's lives and the solutions offered by politicians. Valentim, on the other hand, declares that he is interested in people's spiritual quests and decides to become a preacher and found a religion. The new religion, according to Valentim, will be not only spiritually beneficial but also a successful business venture, given humanity's endless need for lasting beliefs.

Eventually, all four characters become involved in the search for precious mysterious books that may be the repository of transcendental truths. In fact, the axis of Barreno's novel lies essentially in the idea of a pilgrimage or quest for answers to life's crucial questions. She hints that these answers may be located in books, therefore stressing the pivotal role played by writing and literature in this quest. The pilgrimage embarked upon by the various characters mirrors an "internal" search that is carried out by the narrator herself, but also reveals the contours of the author's own "organic" relationship to writing.

The novel *O chão salgado* thematizes the act of writing. Graça, the main protagonist, is witnessed in the middle of assembling various narrative episodes that together will form the greater part of the novel. The fictional space of *O chão salgado* is a chain of various recurring narratives that are intertwined and flow continuously in and out of each other. The borders between the fiction of reality and the reality of fiction appear fluid, and the text invariably comments upon how they inform and affect each other. The everyday life of Graça, the writer, and her family reflect upon the narrative episodes that she happens to be writing, and vice versa, through a constant interplay of texts within texts. By creating such a complex and playful metafictional and intratextual web in *O chão salgado*, Maria Isabel Barreno positions herself at a considerable distance from the narrated facts and allows herself great flexibility to comment on what it means to be a writer, the relationship between the writer and the world, and the ontological status of literature and truth in the world today.

The fictional intratexts continue to meet throughout *O chão salgado* when Graça and her family depart on their own pilgrimage to the heartland of their country, circulating through various specific locations that are reminiscent of the "real" Portugal, such as Fátima. Their journey resembles Gracinda and Valentim's pilgrimage, once again reminding the reader of the constant interplay and symbiotic relationship between fictional levels within the novel, as well as signaling where the author positions herself with regard to her writing, her discrete relationship to the Portuguese nation, and the world at large, and the ways in which they inform her writing. As previously mentioned, in *O chão salgado* there are numerous instances where the narrator or various characters explicitly or implicitly comment on the possibility that literature may be an ultimate repository of lasting truths. Graça, the narrator, asserts that in this novel there is not one secret or revelation or point of illumination. It is a novel that has no redemptive aspirations. All characters of the stories or narrative layers that make up the novel are in search of ultimate secrets and answers that they do not find in books. In a Borgesian fashion, the characters eventually realize that the secrets they discover in the books they read are things they have learned in stories that have already been told in countless forms throughout history. Maria Isabel Barreno, through her narrator Graça, highlights the ways in which human beings are ceaselessly propelled by their fascination with suddenly discovering hidden secrets in literature, though they eventually realize that the secrets lie in the art of storytelling itself.

As much as literature—or, to be more precise, The Book as a symbolic locus of foundationalist narratives (such as the Bible)—is relegated to the precarious relativity of human truths in Maria Isabel Barreno's *O chão salgado,* a similar fate befalls the grand narrative of the nation.[17] In the history of the civilization that is depicted in one of the multiple stories told in *O chão salgado,* the reader can discern traces of the "real" historical Portugal. The history of this "particular" civilization echoes the history of other civilizations in the world that have also experienced cycles of expansion, prosperity, crisis, and decadence. Barreno seems intent with emphasizing the nonsacred and contingent nature of the "national destiny" and how the destinies of nations parallel, in many ways, those of individuals, as they all live through stages of "decadência, sofrimento, implosão de sentimentos, morte e construção de sonhos" (decline, suffering, the implosion of feelings, death and the building of dreams) (186).

Through a self-consciously diffuse and fragmented narrative framework that verges on the mythical-fantastic, *O chão salgado* addresses thematic and philosophical concerns akin to those seen in *Crónica do tempo* regarding the ontological status of the (Portuguese) nation, the postmodern mistrust of utopian ideologies, and the changing positions of female and male subjects in contemporary Portuguese society. Furthermore, in all of Barreno's novels considered here, there is an emphasis on the subject's relationship with the other and its absolute necessity as an ultimate existential horizon for the constitution of the self and society in an era of shattered dreams and accentuated solitudes. This is best symbolized in the final scene of *Crónica do tempo,* which presents a tender image of the embrace between mother and daughter, Manuela and Rosa, after Jorge's funeral. It is an embrace that attempts to grab hold of life, beyond all individual deaths, beyond the fugacity of all nations and utopias. It is a tearful embrace that strives to affirm the affectional ties of each woman with the other—indelible though ephemeral ties among the threads of the time that passes.

CHAPTER FIVE

Worlds in Transition and Utopias of Otherness

The previous four chapters have traced the shift from the grand narratives of nationhood proposed by various currents of Portuguese and Brazilian intellectual thought to a proliferation of micronarratives of nationhood in the realms of literature, popular culture, and the political arena in contemporary Brazil and Portugal. Although this study has focused primarily on Portuguese and Brazilian national cultures, this epistemological shift has clearly been an international phenomenon due to a multiplicity of interrelated factors, namely (in varying order of intensity) globalization, the relative weakening of foundationalist thought structures (for example, nationalisms, Marxism, and Christianity); the affirmation of micro or group subjectivities (along the lines of gender, race, or sexuality, to name some of the most obvious cultural manifestations), and the rise of alternative social movements (ecological, human rights, etc.), among other factors.

This chapter explores the ways in which Portuguese and Brazilian contemporary writers whose fictional production not only redefined in manifold ways the concept of nationhood for Portugal and Brazil, respectively, but also invested itself to varying degrees in utopian or emancipatory causes such as Marxist revolution, women's liberation, or sexual revolution, have since shifted their attention to alternative modes of conceiving the ethical and political realms, thus reflecting the epistemological change outlined earlier. These authors have privileged the subject's relationship with the "other," in the form of family, a loved one, a community, or the "reader." There has been a clear shift of emphasis from national to postnational concerns, where the destiny of "Western culture," or in some cases that of "humanity" in the widest sense, occupies the center stage. It can be argued that this postnational and humanistic reconfiguration has played a major role in the literary production of all the authors considered here. Hence, this chapter is organized into four subsections that discuss the conceptual uses of utopia, the dominant national utopias in modern Portugal and Brazil, the continued need for utopias in contemporary societies, and microutopian expressions in postmodern Portuguese and Brazilian fiction.

So far this study has focused primarily on Brazilian and Portuguese writers Caio Fernando Abreu and Maria Isabel Barreno; however, this chapter incorporates an additional group of Portuguese and Brazilian writers, namely Vergílio Ferreira, Clarice Lispector, Maria Gabriela Llansol, and José Saramago. Here the focus is on the ontological status of "utopia" in a contemporary world where various political and social utopias have been put into question. The authors contemplated here are among those in contemporary Portuguese and Brazilian literatures who have most actively and persuasively engaged the question of utopias and their place within contemporary society.[1] They suggest that in spite of the exhaustion or weakening of utopias that governed the human imaginary (nationally and transnationally) until the late twentieth century, certain strands of utopian thinking are still necessary for the survival of humanity. Therefore, we verify in the writings of these authors an important shift from grand utopian visions to smaller utopian imaginings of a better world. Thus, in a multiplicity of ways they posit new modes of human possibility embodied in subjectivities and communities based on an ethical commitment to and solidarity with "the other" in order to build a more "decent" and humane life. They all share a common belief in the continued need for utopian thinking as a vital principle of hope in human culture (Ernst Bloch, *The Principle of Hope*). But before analyzing various reformulations of utopian thinking within the realms of Portuguese and Brazilian contemporary fiction, let us explore some of the working definitions of the construct referred to as "utopia" throughout history.

Uses and Concepts of Utopia

There has been a recent upsurge of interest in utopian literature and utopian thought, which reveals a continued desire to think of new cultural horizons and new ways of envisioning better societies at the turn of the millennium and after the collapse of communism, as well as in the face of increased dissatisfaction with the market economy as the historical last word. One major example of this particular development has been the publication of Armand Mattelart's *Histoire de l'utopie plané-taire* (1999), a massive history of the ideas of utopia that have governed the Western imaginary since the sixteenth century, which have been driven by the desire for a unified planet, emphasizing a common humanity under the banner of Christianity (at first), and later on of (Western) humanism. According to Mattelart, globalization, along with all of its technological, communicational, socioeconomic, and cultural underpinnings, would be the most successful concretization of such a desire. Meanwhile, the *New York Times* (5 February 2000) carried a long article announcing the publication of two major books on the topic of utopia (*The Utopia Reader* and *The Faber Book of Utopias*), and shortly afterward *Magazine Littéraire* (June 2000) dedicated an entire number to the renaissance of ideas of utopia, featuring the views of writers, philosophers, economists, cultural critics, art critics, and others who coincide in their belief in a continued need for utopias but on a smaller and more human scale than those of the past.

As it is widely known, Thomas More (1478–1535) was the first to coin the term *utopia*. More carved out this neologism from Greek roots, resulting in an ambiguously ironic term that simultaneously combined the notions of "nowhere" and "somewhere good" (the latter meaning was the result of phonological confusion with the Greek prefix *eu-*). Even though More was responsible for inaugurating a literary genre focusing on modern utopias in the early sixteenth century, at first largely inspired by the literature based on the Portuguese and Spanish navigations and "discoveries," it was in ancient Greece and Rome that the earliest forms of what we now call utopias were given literary shape, for example, in the works of Hesiod, Plato, Ovid, and Virgil. Some of the earliest written accounts of utopias point to the myths of a past golden age or earthly paradise, either pagan or Christian. Early Christian culture was in fact a key influence in establishing the contours of religious as well as secular utopianism for the Middle Ages and the Renaissance. As Gregory Claeys and Lyman Tower Sargent have pointed out, early Christianity posited a past utopia (or Eden), a future utopia (or the millennium), and a utopia outside of time (or heaven).[2] In the fifteenth and sixteenth centuries, some of the early images of utopia, such as the earthly paradise or Eden, were projected onto the newly discovered lands in the Americas, for example, Brazil (as is briefly discussed later in this chapter), as an epistemological strategy in order to gain an understanding of these previously unknown human and geographical realities.

Since Thomas More, the idea of utopia has functioned as a projection of time, primarily pointing to a future to be accomplished, as well as a projection of space, positing a better place that is elsewhere. Both types of projections, of (a future) time and (another) space, were dominant features of the various manifestations of utopia from the Renaissance until the nineteenth century. The rise of utopian literature as a genre and of the concept of utopia as a distinct cultural construct can be considered an integral part of a number of different processes and histories that comprised the passage to modernity, such as the shift from a religious to a secular world-view, European maritime and colonial expansion, the rise of mercantilism, the Reformation, the expansion of communication and transportation networks, and the gradual consolidation of faith in reason and science (the latter becoming fully enshrined during the Enlightenment). All these factors signaled, among other things, the birth of a new intellectual and cognitive world (Stuart Hall, ed., *Modernity: An Introduction to Modern Societies*, 8), which provided at the same time an epistemological opening to radically creative imaginings of new worlds and systematic critiques of societies that were still governed to varying degrees by the values and certainties of the Middle Ages.

The uses of the sixteenth-century neologism *utopia* have been manifold throughout more recent Western history, and in its five centuries of existence a complex constellation of meanings has developed around it. Under the rubric of "utopia" we find a profusion of discursive registers: an intellectual product, a form of rhetoric, an abstract ideal, a means to knowledge, a weighty philosophical argument, a fantastic adventure story, a blueprint for an ideal society or city, the work of social theorists, or a literary form put to the service of social analysis and criticism. In general terms, the idea of utopia presents itself as an account of the contemporary predicament of humankind, meanwhile suggesting ways out of it (Krishan Kumar, *Utopianism*). On the other hand, the concept of utopia may also have clear sociopolitical and cultural contours, by its very existence assuming the perfectibility of humankind and nature, along with the validity of institutional and organized means of producing ordered and stable societies (J. C. Davis, "The History of Utopia: The Chronology of Nowhere"). Boaventura de Sousa Santos defines the search for utopia as the exploration through imagination of "new modes of human possibility and styles of will" (*Toward a New Common Sense*, 479), fueled by the desire to create better worlds that are worth fighting for and to which humanity is fully entitled. All three definitions share a common vision of a world that can and must be improved, even today, in an era when there has been an exhaustion of various utopias that have governed modernity. While in agreement with these various definitions, Mattelart points out that though one of the dominant strands in the tradition of utopian thought is a commitment to equality and justice, he finds this lacking in the currently hegemonic neoliberal utopia of globalization.

Even though the definitions that have historically been more commonly associated with the construct of utopia have been connected to grand visions of entirely new worlds that have been given literary form to the point where one can speak of a profuse genre of utopian literature, the way the concept of utopia is used here departs slightly from the traditional definitions. What predominates here are small utopian visionings that are marked by a sense of yearning and hope that have historically characterized the literary representations of utopias, together with a sense of need and urgency to change the nature of human relationships that results from the totalitarian disasters that punctuated the twentieth century (Hitler's Germany, Stalin's Soviet Union, or Pol Pot's Cambodia), but also from an acute awareness of the world's environmental limits, as well as a skeptical view regarding globalization and the hegemony of the market economy. As is illustrated throughout this chapter, the ethical underpinnings of the subject's relationship with the other in the experience of everyday life will be the basis for updated and more humane "utopian visionings."

Within the wide semantic constellation that has historically grown up around the construct of "utopia" one also finds currents of foundationalist thought, otherwise known, in the realm of postmodern theory, as "grand narratives" or "metanarratives." Grand narratives can be defined as totalizing macroperspectives of society and history that are applied universally or, more concretely, as the stories that reflect, among other things, Enlightenment, Hegelian, or Marxist perspectives regarding emancipation and progress that have served to ground and legitimate knowledge about the human experience and the finality of history. Jean-François Lyotard, for example, defined *metanarratives* as those globalizing discourses which have marked modernity: "the progressive emancipation of reason and freedom, the progressive or catastrophic emancipation of labor (source of alienated value in capitalism), the enrichment of all humanity through the progress of capitalist technoscience, and even—if we include Christianity itself in modernity... — the salvation of creatures through the conversion of souls to the Christian narrative of martyred love" (*The Postmodern Explained*, 17–18).[3]

As evidenced by these definitions, grand narratives and metanarratives posit themselves as overarching and universally applicable explanations of humanity's origins, historical evolution, reason for being or purpose, and destiny. They represent discursive-ideological fields that may be secular or religious, that may speak for individual or collective (national or global) lives, or that may attempt to give a full account of the economic forces that govern a given society, determine its course, and have significant ramifications in all aspects of life. Utopian narratives, on the other hand, offer critiques of present life conditions in a given society or in the world at large, as well as projections of a better place in the future, whether locally, nationally, or globally. Moreover, modern utopias are primarily secular and do not offer explanations of the origins of humankind or the reasons for it being. Yet where grand (or meta-) narratives and utopias intersect is in their totalizing perspectives of sociopolitical, economic, and cultural realities; their investment in visions of a historical telos; and their hope for a better future. Ultimately, utopias, grand narratives, and metanarratives, as well as myths, inhabit a common epistemological space as well as a kindred affectional domain, that is, they all presuppose a considerable amount of hope in the human condition. Given its "literariness" from the time of its origin as a cultural construct, the vastness and fluidity of its semantic field, its overwhelming obsession with the future, and its intrinsically secular and humanistic character, "utopia" is the privileged construct throughout this discussion, without losing sight of its conceptual proximity to notions such as grand narratives, metanarratives, and myths.

Portuguese writer and philosopher Vergílio Ferreira has widely addressed the status of "myth" through the content and form of his novels, as well as through his non-fictional production in *Invocação ao meu corpo* (1969) and *Pensar* (1992).[4] Ferreira's definition of *myth* resonates with conceptual definitions of utopia or metanarratives.[5] In *Pensar*, Ferreira defined *myth* as a foundation of thought and being that shapes the human subject but of which the subject remains unaware. Myth, according to Ferreira, not only structures life into a particular purpose but also organizes moral systems, social differentiation, and affectional territoriality—all in all, the inner and outer dimensions of being. Myths are a human invention, but they acquire their own momentum through history, through habit, and through imposition, unconsciously molding human lives. In *Mythologies* (1957) Roland Barthes explored the semiological foundations of the concept of myth by analyzing how a myth is constructed, how it becomes sedimented and subsequently disseminated within bourgeois culture to the point of becoming socially normativized and ideologically naturalized. Barthes and Ferreira coincide in their assessment of the effects of the "naturalization" of myths; while the former focuses on the (re)production of myths in the mass media and the popular culture and the concomitant reification of bourgeois values, the latter devotes his attention to the "grand myths" of Marxism and Christianity and the obstacles they pose in the construction of an autonomous subjectivity. Meanwhile, in Nietzsche's philosophical reflections on the human condition, myths are seen to belong to the order of truths and lies, that is, linguistic conventions that have become embedded in human relations after long use and that eventually seem "firm, canonical, and obligatory to a people" ("On Truth and Lie," 47). Ultimately, they constitute illusions that human beings no longer recognize as such.[6] Though Ferreira and Barthes do not entirely share Nietzsche's cynical bent, there is a clear sense of kinship between Nietzsche's view regarding the nature of truths and lies and the field of definitions advanced by both Ferreira and Barthes regarding the ways in which myths are linguistically and socially constructed.[7]

Moreover, Vergílio Ferreira distinguishes between positive and negative myths: negative myths stifle freedom and human creativity, whereas positive myths affirm and open paths so that the subject may build his or her own truths (*Pensar*, 249). Ferreira's concept of myth here partially coincides with Lyotard's notion of "metanarrative." Lyotard differentiates metanarratives from myths in that the former seek legitimacy not only in an original founding act, as do the latter, but also in a future to be accomplished. Ferreira, for his part, does not make this particular distinction, arguing that myth is also a projection into the future. In fact, Ferreira's own specific definitions of utopia overlap with those of myth, particularly with regard to the notion of an ideological as well as an affectional investment in the future. Ferreira adds that the history of humankind is, at the same time, the history of its utopias, or of that part of the future utopia that has been achieved. Yet there is a surplus of what will never be achieved, and that is the measure of humankind's limitations. Ferreira is interested in emphasizing the fact that myths as well as utopias (here, the conceptual slippage is inevitable) are products of the human imagination. As a consequence, he stresses the fragile and finite nature of myths and utopias and equates them to the fragility and finiteness of human lives. Moreover, he stresses the infinite hope that is placed in them and the insurmountable gap between hope and their actualization. It is from this precariously human location that he relativizes the ontological status of such myths as Marxism and Christianity, though he also argues for the continued need for myths (or utopias), but believes they should be rethought and recast on a more modestly human scale.

Until the nineteenth century, the idea of utopia was most often associated with literary works imbued with philosophical thought (for instance, Thomas More's *Utopia* or Francis Bacon's *New Atlantis*), but during the nineteenth century these were relegated to the margins with the upsurge of utopian social theory (in the writings of Saint-Simon, Fourier, Comte, Spencer, and Marx) and communal experiments (particularly in the United States). Nineteenth-century utopian social theory was rooted in the Enlightenment's critical rationalist mode of thought, which combined the application of reason to social, political, and economic issues with the utopian concern for progress, emancipation, and improvement of society. Thus, utopian thought evolved from the creation of imaginary societies in the sixteenth and seventeenth centuries—where authors such as More and Rousseau did not necessarily expect to change or improve their respective societies—to the consideration of questions of political action in the nineteenth century.

During this period there was a proliferation of blueprints for planned new societies, as well as social experiments on a small scale that aimed at achieving perfect harmony, with the ultimate intent of transforming humankind. Most critics agree that Marxism should be placed within the wide spectrum of utopian ideologies that were borne out of the nineteenth century. Even though Marxism was averse to providing blueprints for a future society (in contrast to the utopian socialists of that era) and even though it rejected the label "utopian" or "ideological" altogether (Paul Ricoeur, *L'Idéologie et L'Utopie*), covering itself instead with a veil of scientific determinism and social praxis, it was as invested as utopian socialism in the desire to transform the present and posit a perfectible future embodied in the concept of a "classless society." Marxism eventually became one of the most powerful utopias and, by extension, one of the grand narratives of the twentieth century. Its unwavering faith in the future as indefinite progress can be considered simultaneously its most powerful source of inspiration and yet the path to its eventual demise, particularly due to the totalitarian practices of state-sponsored Marxism.

Thus, during the first half of the twentieth century socialism—as a concrete material attempt to put Marxism into practice—became simultaneously the archetypal expression of a modern utopia and an antiutopia. In fact, the century saw a proliferation of dystopian types of literature that were largely based on the experience of Stalinism (Orwell's *1984* [1949] was one of the most prominent examples). The United States, as the embodiment of "free-market" capitalism and democracy—where the former has become indissociable from the latter—has had a global utopian appeal that has lasted even longer than that of Marxism, continuing until today. In spite of having "fallen from grace" in the course of the twentieth century and having its utopian appeal relatively tarnished, the United States continues to be regarded by many as a land of political freedom, as well as abundance and opportunity. This is evidenced by the fact that the United States is still one of the primary destinations of emigrants throughout the world. Yet its pitfalls are numerous, among others an unequally distributed economic wealth, racial and ethnic tensions, unfettered violence, excessive materialism, and at times, ruthless exploitation. The latter two examples have inspired antiutopian novels, for instance, Aldous Huxley's *Brave New World* (1932). Furthermore, in terms of foreign policy matters, the United States has had a mixed record; while in many cases it has supported just causes and the promotion of ethical values, in other cases it has utilized its political power for highly questionable, or sometimes even genocidal, purposes. This is exemplified by the overt and covert support given to Latin American right-wing dictatorships between the 1960s and the 1980s, to the Indonesian government in its bloody campaign to forcefully annex newly independent East Timor during the 1970s, or to vastly undemocratic governments such as those in Saudi Arabia or in the Persian Gulf states for blatantly geostrategic and economic reasons (in this case, because of the continued U.S. dependence upon Middle Eastern oil).

Some of the most tragic experiences of the twentieth century have severely shaken the foundations of faith in utopia and in the betterment of humanity if one thinks of the Nazi Holocaust; numerous other horrific examples of "ethnic cleansing" (some of the most recent examples are those of Kosovo, Bosnia, and Rwanda); the threat of nuclear annihilation; the ever-present danger of ecological disasters; countless wars and never-ending cycles of armed conflict in various corners of the globe (Colombia, Angola, the Sudan, and the Congo are some of the most pernicious examples); dramatic socioeconomic gaps; and intractable poverty, which is reflected in the continued hunger, illiteracy, and lack of adequate housing of hundreds of millions of people across the planet. On the other hand, many utopian dreams have been attained, particularly in industrialized societies, as exemplified by major technological advances in the fields of communication, science, medicine, information systems, and transportation, as well as environmental awareness, to name some of the most obvious. There have also been significant cultural changes, more pronounced in the industrialized countries of the West, in terms of women's rights and the rights of sexual and racial or ethnic minorities, the liberation of the body, and the reformulation of the patriarchal heterosexual family unit, for example. In spite of the achievements enumerated so far, there are continued disparities and gaps in levels of social development and welfare, access to technological advances, and economic and cultural opportunities, not only between industrialized and less developed countries, but within given individual countries, that the process of globalization seems to accentuate rather than ameliorate.

In fact, globalization and its corollary, the rise of a market economy, have simultaneously become new utopian as well as antiutopian frontiers. The process of globalization represents the meeting of cultures worldwide on an unprecedented scale (via tourism, migration, the Internet, satellite radio and television, etc.), spawning a growing sense of planetary human interconnectedness, cultural pluralism, and, in the best of cases, an openness to difference. Yet globalization has also given rise to the nearly complete hegemony of the United States in the contemporary world, with all of its economic, political, cultural, and military ramifications in terms of power dissymmetries, increasing identity and standardization (rather than difference across cultures), and, in some of the worst of cases, the wholesale imposition of market economies worldwide through institutional mechanisms such as the International Monetary Fund or the World Bank, regardless of the negative social consequences. There are now clear signs throughout the world of increased discontent and resentment, as well as massive global networking and organizing, particularly in Europe, Latin America, and North America, as demonstrated in the World Social Forum of Porto Alegre in 2002, in relationship to the prevailing socioeconomic disparities of neoliberal globalization and in defiance of the proliferation of discourses that focus almost exclusively on the virtues of the market economy or that view the market economy as a historical inevitability or telos. Still, the most formidable and yet sinister challenge to globalization, and in particular to the United States' ascendance as the hegemonic power in today's globalized order, as was dramatically witnessed in the World Trade Center catastrophe of 11 September 2001, comes from transnational Islamic terror networks, which have brought the contestation of U.S. or Western (neo-)imperial power to previously unforeseen levels of violence and mayhem. This relatively recent development posits new and overwhelming challenges to those living in the twenty-first century, as drastically opposing world-views and political agendas will doubtlessly continue to clash with enormous destructive power and worldwide repercussions.

Portuguese and Brazilian Modern Utopias

What are some of the most powerful national utopias that have governed the cultural horizon in contemporary Portugal and Brazil? In late twentieth-century Portugal, two crucial events sparked a considerable amount of utopian hope: the 1974 April Revolution and the nation's entrance into the European Union in 1986. It can be argued that in both cases some utopian hopes have been fulfilled, while others have not. The April Revolution brought about the downfall of the forty-year-old authoritarian Salazar-Caetano regime, the end of five hundred years of Portuguese colonialism in Africa (and Asia), the emergence of democratic institutions, and Portugal's reintegration into the concert of world nations. At first, the revolution was influenced by Marxist-Leninist ideology and sought to build an egalitarian society through concrete measures such as land reform and the nationalization of key industries.

However, after April 25 Portugal remained a nation deeply divided along class and ideological lines. This situation became further exacerbated by the return of nearly a million Portuguese from the former African colonies and the geopolitical realities of the cold war, which meant that there was enormous pressure (external as well as internal) for Portugal not to align itself with the (former) soviet bloc. Eventually, some of the salient socioeconomic features of the revolution were dismantled, as well as the Marxist rhetoric that had informed the Portuguese polity at the time. Even if the dreams of an egalitarian society were not realized, April 25 opened the door for the democratization and modernization of Portuguese society at the same time as it opened the path toward European integration.

Portugal's entrance into the European Union, by the same token, has signified an important national paradigm shift from the metanarrative of empire to the metanarrative of Europe. In fact, after the revolution and decolonization, it can be argued that the metanarrative of empire has metamorphosed into that of *lusofonia*—that is, the community of Portuguese-speaking nations. *Lusofonia,* a geocultural reality made up of a vastly heterogeneous group of nations united through a common linguistic bond, has become a utopian compensatory space for the Portuguese national imaginary (even if Portuguese is not spoken by all citizens of this pan-Lusophone world, as in parts of Africa or East Timor). However, this space is inevitably a contested one in which Portugal, even though it constitutes the original linguistic matrix, must abandon its claims as the center and instead recognize as well as foster a multipolarity where Brazil, the five African states, and East Timor (where the future of the Portuguese language is still an open question), together with Portugal, can build a community of mutual interests.

Entrance into the European Union has been key to Portugal's promotion from the margins of the contemporary world system to one of its political and economic centers. Yet within this center Portugal occupies a peripheral position from which it must negotiate its own political, economic, and cultural particularities and interests. The end of Portuguese colonialism has not signified the end of the myths associated with maritime expansion and "discoveries" that explain the rise of Portugal as a modern nation, yet the utopian notion of the Portuguese empire as having fulfilled its "manifest destiny" has indeed been superseded by historical reality. Today the myths associated with maritime expansion and "discoveries," (the updated) *lusofonia,* and Europe, together form a Portuguese utopian constellation that shapes the national imaginary now, and will continue to do so for years to come.

In late twentieth-century Brazil, the two most powerful sources of utopian hope were expressed through the myth of modernization and that of "Brazil, country of the future."[8] The two myths are closely intertwined, and, as I pointed out in chapter 2, democratic and nondemocratic regimes have equally embraced them. The utopian investment in the project of modernization and in the myth of Brazil's futuristic potential was embodied in the planning, construction, and inauguration of Brasília during Juscelino Kubitschek's presidency (1956–60). Years later, Brasília's chaotic urban growth and surrounding poverty emblematized the tensions between Brazil's remarkable cultural and architectural achievements; its (justified) ambitions, as well as its potential to become a modern wealthy nation; and its intractable socioeconomic problems. Thus, Brazilian modernity displays a significantly uneven balance between, on the one hand, notable economic and cultural achievements and, on the other, social and political promises vastly unfulfilled. The euphoria of military and civilian governments between the 1950s and 1970s regarding the "manifest destiny" of the Brazilian nation gave way to a sense of popular disillusionment or skepticism in the 1980s and 1990s, as reflected in the notions of "the country that failed" *(o país que falhou)* and "the country that did not make it" *(o país que não deu certo).*

Interestingly, the forcefulness revealed in these expressions of national disappointment convey the suggestive and lasting power underlying the utopia of the "country of the future" and the very high expectations placed upon Brazil given its enormous potential. The utopian notion of Brazil as the "country of the future" is rooted in the vision of the nation as an "earthly paradise," which had been the foundational myth of Brazilian culture since the Portuguese arrival in 1500 (and whose roots have been amply studied by Sérgio Buarque de Holanda),[9] which in turn finds its origins in ancient Christian utopianism (i.e., the idea of Eden rediscovered). In fact, the idyllic vision of paradise that has since prevailed throughout Brazilian history became inscribed during the late nineteenth century in both the national flag and the national anthem, whereby, according to Marilena Chaui, the Brazilian national identity was projected onto the realm of nature and outside of history.[10] This ideological move placed Brazil within a theological time frame as part of God's plan, where its destiny would be guaranteed as that of "the country of the future."

In the late twentieth century, the utopian projection of the notion of "the country of the future," which was metonymically expressed in the project of modernization, did not completely vanish, although it became attenuated and more attuned to the actual socioeconomic realities of the country, including its strengths and weaknesses, as well as its accomplishments and potentialities. Even though the dominant utopias of Brazilian nationhood suffered severe blows in the late twentieth century due to the experience of dictatorship and a frustrating democratization process—particularly with regard to the country's perniciously vast socioeconomic inequalities—they did not altogether disappear. In fact, today in Brazil modernization is seen by a vast number of intellectuals, artists, social activists, and progressive politicians less in messianic terms and more in terms of being inseparable from the need for greater social justice and a continued investment in democratic values. Thus, in contemporary Brazil utopian ideals are being put to the service of a greater collective good and not being used for the sole benefit of the elites, as in the past.

Is There a Future for Utopias?

Despite the postmodern global disillusionment with or suspicion of the idea of utopia—or its discursive and ideological variants in the form of grand narratives, metanarratives, foundationalist thought structures, or myths—critics and scholars of utopia (Holloway, Kumar, Manuel and Manuel, Mattelart, Ricoeur, Santos, Siebers, and Simecka) unanimously agree that there continues to be a need for it and that it should not be abandoned. Michael Hardt and Antonio Negri, in their groundbreaking work *Empire* (2000), unabashedly embrace utopia by positing a globalized, rhizomatic neo-Marxian utopia of the "Earthly City," which would be the result of the reorganizing and redirecting of the oppressive and destructive processes of globalization (or, as they prefer, "Empire") towards new ends, thus unleashing the creative powers of "the multitude" in order to construct a counter-Empire.

Meanwhile, postmodern critics such as Best and Kellner, Hutcheon, Jameson, McHale, and Waugh point out the aporiaristic qualities of Lyotard's narrative of "the end of metanarratives," which in itself has become its own metanarrative. These critics suggest that there is no way of entirely escaping metanarratives. Brian McHale, for instance, calls for demoting metanarratives to "small" or minor" narratives, to be endorsed only provisionally and locally, and for tolerating the anxiety caused by them (*Constructing Postmodernism,* 6–7). Linda Hutcheon points out that knowledge cannot escape complicity with metanarratives or with the fictions that render possible any claim to "truth," however provisional. Ultimately, according to Hutcheon, no narrative can be a natural "master" narrative ("Representing the Postmodern," in *Poetics of Postmodernism,* 253). In agreement with Jameson as well as Ricoeur, Best and Kellner conclude that we are condemned to narrative (be it utopian, mythic, etc.) in that individuals and cultures organize, interpret, and make sense of their experience through story-telling modes (*Postmodern Theory,* 173).

This discussion points to the fact that there has been no end to the narrative investment in and uses of utopia (or any of its discursive correlatives). Utopian thinking has attracted and continues to attract all intellectual disciplines and artistic expressions. Fiction writers and intellectuals from both developing and industrialized nations continue to search and advocate for new and better social possibilities. José Saramago, for instance, has been adamant in stating in countless interviews before and after he won the Nobel Prize for literature in 1998, and in his diaries *(Cadernos de Lanzarote: Diário IV)*, that as long as there is a deficit in social justice throughout the world, there should be no end to our faith in utopias or in the betterment of society. Boaventura de Sousa Santos, on the other hand, stresses the exhaustion of the paradigm of modernity and the consequent need for the invention of a "new common sense" geared toward what he calls "the community principle," based on ideas of solidarity, participation, pleasure, cross-cultural dialogues, and the emancipatory struggles of oppressed social groups, among others.[11] Jurandir Freire Costa calls for an effort to conceive of new forms of family relationships; new modes of affectional, amorous, and sexual relationships; new styles of sociability; and new attitudes toward scientific and technological progress, among other things, in order to build a more ethical life that may also restore moral dignity to the other, in a society such as that of Brazil, which is plagued with violence (although his propositions would be applicable to other nations in the world today).[12]

Vergílio Ferreira, for his part, is reticent to intervene at a wider social or global scale, either through his thinking or through concrete political gestures or initiatives such as we observe in Saramago, Santos, or Freire Costa. Ferreira's reflections on the questions of myth and utopia remain within a more restricted Western bourgeois sociocultural sphere and tend to focus on the individual subject's relationship with the other in the microinstances of everyday existence where questions of love and affection, and especially life and death, are at stake. In spite of these significant differences between thinkers such as Ferreira, Freire Costa, Santos, and Saramago, they all coincide in affirming the continued need for utopias, myths, projects, or narratives that may provide hope for the human condition.

In the late twentieth century, the historical propensity toward utopian thought or hope underwent significant changes. The exhaustion or weakening of various utopias (or myths or metanarratives) that have governed modernity, and the ensuing incredulity vis-à-vis utopian modes of conceiving society or the world at large, for the most part have given way to smaller and more modest accounts or micronarratives that are no less utopian-inspired or concerned with the well-being and destiny of humanity. Thus, from a philosophical standpoint, significant attention has been given to questions of ethics (by writers such as Levinas, Lyotard, Derrida, and Agamben), whereby notions of "alterity," "difference," the ethical relationship of the subject with the other, or the renewed possibilities of co-belonging to a human community, have become paramount. In political terms, greater emphasis has been placed on micrological modes of theorizing society and advancing change instead of contemplating the wholesale transformation of societal macrostructures. Culturally speaking, there has been an emergence into "the speech of the public sphere" (Fredric Jameson, *Postmodernism, or, The Cultural Logic of Late Capitalism*) of a wide range of groups organized around facets of human subjectivity that have been historically neglected or marginalized, such as gender, sexuality, race, and ethnicity, and this has had important repercussions in all aspects of society (economically, politically, etc.), even in Brazilian and Portuguese societies, which have been the primary object of this study. These various epistemological shifts have had decisive effects in the realm of contemporary literature, as well as in the realms of other artistic expressions; in fact, the symbiotic relationship between these shifts and the fields of culture and the arts is quite apparent.

The Portuguese and Brazilian fiction writers contemplated here, while not interested in developing blueprints or establishing paradigms for a new society, are exploring the ontological and ethical parameters underlying the subject's relationship with the "other, in the form of a loved one, family, community, or the "reader." The parameters of this relationship reveal its direct kinship with Bakhtin's conceptions of being and "dialogism," parts of his "philosophical anthropology," where the other plays a key existential role.[13] Most of the writers studied here believe that the relationship of the subject with the other appears not only as a microcosm of a given national society, but also of humanity at large, and it becomes the foundation for building a "more decent" individual as well as collective life. At times, this relationship is conducted in "limit situations" exemplified by the complete breakdown of society as we know it, as in José Saramago's apocalyptic novel *Ensaio sobre a cegueira* (1995), where human beings must search for new ways of relating to each other in order to survive catastrophe and to eventually build a renewed and better life. In other cases, as in various works by Caio Fernando Abreu, Clarice Lispector, and Vergílio Ferreira, we observe the subject-narrator coming to terms with the end of life, either consciously or unconsciously, due to illness or old age. In this context, the emotional and even the physical bond with the other become decisive forces in the quest for a purposeful and fruitful existence at the end of life, as well as for a greater acceptance of death's inevitability. Maria Isabel Barreno, on the other hand, suggests that the foundations of social commitment, social justice, and democracy, far from being based on abstract concepts, lie first and foremost in the subject's everyday interaction with the other in the context of family life, the workplace, friendship, anonymous city life, and so on. For Maria Gabriela Llansol, the literary text is a transhistorical space where "communities of rebels" are formed, united by common cultural and ethical concerns.

The ethical philosophy of Emmanuel Levinas, which in turn was largely based on the dialogical thinking of Martin Buber and Franz Rosenzweig, resonates with the contemporary cultural and political dominants that interest us here, as pointed out in previous chapters. Levinas's definition of being is based on an intersubjective relation premised on the subject's ethical obligation with regard to the other. This ethical modality of subjectivity brings about a sense of *entre nous*, where ontology is defined in a dialogical fashion. The ethical relationship becomes the fundamental relationship between subjects whereby to be oneself is to be for the other. Thus, the encounter with the other entails becoming responsible for the other. In Levinas the other is defined quite fluidly, encompassing the biblical notion of the other as "neighbor" *(autrui* in French, or *outrem* in Portuguese), the "other person" *(l'autre),* as well as God. Ultimately, the subject's relationship with the other as an individuality or collectivity, according to Levinas, is a relationship with infinity. Infinity, by the same token, is manifested by the figure of God. The subject's relationship with God is presented as a relationship with the other *(l'autre homme)* that Levinas posits quite literally. He adds that through the mouth of the other, one hears the word of God (*Entre Nous,* 120).

Levinas's definitions of otherness are inevitably laden with ambiguity, conflating the religious and the secular, the human and the godly. As Jacques Derrida points out, Levinas remains within "the play of difference and analogy, between the face of God and the face of my neighbor, between the infinitely other as God and the infinitely other as another human" (*The Gift of Death,* 83–84). In his essay "Tout Autre Est Tout Autre," Derrida criticizes what he perceives as the lack of differentiation between the orders of the ethical and the religious in Levinas, which is revealed in the ambiguity underlying the notion of the "infinite other" (is it God, my neighbor, or another human?). Derrida wants to call attention to the aporiaristic nature of the confluence between the ethical dimension and the realms of the religious, moral, legal, and political, particularly when confronted with the realities of war. In the face of war, the notion of the "unconditional responsibility toward the other" is put severely to the test, especially with regard to the enemy. Some of the political or socioeconomic limitations of Levinas's utopian ethics become apparent when, for instance, Levinas is questioned about the relations between Israelis and Palestinians or his views regarding moral and ethical responsibility in the aftermath of the Sabra and Chatila massacre in Lebanon in 1982 (Sean Hand, ed., *The Levinas Reader,* 289–97). The abstractness of ethical-philosophical formulations based on a fundamental and all-encompassing notion such as the relationship between the subject and his or her other(s) is tested against the practice of everyday life, which presupposes concrete political, cultural, and socioeconomic scenarios and transactions that in fact demand an ethical positioning or response, and is tested even more in the face of limit situations such as war.

Derek Attridge, for his part, connects otherness to a dimension differ-ent from the strictly anthropomorphic or sociological one commonly associated with the concept of "the other," which is also key to our dis-cussion on literature and ethics. Attridge links otherness—also defined by Levinas as a reality produced in an active or eventlike relation—to acts of creativity and invention. These acts would be akin to the experi-ences of writing and reading, echoing here Derrida's own view of oth-erness as that which is produced through the act of writing, although Derrida is more interested in establishing the singularity of the act where otherness emerges. Writing would refuse to be enclosed or dominated by an economy of the same and would establish a relationship of *différance* between the I (that is, the reader) and the other that emerges (*Acts of Literature*, 342–43). According to Derek Attridge, editor of *Acts of Liter-ature,* the other is also that "which beckons or commands from the fringes of my mental sphere when I engage in a creative act" (23)—a creative act that can be represented by the act of writing or reading. The emer-gence of the other in the act of writing as well as in the act of reading would be the result of one's interaction with the singular otherness man-ifested in a creative and innovative human artifact, such as a journalistic report, a mathematical proof, a painting, a musical piece, or a novel.

The privileging of "the other" as a primary ontological, ethical, and political horizon in the literature and philosophy discussed here points to its emergence as a major utopian frontier within contemporary global culture. We can describe this phenomenon as the appearance of the "utopia of alterity" or the "utopia of otherness." With the exhaustion, weakening, or relativization of the utopias of Marxism, Christianity, nationhood, and globalization, among others, we are left with human-ity as the most basic ontological foundation as well as the source of faith and hope. The utopia of otherness thus situates itself between the condition of being an absolute principle and the condition of being radically fragmented into a multitude of small narratives and relational instances that describe and govern the contemporary human condition. The other—as posited by the fiction writers who are the object of this study—presents a wide constellation of meanings, ranging from vari-ous individualized or collective beings to the objects of eventlike rela-tions, as embodied in the figure of a lover, family, friend, co-worker, or community; the nation; humanity; the "reader"; or the act of writing or reading. At times, the other, in certain characters created by Saramago or Lispector, may appear as "the oppressed other" or "the subaltern," as defined by postcolonial theory (particularly with regard to class). In the cases of Abreu and Barreno, the other tends to appear in the form of a lover, family, friend, or co-worker. In the cases of Lispector, Ferreira, and Llansol, the question of alterity becomes, in multiple ways, the centerpiece of an ongoing reflection on the ontological status of literature, on the acts of writing and reading, and on the symbiotic relationship between living and writing. In the specific case of Llansol, there is also the pursuit of freedom in the context of the mystical experience that is an integral part of the experience of writing and, by extension, of the relationship with the other.

While Saramago, Barreno, and Lispector are concerned with class issues as they reflect upon the subject's relationship with his or her others, and while the issue of freedom of consciousness and of religion is also an important concern in the work of Llansol and Saramago with regard to the question of alterity, none of the fiction writers or philosophers discussed so far explicitly consider racial, ethnic, and/or national differences in their reflections about the other. Even though all thinkers under discussion here are probably aware of the central importance of these differences and their profound impact on human relations at the local, national, and global levels, the issues of race, ethnicity, and nationality are not objects of discussion in their writings. Yet these issues have historically been at the core of human conflict and will continue to be some of the greatest sources of tension and misunderstanding in the quest to defend the primacy of a "utopia of otherness" as an emerging collective practice.

Utopias of Otherness in Postmodern Portuguese and Brazilian Fiction

Vergílio Ferreira was one of the Portuguese authors who most devoted himself to existential questions. His vast fictional and nonfictional production includes ample space dedicated to delineating the ontological contours of human subjectivity with regard to dominant ideological currents (in either the political or the religious sphere), the impending horizon of death, or in the subject's relationship to the other. In Ferreira's fictional works the subject is located at an existential and cultural crossroads beyond universal truths, where the sole ontological horizon is the human subject. It is in solitude, hyperaware of the limits of his body and his language, that the Vergilian subject searches for his own truth in order to fulfill, however briefly, his fragile existence.[14] This cultural and existential crossroads is a consequence of the profound incredulity in relationship to totalizing ideologies or myths, such as Christianity and Marxism, that were dominant in the twentieth century. However, at the end of the century, as state-sponsored Marxism waned, Christianity continued to engage in a dominant set of discourses in various countries of the Western world. Ferreira's novels dramatize this moment by presenting subjects that strive to overcome cultural discourses or myths that frustrate their attempts at constructing their own measures of freedom, their own truths.[15]

Throughout Vergílio Ferreira's fiction a great amount of narrative energy is expended in the subversion of totalizing thought structures or ideologies—Marxism or Christianity, for example—that have historically stifled the human subject in its quest for individual freedom.[16] In his novels the author utilizes formal experimentation, irony, and parody as strategies to subvert those myths, as well as to deflect or weaken his own authority so as to achieve a nontotalizing narrative. However, Ferreira—like many other postmodern thinkers, including Lyotard—cannot completely escape totalizing thought structures or even his privileged position as a prominent intellectual figure of his place and time, which implicates him as a (re)producer of other myths or metanarratives. These are paradoxes that refuse to get resolved, and Vergílio Ferreira is clearly well aware of it. In fact, he plainly assumes these unresolvable paradoxes—on the one hand, by challenging the myths of Christianity and Marxism, but on the other hand, by firmly embracing another myth: that of humankind, which he believes inescapable. This is, in fact, one of the philosophical areas that separates Ferreira from most postmodern theorists, to the point at which he has been called "the last of the moderns" by Maria Alzira Seixo.[17] However, Ferreira could be better described as having been caught between a modernist yearning for stable and lasting truths to serve as a foundation for human existence and a postmodernist skepticism regarding absolute truths. This points to the tension underlying the impossibility of escaping metanarratives, myths, or utopias altogether, and the heightened awareness of their provisional ontological status.

Ferreira believes that humankind represents the ultimate horizon to and from which truths emanate. However, however much Ferreira wrote about the "flight of the gods" and the consequent solitude and contingency that envelops human existence, the gods never completely disappear. They function, rather, as utopian projections of what or where humans are not, but aspire to be. Vergílio Ferreira believes that humankind must confront its own fragility and finiteness, searching for a measure of freedom and happiness, in order to make life more livable and death more endurable. The other—as emblematized by another human being, in this case a loved one—becomes a secularized as well as an anthropomorphic utopian projection that carries a weight commensurate with the precariousness of human existence. Such is the measure of humankind's provisionality as utopia or myth, according to Ferreira.

In 1969, when *Invocação ao meu corpo* was published, Vergílio Ferreira spoke of humankind as the only permanent value after the emptying or death of all other values (*value* here refers to myth—the myth of Christianity or communism, for example). Humankind does not become devalorized, but rather attempts to recognize itself within the limits of its body (*Invocação,* 250). The body and the I are indissociable from one another. The absolute of the body becomes the absolute of the I—the body is the site not of the person but of the "actual" person *(pessoa efectivada):* "Não existo eu *mais* o meu corpo: sou um corpo que pode dizer 'eu'" (253). (I don't exist *plus* my body: I am a body that can say "I.") However, by 1990, when *Em nome da terra* (In the name of the earth) was published, we face (as has been pointed out by Fernanda Irene Fonseca) a subject no longer unified with the body.[18] The irreversibility of death shatters this unity to such an extent that it becomes only a memory. In *Em nome da terra* this memory is made up by the memory of the other (a lover) and the subject's amorous relationship with her. Here the narrating subject calls forth a second person (Mónica, his loved one, who has since passed away) in what constitutes a long, passionate letter, which in essence is the novel itself: "Querida. Veio-me hoje uma enorme vontade de te amar. E então pensei: vou-te escrever. Mas não te quero amar no tempo em que te lembro. Quero-te amar antes, muito antes" (9). (My dear. I've been suddenly overtaken today by a desire to love you. And so I thought: I will write you. But I do not wish to love in the very instant in which I remember you. I wish to love you before, much before.) All events take place in the memory of João, the narrator: Mónica, his absent interlocutor, will be reconstructed, as if from a desire to reconstruct himself through the other—emotionally, spiritually, ontologically—at the edge of life, now that the corporeal is slowly and irreme-diably falling apart. The narrator can exist only as long as he expresses the passion he feels for his loved one, as long as the other's presence is called forth. The force of the novel is therefore extracted from its very dialogical structure: "Meu amor—que amor? Não és tu. És, és. Não és. Na realidade não sei. Na realidade há o que existe, o que se diz um facto, o que se avalia ao quilo ou ao quilómetro. E há o que nos existe, aquilo que está por dentro disso—vou amar o teu corpo como nunca te amei" (155). (My love—what love? It isn't you. Yes it is. No it isn't. I really don't know. In truth, all that exists is what is, that which calls itself a fact, whatever can be measured by the pound or by the mile. And there is also what exists within us and whatever that is—I will love your body as I've never loved you.)

In spite of the decline or weakening of utopias or myths that domi-nated the Western cultural landscape throughout the twentieth century—an epistemological shift that Ferreira so insistently thematized in his later works—there is a detectable nostalgia for "the whole," or lasting myths that may provide an affectional as well as an ideological basis for human existence.[19] This is apparent in the constant search for absolute beauty in *Na tua face* (1993), in spite of the narrator's hyperawareness of living in a time beyond absolute beauty. In *Em nome da terra*, the desire for absolute communicability between the narrator and his forever-lost lover becomes a metaphor of the longing for a time in which the belief in the correspondence between word and object of representation was held to be true. In *Para sempre* (1983), there is an endless desire to achieve a plenitude of being that may be expressed through language. In all three novels, the search and the desire for absolute beauty, communica-bility, and a plenitude of being are invariably framed within the context of the longing for a loved other. The desire for the other as a metonymic expression of the search for lasting truths becomes a propelling force for the act of literary creation, as well as for the act of living—which are both inseparable in the writings of Vergílio Ferreira.

Brazilian writer Clarice Lispector and Vergílio Ferreira are kindred writers in their existential concerns; both see questions of being and al-terity as fundamental at the same time as they are inseparable.[20] On the other hand, the two writers greatly diverge in terms of the attention given to gender and other sociopolitical issues. Lispector's fictional world can be summarized as the site of a continuous search for existential truths that are reflected in the questions explicitly or implicitly posed by author, narrators, and characters: What am I in life? How am I to speak my being? What is women's place in bourgeois society? How can one overcome in life the horizon of life's solitude and finitude? The search for answers to these questions takes place initially as a deeply introspective and individualized experience, but reaches its highest point only in "limit situations" or phenomenological experiences that entail encounters with the other. The other here may be represented by a human being, an animal, nature, an object, or a given event. This play of alterity and difference entails, on the one hand, a philosophical reflection on "being in the world," and on the other hand, a reflection upon women's condition in patriarchal society; thus, ontological and gender issues became inextricably linked in Lispector's fiction.[21]

Lispector's best-known novel, *A hora da estrela* (1977), is a lyrical reflection on the process of writing, as well as a quest for a truth of self in the face of death's inevitability and a meditation on the raw material of writing (that is, language), the role of the writer in a "Third World" society, gender relations, and the dramatic socioeconomic inequities within Brazilian society. This novel presents a dialectic narrative between a female author (Clarice Lispector) and a male narrator (Rodrigo S. M.) that leads to an implicit, and sometimes explicit, debate about the effects of the "genderization" of the narrator in literature and a questioning of the weight of the male authorial voice—itself a manifestation of a restrictive patriarchy.[22] The ultimate focus of *A hora da estrela*, though, is on Macabea (a semiliterate migrant worker from the Brazilian Northeast in the richer Rio de Janeiro), thus calling attention to the painful socioeconomic imbalances in contemporary Brazil. Through her otherness, Macabea becomes the objectified surface onto which the selves of the author/narrator (and even readers) are projected, and in turn refracted. This is the metafictional/ontological network functioning throughout the novel of which Macabea becomes an essential piece. Her material poverty thinly veils the spiritual richness that the author/narrator is keen to uncover and use to nurture himself. As the narrator points out, even if one does not suffer monetary poverty, there is spiritual or emotional poverty—deep human solitude that many share and through which each one identifies himself. We (author/narrator/readers) are bound to Macabea in sympathy, as well as in solidarity.[23] In Macabea we see ourselves; we see life's contingency[24]:

Acho que julgava não ter direito, ela era um acaso. Um feto jogado na
lata de lixo embrulhado em um jornal. Há milhares como ela? Sim, e
que são apenas um acaso. Pensando bem, quem não é um acaso na vida?
Quanto a mim, só me livro de ser apenas um acaso por que escrevo. (52)

(I suspect that she felt she had no right to do so, being a mere accident
of nature. A fetus wrapped up in newspaper and thrown onto a rubbish
dump. Are there thousands of others like her? Yes, thousands of others
who are mere accidents of nature. And if one thinks about it carefully,
aren't we all accidents of nature? I have only escaped from a similar fate
because I am a writer). (Trans. by Giovanni Pontiero as *The Hour of the
Star*, 36)

Writing, then, opens a path for the narrator/subject to attempt to overcome (albeit arduously and ephemerally) his existential fatigue, disquietude, and anguish in the face of life's ever-present horizon of solitude and inexorable death:

Escrevo porque sou um desesperado e estou cansado, não suporto mais
a rotina de me ser e se não fosse a sempre novidade que é escrever, eu me
morreria simbolicamente todos os dias (35–36) [. . .] Se ainda escrevo é
porque nada mais tenho a fazer no mundo enquanto espero a morte.
A procura da palavra no escuro. (88)

(I write because I am desperate and weary. I can no longer bear the
routine of my existence and, were it not for the constant novelty of
writing, I would die symbolically each day] (Pontiero, trans., *The Hour
of the Star*, 21) [. . .] I have grown weary of literature: silence alone com-
forts me. If I continue to write, it's because I have nothing more to
accomplish in this world except to wait for death. Searching for the
word in darkness.) (70)

Lispector's posthumous work of fiction, *Um sopro de vida* (A breath
of life, 1978), was her most radical and "urgent" literary experiment. As
the author suggests, it is a series of "pulsations" *(pulsações)*, whereby the
act of being in the world is coterminous with the act of writing. Lispector stresses in a final breath that writing is a primordial part of being.
Clarice Lispector's pulsations signal that literature, art, and music are
an integral part of the mystery of life, because they are the expression of
it.[25] In fact, according to the author/narrator, the act of writing is an attempt at saving life from death. It is the certainty of death that propels
the act of creation and through which life is affirmed: "Eu escrevo como
se fosse para salvar a vida de alguém. Provavelmente a minha própria

vida. Viver é uma espécie de loucura que a morte faz. Vivam os mortos porque neles vivemos" (17). (I write as if I were saving somebody's life. Maybe my own life. Living is a kind of insanity that death creates. Long live the dead, because we live in them.)

In *Um sopro de vida*, the reader confronts an intensely self-conscious male narrator who overtly thematizes his position as author/narrator (these are fluid notions in *Um sopro de vida*, as in *A hora da estrela*) at the same time as he meditates throughout on what it means to be an author as well as to create a character: "AUTOR: Eu sou autor de uma mulher que inventei e a quem dei o nome de Ângela Pralini. Mas ela começou a me inquietar e vi que eu tinha de novo que assumir o papel de escritor para colocar Ângela em palavras porque só então me posso comunicar com ela" (37). (AUTHOR: I'm the author of a woman whom I invented and whose given name is Angela Pralini. But she made me restless so I realized that I needed to assume the role of the writer and give her words, because that's the only way we can both communicate). Ângela, though, never acquires a fully autonomous life in *Um sopro de vida*, suggesting that a fictional character is never entirely autonomous of the author's subjectivity; in this particular case, many life details related to the character Ângela closely reflect Lispector's own life circumstances (both are writers and painters, both have a close emotional attachment to a dog named Ulisses who nearly disfigures them, both experience frustration with publishers, and so on).

Ultimately, the borders between Clarice Lispector, the male narrator, and the character Ângela are tenuous at best. In fact, Clarice Lispector doubles herself simultaneously as the author and the character Ângela, as she plunges into their beings, each sharing the other's anguish. In *Um sopro de vida* we find many expressions such as: "Eu te respiro-me," "Ela me é eu," and "de mim para si mesma" (I breathe you within myself, She is I within me, from me to her own self), that signal an implosion of identities between author, narrator, and character. At the same time, this implosion dramatizes the need for the author to "other" himself in order to better understand and communicate his own process of "being in the world"—a need so ardently felt and sublimely expressed by poet Fernando Pessoa earlier this century. In the words of the author/narrator of *Un sopro de vida:* "Escolhi a mim e ao meu personagem—Ângela Pralini—para que talvez através de nós eu possa entender essa falta de definição da vida" (24). (I chose myself and my character Angela Pralini so that perhaps through us I may understand the lack of definition in life.)

The author/narrator also thematizes the struggle of bringing a character to life, suggesting the impossibility of fully seizing as well as representing subjectivity. As Lispector writes: "Tentar possuir Ângela é como tentar desesperadamente agarrar no espelho o reflexo duma rosa" (49). (Trying to possess Angela is like trying to take hold of the reflection of a rose in the mirror.) By the same token, the thematization of the constitutive *différend* between the experience of being and its representation has a gender corollary, whereby it is suggested that women's subjectivity cannot be apprehended in the entirety of its truth because it is an "enigma" (113) or because it refuses "domestication" (140).[26] In fact, throughout Lispector's fiction there is a clear oscillation between the notion—implicitly and explicitly expressed—of the impossibility of representing the subject's "being in the world" as it occurs, regardless of gender, and the impossibility of apprehending a specifically gendered (in this case, women's) experience within language. Being, as Lispector's fiction so lyrically and eloquently suggests in *A paixão segundo G. H.* (1964) or *Água viva* (1973), can be expressed only at a preconscious or prelinguistic level; that is, in a deeply paradoxical fashion, the author suggests that it is at the point of most incommunicability of the subject's thinking-feeling that *being* can be apprehended.[27] Hence, the preponderance of nonlinear, non-Cartesian, highly fragmented, and free-flowing narratives within the greater part of Lispector's fictional production, aside from the strong presence of music and painting in her writing, can be seen as privileged nonrational spaces where the experience of being can be expressed (here Lispector overlaps with Vergílio Ferreira and Maria Gabriela Llansol).[28] So in *Um sopro de vida* it is through the thinly veiled *mise-en-scène* of nearly overlapping identities between Clarice Lispector, the male narrator, and the character Ângela, where the struggle for representation is paramount, that the reader also acutely perceives a sense of existential urgency that is not only metaphysical, but eventually physical, in view of the author's health circumstances in the last days of her life.[29]

Vergílio Ferreira, Maria Gabriela Llansol, and Clarice Lispector are key figures in the Portuguese and Brazilian literary and cultural fields who actively engaged in the process of epistemological reconfiguration in Western philosophy and literature throughout the late twentieth century. This reconfiguration was intimately connected to the problematization of the relationship between being and language. This dynamic reveals to varying degrees the kinship between Ferreira, Lispector, and Llansol and the philosophical thought of Nietzsche, Heidegger, Wittgenstein, Foucault, and Derrida, among others. At the center of this epistemological reconfiguration lay, in addition to other factors, the untenability of the Cartesian cogito as the core principle of human subjectivity, as well as the impossibility of a unitary or absolute origin of meaning given the inherent instability of the relationship between signifier and signified. These two key factors alone have had vastly profound consequences regarding definitions of truth, being, and morality, which in turn have affected the act of literary representation. In fact, it has been within the realm of literature that these crucial philosophical problematics have been most dramatically depicted.

The literary practices of Lispector, Ferreira, and Llansol have implicitly and explicitly thematized the struggle between being and language.[30] The phenomenological constitutes an integral dimension within this struggle, because it entails the subject's interaction with the other.[31] These authors have thematized the act of creation as an event where otherness emerges in a multiplicity of registers. Thus, literature, music, and art are posited as creative spheres where identity is seen as inseparable from alterity. This interaction brings about an unsolvable yet endlessly exciting paradox where the subject approaches the heart of being and yet remains farthest away from its communicability. This dynamic propels the subject (the writer, in this case) to live and create, and even more passionately so, in the face of death. The later novels of Clarice Lispector *(A hora da estrela* and *Um sopro de vida)* and Vergílio Ferreira *(Para sempre* and *Em nome da terra),* for instance, were written with a sense of urgency at the edge of life. They all express the need to overcome life's contingency in order to make life more livable, and perhaps death more acceptable.

Maria Gabriela Llansol, together with Fernando Pessoa, Clarice Lispector, and Vergílio Ferreira, as well as Brazilian fiction writer João Guimarães Rosa, is part of a common lineage that encompasses the most highly philosophical literature written in the Portuguese language throughout the twentieth century. Although Llansol's concerns regarding subjectivity and literary representation overlap with those of this group of writers, her view of subjectivity as indissociable from the subject's relationship with "the other" brings her much closer to Lispector and Ferreira. At the same time, Llansol's reflections on the literary space, on the act of writing, and on the relationship between the subject and "the other" and its bearing upon the act of literary creation take her to an almost entirely new place and one distinct from that inhabited by Ferreira or Lispector.

Critics unanimously consider Llansol's writing practice groundbreaking in that she completely redefines the parameters of fiction and even the nature of literature itself.[32] Her work has been deemed "unclassifiable," constituting a hybrid genre of free-floating diaries, fiction, dialogues, essays, and poetry, with no particular sequential logic or strict chronological order.[33] In Llansol's "novels" she has radically reformulated notions of space and time within the literary text. There is a geographical deterritorialization where "events" (or "textual moments of being") take place in undetermined locations or they occur simultaneously in time in more than one location or within an interior plane. As Lúcia Helena points out, time becomes "de-historicized" and space "de-geographized" ("Estratégias narrativas na obra de Maria Gabriela Llansol," 39). Space, moreover, is freed from the contingencies of time. The reader is confronted with numerous purposeful gaps in the narrative sequences, a proliferation of contingent facts, and language that is scarcely metaphorical. The semantic field is radically transformed, and signifiers are displaced from their usual contexts, acquiring new meanings at the same time as new associations of meaning between signifiers are formed. Llansol's writing is deconstructive in itself vis-à-vis the uses of language and the ontological status of literature, displaying "the open-ended indefiniteness of textuality" that Spivak talks about in describing Derrida's deconstructive hermeneutics (*Of Grammatology*, lxxvii). Here, though, it is Llansol (the writer/narrator) who through her texts inaugurates a process of productive reading of the world that underlies deconstruction, where metaphysical and rhetorical structures are dismantled, transfigured, and reinscribed.

The reality principle in Llansol's texts tends to exclude everyday events while confronting the reader with the uncommon, the unconventional, or the nonhabitual (Augusto Joaquim, "Posfácio" to *Um falcão no punho*). Llansol stages a transhistorical and intertextual dialogue between her fictional characters (Aossê, Infausta, Isabôl, and Ana de Peñalosa, among countless others) and a large cast of major Portuguese as well as western European cultural figures (Ramón Llull, Copernicus, Spinoza, Camões, Pessoa, Bach, Virginia Woolf, Hadewijch, Vergílio Ferreira, Nietzsche, and Müntzer, among many others).[34] These figures become part of a series of heterogeneous fictional, cultural, and historical communities through the deployment of "clusters of companions" *(dispositivos de companheiros)*, that is, mythical or historical figures united by common cultural problematics, for instance, the relationship between the exercise of power and the freedom of consciousness, or the capacity of human beings to "live in each other's proximity" (*Lisboaleipzig 1: O encontro inesperado do diverso*, 95). What also unites these figures is having been protagonists of dramatic moments in the course of Western history in which they revolutionized mentalities and cultural paradigms, and because of this were either marginalized, ostracized, or persecuted by the established powers. Llansol considers these figures rebels or heretics who struggled for the right to exercise their freedom to think and to create, and therefore they play a central role in Llansol's cultural project. Ultimately, beneath the density, abstraction, intertextuality, and self-referentiality that permeate Llansol's texts, there is an ongoing ethical reflection on the human condition or the destiny of humanity, the ontological status of literature and its future within contemporary Western society, the place of Portugal within Western culture, the relations between the sexes, the relationship between power and freedom of consciousness, and the place of the mystical experience within daily life, among other topics.

Llansol's literary production is essentially a self-conscious fiction of fictions that flows without following any prescribed teleological progression or without a predetermined addressee. Her texts are made up of fragments and variations, emulating the structure of classical music compositions. Truth is posited at a dialogical level through the relationship between the I and the other. Thus, the world is defined as primarily relational. Human lives, according to Llansol, are governed by libidinal and affectional forces (much as in the writings of Deleuze) that reach their highest point in the face-to-face encounter with what she terms "the Lover" (we could interpret this being or entity as a human loved one or as God). Llansol's concept of alterity is profoundly heterogeneous, simultaneously encompassing not only a concrete material as well as historical basis, but also a spiritual, affectional, and carnal substratum. The combination of these various elements in moments of the emergence of otherness produces an effect of abstraction that may be seen to make Llansol's definition of alterity approximate that of Levinas; however, her attention to sex-gender matters, her penchant for a panreligious mysticism (as opposed to being enclosed within one theological system, as Levinas was in that of Judaism), and the concrete cultural and historical problematics underlying her philosophical thought/literary writing distance her from many of the specifics of Levinasian ethical philosophy. For Llansol, ultimately, being human would be defined by the principle of "the eternal return of the mutual" (*Lisboaleipzig 1*, 130). These various definitions of the world or human lives are akin to Llansol's own definition of literature itself, and they are the driving force of her cultural project. Writing becomes life's double: a daily act inextricably linked to "the unexpected encounter with the diverse" (*o encontro inesperado do diverso*).

In Llansol's "fictional world," desire and sensuality reveal themselves in multiple registers and varied sex-gender permutations. Some characters, in fact, may shift between genders, such as Aossê in *Lisboaleipzig 2: O ensaio de música* (Lisboaleipzig 2: The essay on music, 1994), and some characters may shift between male and female objects of sexual desire, such as Isabôl and Hadewijch in *Contos do mal errante* (Stories of the wandering evil, 1986). Thus, Llansol presents a wide and fluid spectrum of male and female characters, without privileging one gender, or even sexuality, over another. For Llansol, the co-existence and interaction between the genders can take place only on the basis of equality. Only from such basis can there be a possible "neutralization" of gender differences for the creation of a more human society. On the other hand, regarding the question of a specifically "feminine" writing, Llansol believes that once the text acquires a certain "potency," it ceases to be specifically male or female (*Um falcão no punho* [A falcon in the fist], 140). Yet, in spite of these statements, one can detect a certain preponderance of female characters in Llansol's writing, more specifically a certain privileging of female companionship in the act of writing/reading, that is, the presence of women who "illuminate the text with their profound beings" (*Lisboaleipzig 1*, 17), to the point of becoming a vital force within the text itself. This can be better understood in reference to the Beguines, who play a key role in Llansol's writing, as well as in her own life experience.[35] The communities of female characters who populate Llansol's fictional world are manifestations of the Beguines in their mystical pursuit of the divine in a context of freedom, simplicity, and companionship.

However, even though we speak of "characters" within Llansol's writing, the author ultimately does not create actual fictional beings, but instead delineates "modes of being." In Clarice Lispector's *Um sopro de vida* we encounter her most tenuous of characters, Ângela, who appears as the author's double or semiheteronym and functions as a springboard for urgently felt or thought reflections regarding the symbiotic relationship between being and writing, but Llansol steers away from representational writing altogether. In fact, instead of basing her texts on thematic, character, or plot development, Llansol creates "constructive nodes" (or *nós construtivos*), each of which may consist of a historical figure; a sentence, such as "Este é o jardim que o pensamento permite" (This is the garden that thinking allows) (*Um falcão no punho*, 130); or a dream. The logos of Llansol's text is constituted by these nodes, which are also called "luminous scenes" *(cenas fulgor)*. These scenes are phenomenological instances based on the relationship between the subject and a multiplicity of "beings" (human, animal, or plant), a place, a landscape, or a hidden source of vibration and happiness. Vergílio Ferreira, as the author herself has noted (in *Inquérito às quatro confidências* [Inquiry to the four confidences], 26–27), has said that Llansol's writing is based upon meetings or encounters between textual figures in pursuit of particular affectional-mental experiences.

Through her writing Llansol desires to "emigrate to a LOCUS/LOGOS or landscape where power is not exerted over the body, reminding us of the ancient experience of God, outside of all religious or sacred context" (uma emigração para um LOCUS/LOGOS, paisagem onde não há poder sobre os corpos, como longínquamente, nos deve lembrar a experiência de Deus, fora de todo contexto religioso, ou até sagrado") (*Lisboaleipzig 1*, 121). In other words, the author suggests that the principle governing her experience of writing is akin to the mystical experience, where the division between body and spirit or between reason and the senses collapses. Here freedom is exercised beyond any one particular enclosed theological system, even if at times Llansol's texts may include references to Christian theology, as in *Ardente texto Joshua* (Ardent text Joshua, 1998)—though, like all cultural material that enters Llansol's fictional universe, these references appear transfigured and recontextualized. Thus, through her writing Llansol wishes to mutate "narrativity" into "textuality." According to the author, "*textuality* may allow us access to the poetic gift, the distant example of which would be the mystical experience" (a textualidade pode dar-nos acesso ao dom poético, de que o exemplo longínquo foi a prática mística) (*Lisboaleipzig 1*, 120). Llansol defines the poetic gift (as a contemporary manifestation of the mystical experience) as creative imagination that is unleashed through the interaction of affectional, rational, bodily, and intellectual forces. These forces intervene in the act of writing, which, as has been pointed out, entails "the unexpected meeting of the other." The poetic gift, by the same token, is inextricably linked to freedom of consciousness. Thus, writing becomes an act of affirmation of freedom beyond cruelty and selfishness (*Um falcão no punho*, 101). Llansol, in fact, believes that the goal today, in the context of the contemporary Western world, is "no longer to attain freedom but to enlarge its scope, to bring it to all that lives, *to bring us to life among all living beings*" (não é fundar a liberdade, mas alargar o seu âmbito, levá-la até ao vivo, *fazer de nós vivos no meio do vivo*) (*Lisboaleipzig 1*, 120).

For Maria Gabriela Llansol, the text essentially becomes a living being of a sacred order, while it is suggested that the act of writing itself is coterminous with living, where there is a symbiotic relationship between one and the other, as we have witnessed among all writers considered in this study. In the case of Llansol, however, the isomorphic relationship between writing, textuality, and living is radicalized. Even if in her texts we are not confronted with an impending horizon of death as in the later works of Clarice Lispector, Vergílio Ferreira, and Caio Fernando Abreu, in Llansol's writing, as in that of countless other writers throughout the world, there is a keen awareness of the fact that she is affirming life as much as affirming freedom of consciousness. It can be argued that Llansol's text constitutes in itself a space upon which a utopia of a kind is built. Even if it is not necessarily a "projection into the future," because its temporal framework is profoundly transhistorical, and even if it is not exactly "nowhere" from a spatial point of view (though it dramatically defies spatial/geographical boundaries), Llansol's text posits a world that goes beyond established conventions of time, space, language, sex-gender, and literature itself. It is a fictional attempt to create an entirely new world. Llansol desires to create a space for the evolution of what is possible, and above all, of what is unpredictable (*Lisboaleipzig 1, 92*). In spite of its apparent hermeticism and its high level of abstraction, Llansol's fictional world reflects back upon key cultural questions that have defined the history of Europe or of the West (as the author herself asserts). Thus, the space of literature becomes indissociable from an ethical dimension that hinges upon a transhistorical human destiny where the exercise of freedom in the face of the "power of the Princes" is paramount. The exercise of writing, then, is the equivalent of the exercise of freedom, at the same time as it is the expression of a vital principle of hope in human culture.

From a structural and stylistic point of view, Maria Gabriela Llansol's literary project could not seem more far removed from that of her contemporary José Saramago. Nevertheless, both authors are profoundly invested in questions of free will and freedom of consciousness within the purview of religious faith, more concretely throughout the history of Christianity (the ability and the freedom of the human subject to search or construct his or her own truths beyond the scope of the dominant myths of Christianity or Marxism were also fundamental concerns of Vergílio Ferreira). Llansol and Saramago, in fact, coincide in their interest vis-à-vis rebellious, heretical, or marginal figures, either historical or fictional, who have defied the established order in the pursuit of truth, freedom, or utopia. This is clearly illustrated by their interest in the Reformation movements of sixteenth-century Europe, most particularly of the independent Anabaptist movement in the city of Münster, Germany, in 1534–35, which ended in tragedy. Both Saramago and Llansol see the Münster episode as a "limit case" of religious faith, where the most heinous of crimes are committed in the name of God, in this case by Catholics, Lutherans, or Anabaptists. A rebellion that may originally have been justified on the grounds of freedom of consciousness as well as religious freedom, with the ultimate aim of creating a utopian community of equality and justice, became instead a dystopia where power was abused to macabre extremes. While Saramago critically reconstructed the historical facts surrounding the siege of Münster in his play *In Nomine Dei* (1992), in her *Contos do mal errante* Llansol staged a transhistorical existential, erotic, spiritual, and intellectual encounter between Copernicus, Meister Eckhart, Hagewijch, and Isabôl (a transfigured version of Portugal's Queen St. Isabel), who are in the process of defiantly exercising their freedom of being at the same time as Münster looms hauntingly on the horizon as a tragically dystopian reality in six-teenth-century Europe.[36]

Throughout most of his career, from *Levantado do chão* (Lifted from the ground, 1980) to *A caverna* (The cave, 2000), Saramago has placed an emphasis on characters who are representative of common, anony-mous, or even oppressed peoples in a concerted effort to subvert the grand narratives of history that privilege dominant social groups and their versions of the facts. This is also evident in Saramago's tendency to place women characters in key roles within his novels. Women invari-ably appear as a locus of wisdom and clairvoyance in a male-dominated world gone awry. Ultimately, Saramago reveals an endless hope in the betterment of the human condition that brings him close to all the authors contemplated in this study, and yet his unwavering commit-ment to social justice on a global scale, and especially his activist profile, even before he was awarded the Nobel Prize in 1998, place him in an al-together distinct location, not only within Portuguese or Brazilian cul-ture but internationally as well.[37] Saramago has now been catapulted onto a world stage where his humanistic convictions and political ac-tivism have a resonance that writers are rarely afforded.

In the 1980s José Saramago built a literary corpus that confirmed him as one of the major Portuguese writers of the late twentieth century, and certainly one of the better known Portuguese-language writers world-wide. His novels of this particular period are representative of what has been termed "historiographical metafiction" (Hutcheon, *Poetics of Post-modernism*) in the context of postmodern literature.[38] For instance, Saramago's best-known novel, *Memorial do convento* (1982, translated as *Baltasar and Blimunda* in 1987), is a fictionalization of eighteenth-century Portugal at the height of its monarchical opulence as a result of the massive influx of Brazilian gold. It dramatizes vividly the horrors of the Inquisition during this period, and above all the construction of the gargantuan Mafra convent (the Portuguese equivalent of El Escorial), which became the embodiment of absolute power. In the midst of it all, Baltasar, a humble construction worker, and Blimunda, a peasant woman with the power to read human wills, consecrate a love affair against all odds at the same time as a Franciscan priest, Bartolomeu Gusmão, cre-ates a flying device to take him as well as Baltasar and Blimunda on a voyage above the earth. In this novel we witness a confluence of the fantastic (exemplified by the flying device and Blimunda's ability to read human wills) with subaltern subjectivities (represented by the figures of Blimunda and Baltasar themselves and the marginality of the heretical priest). This particular confluence allows the novel to posit a utopia of freedom that aims at realizing the most extraordinary of human dreams during one of the most oppressive times and places in history.

O ano da morte de Ricardo Reis (The year of the death of Ricardo Reis, 1984), on the other hand, is a fictional tour de force where the author deconstructs the grand narratives of Portuguese nationhood at the same time as he reconstructs the year 1936, which represented the moment of consolidation of Portuguese fascism under Salazar, as well as that of Nazi Germany and Fascist Italy, and the beginning of the Spanish Civil War. Through this novel the author suggests a paradigm shift for Portuguese culture from the myths of navigation, "discoveries," and empire to a postfascist and postcolonial era based on democratic values and a vision that accounts for the actual potentialities of Portugal on the political and economic fronts, echoing here the concerns expressed by Boaventura de Sousa Santos, Eduardo Lourenço, José Mattoso, and numerous female and male postmodern fiction writers and poets (Isabel Barreno, Maria Gabriela Llansol, Maria Velho da Costa, Lídia Jorge, Al Berto, Luiza Neto Jorge, and António Lobo Antunes, among others) who have endeavored to deconstruct the metanarratives of Portuguese nationhood based on the nation's experience of the sea and empire. In *A jangada de pedra* (The stone raft, 1986), through a lyrical and symbiotic transfiguration of geopolitics and the fantastic, the Iberian Peninsula detaches itself from Europe and sets sail toward the South Atlantic somewhere between Africa and South America, signifying through a powerful symbolic gesture the author's rejection of the utopia of the European Union and his (no less utopian) embrace of the "South" as a geocultural and affectional metaphor as well as a concrete geopolitical context.

In the 1990s there was an important shift in Saramago's thematic focus from a mostly national context to a postnational arena whereby the author's investment in marginalized existences suddenly acquired human contours that defied national specificities.[39] *Ensaio sobre a cegueira* is a disturbing novel in which human society is suddenly overtaken by an epidemic of blindness. Everyone in the novel is mysteriously "contaminated" to the point at which society collapses materially, institutionally, and emotionally. In view of these extreme circumstances, the protagonists become the most absolute other of themselves. This leads them either to self-destruction or to a radical transformation in which they must forge ties of profound solidarity with their fellow humans in order to survive. Saramago's novel presents itself as a devastating allegory of the human condition at the turn of the millennium, where various localized apocalyptic scenarios have emerged in places such as Rwanda, Bosnia, the Congo, Kosovo, and East Timor, where human solidarity has almost vanished and reason is no longer a determining factor in human relations.

The tragedy that befalls the protagonists of *Ensaio sobre a cegueira* leads to their gradual dehumanization as each individual is stripped of the layers—socioeconomic, professional, cultural, and age- or gender-related—that inform his or her being. Women and men are reduced to a barebones existence where survival becomes the sole reason for living. The catastrophic event of universal blindness also produces a leveling of differences whereby human beings are equalized in being reduced to their animal-like qualities, which means taking care of basic physical needs, such as eating, sleeping, urinating, and defecating. In fact, Saramago's novel highlights the scatological aspects of human existence as it reflects upon the ultimate meaning of human life on the verge of apocalyptic self-destruction; human beings are literally condemned to dwelling physically (and spiritually) amid their own excrement (because there is a complete breakdown of infrastructures such as sewers and sewage treatment plants).

The most dramatic example of the collapse of reason as well as human dignity and its devastating consequences for humanity is a mass rape scene that involves the female protagonists, who are victimized by a group of rogue blind men in exchange for food that these men are monopolizing in the compound where they are all quarantined. The novel makes a powerful statement that rape is the equivalent of the violation of humanity as a whole. Saramago stresses the inescapably collective dimension of the tragic events that take place in this novel, including the most ignominious of crimes, such as mass rape, and he argues that it is out of this collective trauma that a profound transformation of human consciousness must emerge alongside a renewed sense of community for the betterment of humanity. In his conversations with Carlos Reis (*Diálogos com José Saramago,* 150), Saramago spoke of the need for human responsibilities, not just human rights. Here he referred to the obligations of each human toward the other and the need for solidarity between human beings. The anguish that permeates the novel *Ensaio sobre a cegueira* stems from the realization that the cruelty of humanity toward humanity is still rampant throughout the world at the dawn of the twenty-first century.

Saramago, on the other hand, disagrees with notions such as the "death of ideologies" or the "exhaustion of utopias." Instead of the notion of the "death of ideologies" the author posits the weakening of Marxism and Christianity as ideological monopolies through which to interpret reality, while he views the "exhaustion of utopias" as misconceived if the idea of social justice is to be considered "utopian" (here the author is parting from a narrow definition of *utopia* as "no where").[40] If *utopia* is defined more widely, we can argue that Saramago remains firmly committed to those aspects of utopian thinking that point to the need for the enlargement of democracy and for an increase in social justice, as well as the urgent need for greater solidarity among human beings for our basic survival. Even though he continues to be a member of the Portuguese Communist Party, Saramago acknowledges the excesses of soviet-style communism and is skeptical of dogmatic teleological progressions, be they of a religious or a political nature. At the same time, he believes that the hegemony of globalized market economies throughout the world today has brought material well-being to only a relatively small portion of the planet's citizens, while the vast majority still suffer from social injustice that in the worst of cases is exemplified by hunger, illiteracy, and misery, in spite of the fact that there is sufficient accumulated wealth in the world to take care of humanity's basic needs.

Saramago's view of alterity and the subject's responsibility to the other reveal very specific historical and material contours that distance him considerably from definitions of alterity advanced by Levinas or even Maria Gabriela Llansol. Saramago's engagement with the social brings him closer to the work of Isabel Barreno, and to a lesser extent Caio Fernando Abreu (given the latter's attention to alternative sexualities and lifestyles or to global pop culture, facets of culture that are unknown to Saramago). The writing practices of Saramago, Barreno, and Abreu represent, in palpable terms, the historical "real" and the everyday circumstances where fictional characters happen to find themselves. Although significant attention is paid to existential matters, particularly in the work of Abreu, this attention is rarely divorced from key issues related to class (Saramago), gender (Barreno and Saramago), or sexuality (Abreu and, to a lesser degree, Barreno). On the other hand, the works of Clarice Lispector, Vergílio Ferreira, and Maria Gabriela Llansol reveal a greater propensity toward philosophical abstraction (especially in the case of Llansol), where everyday events undergo substantial transfiguration to reveal the metaphysical substratum of the subject's "being in the world." Nevertheless, these three authors are attentive to the ideological underpinnings of historical currents in the Western world, as well as to various facets of human identity, such as gender (Lispector and Llansol), sexuality (Llansol and, to a lesser extent, Lispector), and class (Lispector, to a limited degree). Where all the authors discussed in this chapter coincide is in their definition of subjectivity as inseparable from the subject's relationship with the other. This relationship is a reason for writing at the same time as the act of writing provides a reason for living. The literature produced by this heterogeneous group of writers dramatizes the notion that our individual and collective destinies are inextricably linked to a sense of ethical responsibility vis-à-vis the other. This notion constitutes a final utopian frontier, as well as an ultimate harbinger of hope.

Conclusion

The preceding chapters stress the weakening of the nation-state at the dawn of the twenty-first century in a multiplicity of arenas such as the economic, the political, and the cultural. However, national questions have not entirely disappeared from the horizon of interests of the Portuguese and Brazilian fiction writers discussed throughout this study, although they have been progressively deemphasized. Interestingly, throughout their respective writing careers, Vergílio Ferreira and Clarice Lispector tended to avoid an explicit treatment of national questions altogether.

From the early part of his career in the late 1940s, Ferreira felt increasingly marginalized in a Portuguese national context that was dominated politically by a right-wing authoritarian regime and where the countercultural hegemony was exerted by a Marxist-Leninist intelligentsia. The existential concerns toward which Ferreira was strongly inclined, though intrinsically humanistic, were most decidedly non-Christian and non-Marxist, which put him at odds with those at the dominant ideological poles of the time. The modes of subjectivity posited by Ferreira are an integral part of an ongoing reflection regarding the human condition that goes beyond national borders and aims at establishing the ontological coordinates of what the author would have defined as a "universal subject," but that we could interpret as a Western or western European (bourgeois and predominantly white male) subject. According to Augusto Joaquim, Vergílio Ferreira was one of the first Portuguese thinkers/writers to successfully delink (individual) subjectivity from (Portuguese) nationhood, in a literary tradition where both have been closely intertwined since the sixteenth century (*Interrogação ao destino, Malraux,* 311). This is corroborated by Ferreira's search for a literary and philosophical lineage that was largely outside the Portuguese national space (from the pre-Socratic philosophers all the way to Dostoyevsky, Nietzsche, and Heidegger, among countless others).

On the other hand, throughout most of her career, Clarice Lispector was one of exceedingly few women writers in a male-dominated Brazilian literary tradition who happened to be at the same time Jewish and foreign-born and, by virtue of having been married to a diplomat, spent significant periods of time abroad. These various factors in differing degrees informed her relationship to Brazil, thus conferring on Lispector an aura of otherness within Brazilian culture. Although she always identified herself as Brazilian, Brazil as a national reality appears only discretely in Lispector's writings. This can be attributed to the fact that Lispector was greatly interested in a series of ontological questions that could not be contained within specific national borders and instead resonate with those engaged in philosophical debates in a wider contemporary cultural framework encompassing the Western world, to which Brazil—through Lispector—fully belongs.

Regarding national questions, Maria Gabriela Llansol is located at a liminal place between Portugal and Europe. She argues that the cultural development of Portugal cannot be understood outside the history of Europe, and vice versa. Llansol thus situates herself simultaneously inside and outside Portugal and Europe, staging a dynamic transhistorical and crosscultural dialogue between them. In her writing she appears to be hyperaware of not belonging to the center of any geopolitically defined cultural sphere and of speaking from the margins of a language that is in itself marginal within the context of Europe. Yet the cultural problematics we encounter in Llansol's texts (the questions of power and freedom of consciousness, among others) are central to the understanding of both Portugal and Europe (as well as other Western and non-Western cultures in general). Llansol, moreover, writes against the current of Portuguese cultural paradigms related to the sea with the intent of surpassing them. She defines her writing as a "garden-text" that is, at the same time, the territory of the word, of everything, and not solely the territory of one nation (*Um falcão no punho,* 51). Llansol attempts, at least temporarily, to divorce herself from the national and cultural trappings of the Portuguese language and instead to privilege the dialogical nature of the uses of language in her pursuit of the "other." This pursuit leads her to stage an encounter between Lisbon and Leipzig, Pessoa and Bach, in a literary-utopian gesture where borders remain within a dialectical cycle of dissolution and reconfiguration.

Of all the writers studied here, Caio Fernando Abreu was undoubtedly the most intimately connected to global media and popular culture. In his fictional works, he portrays Brazilian national culture as actively engaged in a process of "cultural anthropophagy"—the privileged metaphor utilized by modernists and tropicalists alike—with global cultural forces. Yet Abreu also gives considerable attention to existential concerns that derive from the crisis of utopias in the late twentieth century, from a sense of unrealized or conflictive (homo)sexuality, and, toward his later years, from the experience of AIDS. These concerns were invariably permeated by concrete socioeconomic and political circumstances that reflected the Brazilian crisis of the 1980s and early 1990s, whereby metaphors of disease were conflated with the idea of the nation as a whole.

Analogous to José Saramago, Isabel Barreno has cultivated a brand of postmodern historical fiction that is deeply concerned with the development of the Portuguese nation (most particularly in *Crónica do tempo,* *O senhor das ilhas,* and *O chão salgado*). The revolutionary *Novas cartas portuguesas* has a place of its own, because it was collectively written and produced. While the authors of *Novas cartas portuguesas* paid attention to the historical particularities of the experience of women's oppression in Portugal, the ideological underpinnings of their work transcended national borders and spoke about a common experience of women throughout the world. Nevertheless, as committed to national and feminist questions as Barreno has been (and still is), she has not confined her writing solely to these questions. In fact, what is also noticeable in her writing is a particular interest in the notion of the weakening of myths and utopias that governed not only the Portuguese imaginary, but the Western imaginary, throughout the twentieth century (myths such as those of Marxist revolution, nationalism, women's liberation, and so on). Barreno, along with all the writers considered here, maintains that there is a continued need for a dosis of utopian hope but projects this hope toward the subject's relationship with the "other" in the public and private spheres of everyday life. She does not necessarily believe in an automatic solidarity between all women or all human beings in general, but realizes that, as imperfect or as potentially fraught with misunderstanding as this relationship may be, it is our primary ontological horizon and ultimate destiny as a human community, a position that is fully shared by José Saramago.

In fact, Saramago worries about what he perceives as the negative effects of globalization over the realities of citizenship and community. He is concerned about whether human beings are being stripped of the possibility of becoming active citizens in favor of becoming passive consumers. Saramago's concerned pessimism extends to the contemporary status of the nation. He views nations today as more than ever subordinate to the interests of multinational corporations and supranational organizations. While Saramago does not necessarily suggest an alternative to this particular state of affairs, and is willing, at least implicitly, to admit that in the particular case of Portugal there have been more advantages to this situation than disadvantages, he generally views it with a great deal of skepticism. His primary contention is that, overall, there is still not an equal distribution of social justice around the world and that globalization has not necessarily attenuated that fact. Ultimately, Saramago stresses that social justice is a "utopia" worth struggling for and calls on writers as well as critics to play a more active role in ensuring that it becomes a universal good.

This study of contemporary Portuguese and Brazilian cultures and literatures has repeatedly stressed the relativization of the nation in favor of micrological ways of positing the political and the social, at the same time as it recognizes that the nation-state has been weakened by numerous economic, political, cultural, and technological forces that are an integral part of the phenomenon of globalization. By the same token, many of the utopias that shaped the twentieth-century imaginary have been either severely questioned or weakened by historical realities or have been reformulated so as to attain a more modestly human dimension. This study has argued that the literary space has been a privileged locus from which to reflect upon these significant social and cultural shifts, which have also affected contemporary Brazil and Portugal in manifold ways. In spite of the lamentation of Vergílio Ferreira over the notion of "literature in crisis" or the profound skepticism expressed by José Saramago regarding the impact of literature in society at large, most writers considered here have revealed a lasting faith in literature as a vehicle for representing a drastically changing world where the destiny of humanity—individually and collectively—is more than ever at stake.

Notes

Introduction

1. Pêro Vaz de Caminha, *Carta de Pêro Vaz de Caminha a El-Rei D: Manuel sobre o achamento do Brasil.*

2. The Pataxós are the current indigenous inhabitants of this region of the state of Bahia but are not considered descendents of the Tupiniquim Indians who were first encountered by the Portuguese in 1500 and are believed to have practically disappeared.

3. In "FHC pede tolerância com divergências."

4. There are also Portuguese-speaking enclaves in Asia (Macao and Goa), as well as immigrant communities from Portugal, Cape Verde, and Brazil throughout North America, Europe, South Africa, Australia, and Venezuela.

5. Although in this study I have made a conscious choice not to place the five Lusophone African countries at the center of my analysis for reasons of space, I am highly aware of their importance with regard to the development of both Brazil and Portugal. Thus, whenever pertinent, Lusophone African cultures are mentioned throughout this discussion in connection to Portugal and Brazil. However, the need for future comparative pan-Lusophone studies in the realms of literature, popular culture, history, and anthropology, among others, clearly remains.

6. In Portugal there are immigrant communities from all over its former colonial empire: Angola, Brazil, Cape Verde, East Timor, Goa, Guinea-Bissau, Macao, Mozambique, and São Tomé. Unofficial figures point to approximately one hundred thousand Brazilians and more than one hundred thousand Africans of various nationalities. Today there are tens of thousands of recent arrivals from eastern Europe (particularly from the former Soviet Union).

7. *Público,* 27 Aug. 1998, http://www.publico.pt.

8. A recent publication offers an exhaustive account of modern Luso-Brazilian relations, focusing on the history of diplomatic ties, immigration, and economic relations between Brazil and Portugal. See Amado Cervo and José Calvet de Magalhães, *Depois da caravelas: As relações entre Portugal e Brasil, 1808–2000* (2000). On the

other hand, *Brasil e Portugal: 500 anos de enlaces e desenlaces, 1 e 2* (2001) includes a series of essays written by academics and writers from Lusophone Africa, Brazil, and Portugal, focusing on the cultural relations within the Portuguese-speaking world.

9. In the nineteenth century, Brazil was the primary destination for Portuguese emigrants. Toward the end of the nineteenth century, the numbers averaged twenty thousand per year (José Hermano Saraiva, *História de Portugal*, 318). Between 1884 and 1939, Portuguese constituted the largest contingent of immigrants in Brazil (1,502,394), followed by Italians, then Spaniards (Maria Yedda Linhares, *História geral do Brasil* [General history of Brazil], 217). Between the Second World War and the Portuguese Revolution of 1974, there was a steady wave of tens of thousands of Portuguese emigrants per year moving toward Brazil, the United States, Canada, and Europe (primarily France) (A. H. de Oliveira Marques, *Breve história de Portugal*, 665). In fact, according to Maria Ioannis B. Baganha, "Until the 1950s, Brazil received more than 50 percent of Portuguese migratory flows, and France approximately half from that period on" ("Portuguese Emigration after World War II," 189).

10. Until the rise of Brazilian modernism in 1922, the Portuguese and Brazilian literary fields were closely intertwined, because poets from both countries were known on both sides of the Atlantic, featured in anthologies that included poetry written in both countries. Brazilian authors were regularly published in Portugal, as were Portuguese authors in Brazil, and between the late nineteenth century and the early twentieth century, writers from both countries often jointly contributed to Portuguese literary journals or were regularly featured in Brazilian newspapers, such as Eça de Queiroz and other Portuguese intellectual figures of the nineteenth century, such as António Castilho, Pinheiro Chagas, and Ramalho Ortigão. In fact, it can be argued that until 1922 Portuguese literature (alongside French and English) exerted an enormous influence among Brazilian elites. Nevertheless, even if Brazilian modernism broke culturally and linguistically with Portuguese literary influences, joint collaboration between Portuguese and Brazilian writers or attempts to foster cultural exchanges between the two countries never entirely ceased. For more information on this subject, see Arnaldo Saraiva, *O modernismo brasileiro e o modernismo português*, as well as João Almino, "O diálogo interrompido."

11. Alfredo Bosi distinguishes between the Portuguese chronicles that center on the "discovery" and description of Brazil and actual histories that reflect the experience of a colonial subject engaged in the construction of a new Luso-Brazilian reality (*História concisa da literatura brasileira*, 24–25). In the first category, the most notable examples are the "letter of discovery" or *Carta a El-Rei D: Manuel sobre o achamento do Brasil* (1500) by Pêro Vaz de Caminha, as well as Pêro de Magalhães Gândavo's *Tratado da terra do Brasil: História da Província de Santa Cruz a que vulgarmente chamamos Brasil* (1576) and Gabriel Soares de Sousa's encyclopedic *Tratado descritivo do Brasil em 1587*. In the second category, where a "proto-Brazilian" consciousness can already be detected, we find Frei Vicente do Salvador's *História do Brasil* (1627), and André João Antonil's *Cultura e opulência do Brasil* (1711).

12. The most prominent critics of Machado de Assis (Roberto Schwarz and John Gledson) consider him the first major Brazilian writer who has succeeded in transcending national borders, not only due to his masterfully subtle art, but also through the "universal" resonance of his thematic concerns.

13. The stereotype of the "Brazilian" (i.e., the Portuguese emigrant who goes to Brazil and eventually returns home rich) is particularly present in the works of one

of the greatest nineteenth-century Portuguese novelists, Camilo Castelo Branco. See, for instance, the novels *Eusébio Macário* (1879) and *A brasileira de Prazins* (1882), among others.

14. The most virulent manifestations of lusophobia appear in Brazilian natural-ist novels of the late nineteenth century, namely those of Aluísio Azevedo (*O mulato* [Mulatto], 1881, and *O cortiço* [The slum], 1890) and Adolfo Caminha (*Bom-Crioulo*, 1895). Raúl Pompéia, another prominent Brazilian naturalist, was notorious for his caustic journalistic attacks against the Portuguese (Vieira, *Brasil e Portugal*, 127–29). They all reveal a profound resentment of the large presence of Portuguese im-migrants in Brazil during this period, where they held a virtual monopoly over the small business sector of the economy (i.e., small grocery stores, bakeries, restaurants, etc.). This was seen as a pernicious extension of Portuguese colonialism, even though Brazil had been independent for almost a century. This dynamic also attests to the amount of frustration on the part of Brazilian intellectuals with the lack of progress in Brazil. Thus, the Portuguese element became a convenient scapegoat, represent-ing a possible cause of Brazil's socioeconomic ills (122).

15. One of the most highly publicized cases of diplomatic tension between Brazil and Portugal in the recent past had to do with the professional status of Brazilian dentists in Portugal. The tension over this particular issue essentially arose due to the differing educational requirements in the two countries for dental degrees (in Portugal dentists must go through medical school, while this is not the case in Brazil). This misunderstanding may also be seen to underscore the difficulties that Portugal has encountered in absorbing newcomers who are competing with na-tionals in the labor market. Immigration to Portugal is in fact a new development in the nation's history.

1. Portugal

For English-language histories of Portugal or of the Portuguese empire, see Charles Boxer, *Portuguese Seaborne Empire, 1415–1825;* Bailey W. Diffie and George D. Winius, *Foundations of the Portuguese Empire, 1415–1580;* David Birmingham, *A Concise History of Portugal;* Douglas Wheeler, *Historical Dictionary of Portugal;* José Hermano Saraiva, *Portugal: A Companion History;* and James M. Anderson, *The History of Portugal.*

1. Technically speaking, Macao was not considered a "colony" per se. In 1979, the People's Republic of China and Portugal signed an agreement in which Macao was declared a "Chinese territory under Portuguese administration." In 1999, Macao returned to Chinese sovereignty as an autonomous territory within China, much like Hong Kong.

2. Identifying Portugal along with Spain as pioneers in the rise of the first global system, and thus, of modernity, places my argument slightly at odds with Enrique Dussel's Hispanocentric diachrony of the rise of modernity (in "Beyond Eurocentrism: The World-System and the Limits of Modernity," 3–9), which he de-scribes as being the exclusive purview of Spanish maritime and colonial expansion. Dussel's argument is based on a diachronic sequence of the passage from the Renaissance to modernity that privileges Columbus's arrival in the Americas as the landmark for the rise of modernity. He identifies Portugal as a premodern antecedent to European planetarization and centralization within the world system, mostly

because of its westernmost location within a previous interregional system that would have involved only Europe, Africa, and Asia. Yet he seems to ignore the facts that Portugal's westernmost location, facing the Atlantic Ocean, greatly aided its expansion toward the south and the east and that Portugal's involvement in Africa and Asia between the fifteenth and sixteenth centuries, and eventually in Brazil after 1500, was prior and synchronous to Spain's involvement in the Americas after 1492. Both equally contributed to the rise of a world system that would have Europe as its center.

3. After the expulsion of the Jews from Spain in 1492, approximately one hundred thousand sought refuge in Portugal, where there was already a Jewish population of thirty thousand (Oliveira Marques, *Breve história de Portugal,* 155). In exchange for hefty sums of money, King João II allowed Jews to stay in transit before reaching other destinations. Those who were unable to afford the given sums were enslaved, and some children were sent to the African island of São Tomé, where few survived. In 1496, under pressure from Castille, King Manuel I ordered the expulsion of all remaining Jews (both Portuguese and Castillian), but he surreptitiously stopped them from leaving by forcing them into a mass conversion to Catholicism and guaranteeing that for twenty years Jews would not be persecuted for religious reasons. Unfortunately, Portuguese culture during this era was not as tolerant as Manuel's rhetoric may have wished. For more details, see José Hermano Saraiva, *Portugal;* José Mattoso, *A identidade nacional;* and Oliveira Marques, *Breve história de Portugal.*

4. The Inquisition became functional in Portugal in 1534–36 (José Hermano Saraiva, *Portugal;* Oliveira Marques, *Breve história de Portugal*).

5. There are two recent English translations of *Peregrinação:* a complete version by Rebecca D. Catz (*Peregrination,* 1989) and an abridged one by Michael Lowery (*Peregrination,* 1992). Charles R. Boxer first translated and edited Bernardo Gomes de Brito's *História Trágico-Marítima* (*The Tragic History of the Sea,* 1959). This work has now been republished in paperback with a new translation of the heart-wrenching tale of Captain Manuel de Sousa Sepúlveda and his family by Josiah Blackmore, as well as a compelling foreword (2001).

6. Brazilian literary and cultural critic Alfredo Bosi closely analyzes the etymology of the terms *colonization, culture,* and *cult.* The Latin term *colo,* the root of *colony,* signifies "the land that is occupied, a land that can be settled and worked upon, or a people that can be subjected" (*Dialética da colonização,* 11–15). Here we have three elements that characterize the Portuguese colonization of Brazil: the new land that was to be occupied and cultivated, the extraction of its resources, and the subjugation of its natives. In contrast, the Portuguese presence in Asia was more nomadic and was primarily focused on controlling sea trade routes rather than on settling, as in the case of Brazil.

7. The Portuguese Asian colonies of Goa, Macao, and East Timor have played a relatively minor role in the larger framework of the Portuguese colonial empire since the seventeenth century. Goa was conquered in 1510 by Afonso de Albuquerque and soon became the administrative capital of Portuguese Asia, as well as a major commercial outpost, military base, and (Christian) religious center. The Indian Union incorporated the Portuguese enclaves of Goa, Diu, and Daman in 1961.

Macao, on the other hand, was donated by the Mandarin of Canton (Quangdong) in 1557 so that the Portuguese could serve as commercial intermediaries with both

China and Japan. Direct trade between Japan and China was prohibited between 1543 and 1639. After the British conquered Hong Kong in 1842 (as a result of the Opium War), Macao suffered a significant decline, given Hong Kong's more favorable geographical conditions for trade, and eventually its prosperity as a world financial center (Government of Macao, Aug. 1998, http://www.macau.gov.mo).

Timor was initially contacted by the Portuguese about 1515–16 (Luís de Albuquerque, ed., *Dicionário da História dos descobrimentos portugueses*. 1034). The Portuguese conquest of the strategic port of Malacca (Malaysia), in 1511, enabled direct trade with the south islands (which mostly comprise today's Indonesia). Timor became a distant outpost that supplied primarily fine sandalwood (along with wax and honey). Throughout the sixteenth century, Malacca, Macao, and Timor formed a closely integrated trade network between Portugal, Southeast Asia, and China. Timor also attracted Christian missionaries, whose influence is still felt today in East Timor, and accounts as one of the primary differentiating factors (aside from other important cultural, linguistic, ethnic, and racial factors) between East Timor and predominantly Muslim Indonesia.

8. The Berlin Conference of 1884–85 among European colonial powers established the modern borders of Africa. Portugal dreamed of conquering the territory located between Mozambique and Angola (roughly, today's Zambia). In 1890 the British issued an ultimatum to Portugal, urging it to withdraw all military forces from this particular region.

9. The coup d'état of 1926 was led by Generals Gomes da Costa and Carmona. António de Oliveira Salazar, originally a professor of economics at the University of Coimbra, was called to serve as Finance Minister in 1928. In 1932, after major accomplishments under his administration, he became head of state, and in 1933 Salazar became dictator of Portugal.

10. After traveling throughout the Portuguese African colonies in the early 1950s, Gilberto Freyre first formulated his theorization of Luso-tropicalism during a series of lectures in Goa and at Coimbra that were eventually published in *Um brasileiro em terras portuguesas* (1954), and later on he systematized this in *Integração portuguesa nos trópicos* (1958) and *O luso e o trópico* (1961).

11. Interestingly, as Castelo points out, the Salazar regime appropriated only those aspects of Freyre's thought that highlighted the unique contributions of the Portuguese to the world while purposefully ignoring Freyre's celebration of cultural and racial hybridity, as well as the individual contributions of African and Amerindian peoples to a purportedly common luso-tropical civilization (*O modo português de estar no mundo*, 139).

12. There is no consensus as to whether the events that took place on 25 April 1974 in Portugal can actually be described as a "revolution" as opposed to a coup d'état that ended a forty-eight-year right-wing authoritarian regime. Various social scientists and historians (e.g., Phillipe Schmitter, Maria Carrilho, and Carlos Espada) prefer the notion of "democratization," since what occurred was the reestablishment of a political structure akin to those found in liberal (democratic) societies (Richard Herr, ed., *The New Portugal*, 2–3). By the same token, the governments that took power immediately after April 1974 were intent on establishing a left-wing socioeconomic and political program imbued with Marxist-Leninist rhetoric. Even as center-left and center-right parties reached power thereafter and slowly dismantled key programmatic aspects of 25 April such as land reform and the nationalization of

state enterprises, the events of 1974 did in fact revolutionize Portuguese society and paved the way to decolonization and democratization.

13. Popularly, the wars between the Portuguese colonialist forces and liberation movements in Angola, Guinea-Bissau, and Mozambique between 1961 and 1974 are referred to as the Colonial War in Portugal, or the Liberation Wars in Africa.

14. It could be argued whether the newly forged (post)colonial relations between Portugal and its former African colonies are a gently disguised form of neocolonialism, as in the case of the particularly active involvement of France, Britain, and increasingly the United States, in the economic and political affairs of Africa. The precarious economic reality and continued political instability of many African nations have brought about a relationship of dependence upon former colonial powers, as well as other rich industrialized nations outside of Africa, and regional powers within the African continent (South Africa or Nigeria, for example). Furthermore, the process of globalization can also be viewed as a diffuse, fragmented, and decentered form of neocolonialism, where one particular state no longer solely dominates other nation-states—even though the United States does constitute the most powerful nation in the post–Cold War era—where multinational corporations and transnational capital greatly influence national economic and political outcomes. This discussion points to the continuing debates in the realm of postcolonial studies regarding the appropriateness of using the prefix *post* in postcolonialism.

15. Shortly after East Timor achieved independence from Portugal in 1975, Indonesian military forces invaded and annexed the territory. It is believed that a third of the population died as a result of this invasion (approximately two hundred thousand people). These numbers were first published by Amnesty International, then confirmed by the Indonesian army intelligence chief for Timor, and confirmed again in 1994 by the Indonesia-appointed governor (*East Timor Action Network,* Aug. 1998, http://www.etan.org.

The United Nations never recognized Indonesian sovereignty over East Timor, since Portugal was still considered its legal governing power. East Timor became a major human rights cause internationally in the 1990s, and the Nobel Peace Prize awarded to East Timorese Bishop Carlos Filipe Ximenes Belo and activist José Ramos Horta in 1995 became a vital recognition of the urgency of peacefully resolving the East Timor question. By the same token, East Timor had become a great embarrassment to the Indonesian government, which has attempted to gain international stature as a rising economic power in Southeast Asia. Sudden and rapid political changes on the Indonesian political scene in 1998–99 opened the path to a fair resolution of East Timor's political status. Indonesia and Portugal agreed on a United Nations–sponsored referendum on autonomy that was to be held in August of 1999. If autonomy within Indonesia were voted down, Indonesia would agree to grant independence to East Timor. After an astonishing 99 percent voter participation, close to 80 percent of East Timorese voted against autonomy, therefore implicitly voting in favor of independence. Immediately after the announcement of the election results, pro-Indonesian militia forces—trained and supported by the Indonesian military and police—went on a killing and burning rampage throughout the territory, destroying most cities and towns and leaving thousands dead and tens of thousands displaced (thousands of East Timorese were forcibly sent to West Timor and other islands within Indonesia).

The overwhelming international outcry against the atrocities committed in East Timor and imminent economic threats to Indonesia by world powers forced Indonesia to accept a multinational military force headed by Australia in order to pacify the territory and prepare it for a U.N.-led transition period before it would be granted full independence. In late October 1999, the Indonesian Parliament recognized the outcome of the referendum in East Timor and officially rescinded its annexation.

16. Due to the Indonesian annexation of East Timor immediately after it achieved independence from Portugal in 1975, the postcolonial relationship between East Timor and Portugal developed in synchronicity with a new colonial relationship between East Timor and Indonesia. The neglectful colonialism of Portugal gave way to the genocidal colonialism of Indonesia. In this context, the cultural, historical, linguistic, and above all, the religious ties of East Timor to Portugal became a bulwark against Indonesian attempts to conquer the East Timorese. East Timorese poetry written in Portuguese, for instance, borrowed cultural motifs from the Portuguese Renaissance in order to represent the struggle for liberation from Indonesia as a conflict between righteous Christians and oppressive Moors. Practicing Catholicism, speaking Portuguese, or brandishing Portuguese national symbols such as the flag became powerfully subversive (and yet, inevitably ironic) strategies to affirm the East Timorese difference and to defy Indonesian authoritarianism. The "affection" between the East Timorese and Portuguese cannot be understood outside of this context.

17. Besides *O labirinto da saudade*, see also *Nós e a Europa* (1988) and *O esplendor do caos* (1998). In English, see *We the Future* (1997).

18. The miracle of Ourique took place during the battle of the same name in 1139. In the process of reconquering Portugal and taking it from the Arabs, D. Afonso Henriques (the founder of Portugal) and his forces were vastly outnumbered by the enemy. Legend holds that during this battle Christ appeared to him and helped him win. This myth eventually metamorphosed into an anti-Castillian legend.

Young King Sebastian, on the other hand, was said to have been killed in the disastrous battle of El-Ksar-el-Kebir (1578) in Morocco, never to be found again. His disappearance became a messianic myth (with Judaic undertones); it was believed that he would return one day and save Portugal. This myth has had lasting repercussions in the Portuguese collective unconscious and has been transplanted into Brazil as well, where it has played a major role in messianic communities in the Brazilian Northeast.

The Portuguese debacle in Morocco in 1578 and the subsequent loss of independence to Spain in 1580 spurred a wealth of messianic myths that involved the return of King Sebastian and the establishment of a Fifth Empire. In the seventeenth century, at a time when Portugal's hegemony was being severely contested by competing world colonial powers, Jesuit Father António Vieira's version of the Fifth Empire entailed a mixture of Jewish and Christian theological erudition, as well as delirium and a concrete political agenda that involved the reestablishment of Portuguese independence from Spain and the legitimation and further consolidation of Portuguese colonialism around the world. For Fernando Pessoa in the early twentieth century, the Portuguese Fifth Empire was related not to the sequence of empires described in the Bible (Babylon, Persia, Greece, and Rome), but to a sequence of empires composed of Greece, Rome, Christianity, and post-Renaissance secular

Europe. Pessoa's messianism combined a cultural agenda that envisioned a transfiguration of Portugal's colonial-material decline into a spiritual-cultural empire of Portuguese-language poetry with a significant *dosis* of esoteric mysticism, as expressed in his poetic work *Mensagem* (Message, 1934).

19. See *Pela mão de Alice* (1994) and *Toward a New Common Sense* (1995).

20. See Teixeira de Pascoaes's *Arte de ser português* (1915); Agostinho da Silva's *Um Fernando Pessoa* (1959), *Dispersos* (1988), and *Reflexão* (1990); and António Quadros's *Portugal: Razão e mistério* (1986), and *A ideia de Portugal na literatura portuguesa dos últimos 100 anos* (1989).

21. In a recent interview, Santos nuanced his reading of Portugal's particular geopolitical location by stating that not only did it consolidate its "semi-peripheral" condition in the late 1990s, but that it still remains quite behind the core of the European Union in socioeconomic terms. To illustrate this, Santos points out that, comparatively speaking, Portugal's productivity level is 37 percent and its labor cost 36 percent those of Germany (see Rodrigues da Silva's interview, "Visionar o futuro, já," 18–20).

22. The metaphor-concept of "border" is a centerpiece of what has been called "borderlands theory" in the realm of cultural and literary criticism since the 1990s. Its origin lies in the work of U.S. Chicana writer Gloria Anzaldúa, *Borderlands/La Frontera* (1987). In this work, the site of the "borderlands" presents a multitude of meanings and layers of signification. For Anzaldúa, it is first and foremost the actual physical border between the United States and Mexico, more specifically the Texas-Mexico border regions. At the same time, it is the collective and individualized cultural, linguistic, socioeconomic, historical, and (geo)political dynamics associated with that particular region of the world. But for the author the borderlands have psychological, sexual, and spiritual dimensions as well. She herself is the embodiment of a multiplicity of borders that she has had to negotiate throughout her life as a woman who is Chicana (Mexican American), lesbian, and of working-class background (though she only implicitly thematizes this last element).

The notion of borderlands has now migrated to many other discourses and cultures within the humanities and the social sciences—for instance, in the case of Boaventura de Sousa Santos or postcolonial critic Homi Bhabha. The borderlands as physical space as well as psychic reality and cultural experience illustrate the hybrid and finite character of the nation. They are the death-in-life of the idea of the nation as an "imagined community." The borderlands are also illustrative of the liminality and contingency of cultural identity. What is so powerful about the figure of the borderlands, not only as material existence and literal experience but also as life metaphor, is that it involves all citizens of the world. It encompasses all layers of individual and collective subjectivities that are brought to bear when confronting difference, in whichever form or shape it may present itself (from physical ability, age, and physical appearance—which are less talked about and theorized upon—to the more obvious and often theorized gender, race, sexuality, class, nationality, language, etc.). The borderlands are a perpetual psychic state, a ground that is contested, in urban spaces most particularly.

23. See Rodrigues da Silva's interview, "Visionar o futuro, já," 18–20.

24. At the time of the death in 1999 of one of Portugal's most revered cultural icons of the twentieth century, fado diva Amália Rodrigues, fado was already experiencing a veritable renaissance and transformation through the emergence of at

least a dozen new or relatively new singers (mostly female) who have injected a great deal of vitality and creativity into the Portuguese national song: Mísia, Dulce Pontes, Teresa Salgueiro (from Madredeus), Nuno Guerreiro (from Ala dos Namorados), Mafalda Arnauth, Cristina Branco, Camané, Paulo Bragança, Ana Sofia Varela, Marta Dias, Ana Maria Bobone, and Mariza.

2. Brazilian National Identity

1. The ideology of whitening became widespread among the Brazilian elite between the late nineteenth century and the early twentieth century and was the result of the absorption of European scientific racist thought and its adaptation to Brazilian reality. In essence, it was a belief in the irrevocable whitening (read, improvement) of the Brazilian population through miscegenation, which meant the absorption of blacks, Indians, and peoples of mixed blood into the white race. As Thomas Skidmore points out, the Brazilian ideology of whitening entailed a paradoxical twist that contradicted European racist thought in that it held that "racial purity" could be achieved through miscegenation. Regardless of the contradiction and in spite of the critiques advanced by a few enlightened intellectuals of the time, such as Sílvio Romero, the Brazilian elites fully embraced whitening as a national Brazilian ideal and made sure it was codified into immigration laws, thus encouraging European immigration at the same time as prohibiting black immigrants from entering Brazil (regardless of place of origin) and discouraging Asian immigration (which essentially meant Japanese immigration). For an exhaustive historical analysis of race and the ideology of whitening in Brazil, see Thomas E. Skidmore's *Black into White: Race and Nationality in Brazilian Thought* (1995).

2. See Johann Baptist von Spix and Phillip von Martius, *Travels in Brazil in the Years 1817–1820 undertaken by command of his Majesty the King of Bavaria;* Capistrano de Abreu, *Capítulos da história colonial do Brasil 1500–1800* (Chapters of Brazil's colonial history 1500–1800); and Paulo Prado, *Retrato do Brasil.*

3. Since the quincentennial of the Portuguese arrival in Brazil there has been a publishing boom that has focused on essays dealing with Brazilian national identity, intellectual tradition, historiography, sociology, and cultural criticism. Many classic essays by canonical thinkers of the past two centuries have been republished, while new interpretations of the intellectual production of these established thinkers have vigorously surfaced. Some of the most outstanding are Lourenço Dantas Mota, ed., *Introdução ao Brasil: Um banquete nos trópicos* (1999); Carlos Gulherme Mota, ed., *Viagem incompleta: A experiência brasileira,* vols. 1 and 2 (2000); José Carlos Reis, ed., *As identidades do Brasil* (1999); and Silviano Santiago (*Intérpretes do Brasil,* vols. 1, 2, and 3 (2000). In the same vein but in English translation, special mention should be made of *The Brazil Reader: History, Culture, Politics* (1999), edited by Robert W. Levine and John J. Crocitti.

4. According to Randal Johnson, the search for Brazilian modes of expression in literature, or definitions of Brazilian national identity in literary as well as other cultural discourses, is consonant with the rise of nationalistic and authoritarian thought currents in Brazil after the revolution or coup of 1930 that brought populist Getúlio Vargas to power. Some of the most outstanding intellectuals and artists of this period became (in most cases) willing accomplices to the Vargas regime, which

sought to sediment its power along nationalistic lines, at the same time as it became intellectually legitimated.

5. The idea of cultural "originality" and "distinctiveness" is shared by Spanish American critics when referring to Latin America as a whole (even though, more often than not, among Spanish Americanists Latin America stands metonymically for Spanish America at the expense of Brazil). Here they emphasize a regional or continental identity, even though most Brazilian critics, while cognizant of the commonalities with the former Spanish colonies of the Americas, tend to privilege Brazil as a separate cultural entity that is also distinct from the rest of Latin America.

6. Freyre, Buarque de Holanda, and Prado also point out the propensity of the Portuguese colonizers to mix with "peoples of color" and their adaptability to the tropics. These particularities (expressed by intellectuals of differing political beliefs) interestingly would become the ideological basis for the legitimation of Portuguese colonialism by the right-wing regime in Portugal after the 1930s.

7. Brazil was one of the last countries to abolish slavery. The abolition of slavery was a very slow process that entailed several different stages. It was entirely accomplished only in 1888. While Britain prohibited slave trade across the Atlantic in 1845, Brazil (formally) eliminated slave trade only in 1850 (Lei Eusébio). Meanwhile, as of 1871 all children of slaves were considered free (Lei do Ventre Livre).

8. See, for instance, Fernando Novais, ed., *História da vida privada no Brasil* (1997); Mary del Priore, ed., *História das mulheres no Brasil* (1997); James Green, *Beyond Carnival: Homosexuality in Twentieth-Century Brazil* (1999); and Jeffrey Lesser, *Welcoming the Undesirables: Brazil and the Jewish Question* (1995).

9. Gilberto Freyre's magnum opus is the trilogy of works focusing on the formation of Brazilian patriarchal society: *Casa-grande e senzala* (The masters and the slaves, 1933), *Sobrados e mucambos* (The mansions and the shanties, 1936), and *Ordem e progresso* (Order and progress, 1959).

10. Darcy Ribeiro's *O povo brasileiro* (1995) is a rarity in contemporary intellectual thought in that it presents a totalizing view of Brazilian culture, much in the vein of the canonical works by Gilberto Freyre, Sérgio Buarque de Holanda, and Caio Prado, Jr., earlier this century. Ribeiro adopts a macrological approach as he formulates what he describes as "a social and empirically based theory" of Brazil (15). In essence, he presents a historical, anthropological, and sociological study that focuses primarily on issues of race, ethnicity, nationality, and class. The critic aligns himself with "the people," abandoning any pretense of objectivity as he overtly expresses an ethical commitment vis-à-vis his object of study, in this case the most oppressed and marginalized of Brazilian people: the Amerindians. Darcy Ribeiro practically assumes the point of view of the Amerindians and becomes their staunchest defender; thus the Portuguese colonizer is clearly seen as an "invader." Echoing common themes expressed throughout this century, Ribeiro sees Brazil as an example of a "new people" or a "new human type," which is the result of the trauma of colonization as well as subsequent migratory waves. He points out how unified the Brazilian nationality is today as a result of urbanization, industrialization, the technological revolution, and the mass media. By the same token, the critic stresses how the highly unified Brazilian nation is also the result of long-lasting social repression. Equally, he views ethnic-cultural unity as disguising deep social class divisions.

Darcy Ribeiro's most important contribution is to have updated the debate around Brazilian national identity while bearing in mind the social conflicts of contemporary Brazil, at the same time as he privileges the Amerindian experience and contribution to Brazilian culture, even if his approach may occasionally seem romantic and hyperbolic regarding his object of study.

11. Antonio Candido is largely responsible for the resurging interest in Freyre, Buarque de Holanda, and Caio Prado in recent years due to his preface ("O Significado de *Raízes do Brazil*," 9–24) to the new editions of Buarque de Holanda's *Raízes do Brasil*.

12. See the enormous dossier dedicated to the hundred-year anniversary of the birth of Gilberto Freyre published in the weekly "Mais!" section of *Folha de São Paulo Online* (12 March 2000).

13. For more details on Eduardo Portella's reading of Freyre's intellectual contribution, see "Gilberto Freyre, além do apenas moderno," *Rumos* 1 (1998–99).

14. Other important works by Sérgio Buarque de Holanda, aside from his monumental *História geral da civilização brasileira* (1960), include *Caminhos e fronteiras* (1956), which focuses on the exploration and settlement of the Brazilian hinterland, and *Visão do paraíso* (1958), which subtly contrasts the Portuguese and Spanish "baroque" mentalities.

15. The metaphor-concept of "misplaced ideas" is one of the central pieces of Roberto Schwarz's intellectual contribution (see his "Misplaced Ideas"). Based on his reflections on nineteenth-century imperial Brazil and the fiction of Machado de Assis, Schwarz delineates the essential contradiction between the liberal ideals that were being imported to Brazil—progress, equality, the right to work, and the freedom to work—and slavery. Schematically, Schwarz points out that colonialism created three social groups: landowners, slaves, and "free men." The members of this third group, though "free," were dependent upon the "favors" of the powerful landowners. The dynamic of "favors" thus became a mechanism of social reproduction for an entire class of people that would soon spread to the whole of Brazilian society (government, commerce, the liberal professions, etc.). In short, it became an instrument of mediation that was less odious than slavery, but nevertheless undemocratic. If slavery was absolutely incompatible with the liberal ideals of the late nineteenth century, the system of "favors" absorbed and displaced them, creating a novel and peculiar social system that came to characterize Brazil.

16. By focusing on the cultural rituals and social dramas of Brazilian contemporary life, anthropologist Roberto DaMatta sheds light on what he terms "the Brazilian dilemma," which entails essentially the authoritarian, hierarchical, and even violent strands that collide with the desire for a democratic, harmonious, and nonconflictive society, resulting in a contradictory and liminal national reality (*Carnavais, malandros, e heróis*, 1981). In this context, *carnaval* appears as the emblematic Brazilian ritual where the nation as a collectivity identifies itself as a cohesive cultural unit at the same time as it inverts and reifies hierarchical and authoritarian structures, while it enacts the relatively egalitarian—albeit ephemeral—rite of passage that *carnaval* represents.

DaMatta's intellectual project marks an important transition in Brazilian thought on the nation or national identity vis-à-vis the "great" thinkers of the 1930s by shifting the focus from the colonial past to contemporary Brazilian society and from a macrological vision of the "infrastructure," the "national character," or the racial or ethnic roots of the nation to micrological instances of everyday life rituals and cultural practices that do indeed underscore the authoritarian strands present in Brazilian culture that intellectuals such as Sérgio Buarque de Holanda or Caio Prado, Jr., accounted for through differing yet totalizing conceptual models.

17. Intellectuals such as such as Fernando Ortiz, Angel Rama, and Antonio Cornejo-Polar have studied the dynamics of "transculturation" as they pertain to the colonial experience of Spanish-speaking Latin America and its continued relevance to understanding the geopolitical contours of Latin America's cultural production today. The underlying concerns of Spanish American intellectuals generally coincide with those of Brazilian thinkers in terms of the dialectic between center and periphery, local and cosmopolitan, and national and foreign and the ways this varyingly defined dialectic has shaped Latin American forms of knowledge and their relationship to centers of intellectual production in Europe and North America. Josh Lund provides a lucid comparative reading between Antonio Candido and Cuban sociologist Fernando Ortiz (see "Barbarian Theorizing and the Limits of Latin American Exceptionalism"). Lund suggests that both critics displayed a modality of "hybrid thinking" that defied expectations of scientific objectivity predominant in "Western" epistemology, at least until the advent of poststructuralism. This intrinsic discursive hybridity would constitute its strength and originality, but also has provided the justification for its marginalization from major intellectual currents in the "West." We could argue that this marginalization is the result of geopolitical dynamics and their economic underpinnings that have limited the circulation and legitimation of bodies of knowledge produced by the peripheries as much as it may be a strictly "epistemological problem." On the other hand, we could add that the constitutive interdisciplinarity in the work of both Candido and Ortiz, perhaps in an inadvertently "performative" fashion, reveals the (inevitably) liminal space occupied by Latin American cultures, which are simultaneously Western and non-Western from an epistemological as well as a geopolitical standpoint.

18. Among contemporary Brazilian intellectuals, particularly Candido, Santiago, and Schwarz, there is a constant slippage between constructs of "Brazil" and "Latin America." Even though previous intellectuals such as Freyre, Buarque de Holanda, and Caio Prado, Jr., were aware of the commonalities in the cultural experiences of Brazil and various Spanish-speaking American countries, due to their personal and intellectual commitment to the project of "Brazil," as well as the particularly nationalistic political context under Getúlio Vargas, their geopolitical emphasis was clearly national and not regional, transnational, or pan–Latin American. A pan–Latin American perspective in Brazilian intellectual thought is a more recent phenomenon, dating from the 1960s and partly due to the Cuban Revolution and its international(ist) impact, especially throughout Latin America.

19. "O entre-lugar do discurso latino-americano" (Latin American discourse: The space in between), recently published in English as The Space In-Between: Essays on Latin American Culture (2001)], 12.

20. For an English translation of the "Manifesto Antropófago," see Leslie Bary's annotated version, "Oswald de Andrade's 'Cannibalist Manifesto'" (1991).

21. This essay was first published in Portuguese as "Nacional por substração" in Folha de São Paulo (7 June 1986) and then published in English as "Nationalism by Elimination" in New Left Review 167 (1988). It is also included in the first English-language collection of Roberto Schwarz's essays, Misplaced Ideas (1992).

22. Roberto Schwarz's intellectual contribution is of particular interest to neo-Marxian critics such as Neil Larsen who wish to retain an economically informed

and class-based reading in contemporary debates regarding the effects of globalization on the national cultures of Latin America. Larsen vehemently criticizes Latin American(ist) "postnational" cultural studies, as represented by Nestor Canclini, for locating themselves in isolation from the economic basis and from labor and class relations within the nation-state. He feels that Schwarz correctly maintains the centrality of the notion of "alienation" in explaining the relations between intellectuals and the social field, as well as the continued unequal flow of ideas between cores and peripheries, whereas postmodern concepts such as "transculturation" or cultural "reconversion" are inadequate to explain these socioeconomic and geopolitical dynamics. The conflict here arises essentially from the excessive weight given by critics such as Larsen to issues of class in analyzing national cultural phenomena as they pertain to the process of globalization and from the insufficient weight given to class concerns by some cultural studies critics. Nestor García Canclini, however, does not ignore class dynamics, but favors a heterogeneous reading that also incorporates other cultural, sociological, and geopolitical variables in analyzing questions of nationhood and globalization (*Consumidores y ciudadanos: Conflictos multiculturales de la Globalización,* xvi). The overemphasis on class matters or on the possibility of a utopian social revolution in Larsen's discussion occludes areas of cultural production where Brazilian artists and intellectuals reveal a heightened degree of pragmatism, creativity, and dynamism in relationship to international cultural currents without necessarily losing sight of Brazilian national specificities that entail, among others, intractable socioeconomic problems that may or may not be directly connected to a larger geopolitical context.

23. Malcolm McNee has written a pioneering dissertation focusing on the cultural underpinnings of the Brazilian landless rural workers' movement and its key contribution to the struggle for a more democratic and just society for Brazil ("The Arts in Movement: Cultural Politics and Production in Brazil's Landless Rural Workers Movement [MST]").

3. Subjectivities and Homoerotic Desire in Contemporary Brazilian Fiction

1. The first conference on literature and homoeroticism in Brazil took place in May 1999 at the Universidade Federal Fluminense in Niteroi (near Rio de Janeiro). Of a total of twenty-seven papers presented, Caio Fernando Abreu was the author who received the greatest amount of attention (there were at least half a dozen papers focusing on his work). In subsequent conferences in 2000 and 2001, there have been signs of a sustained critical interest in Abreu's work. These examples are sure signs of the emergence of Abreu's work as part of the canon of Brazilian literature.

2. The work of Caio Fernando Abreu has already been widely translated in Europe, particularly into French, Italian, and German. So far only two full works have been translated into English *(Os dragões não conhecem o paraíso,* translated as *Dragons,* and *Onde andará Dulce Veiga?* translated as *Whatever Happened to Dulce Veiga?),* along with two short stories ("Sergeant Garcia" and "Those Two," included in Leyland Wilson's anthology *My Deep Dark Pain Is Love: A Collection of Latin American Gay Fiction,* 1983). With the added visibility and recognition that Abreu has gained inside and outside of Brazil since his death, it is highly probable that we will see

more of his works translated into English in the United States. Meanwhile, in Brazil practically all of his works (those written from 1970 until his death) are being re-published. Several of his short stories have also been adapted into performance pieces, and several of his plays have been produced with great critical success. In addition, a major anthology (Paulo de Tarso Riccordi's *Caio de amores,* 1996) including short stories written by twenty authors from Caio Fernando Abreu's home state of Rio Grande do Sul was published as a tribute to the author who is considered, in his region as well as in Brazil, one of the most important voices of his generation.

3. Former Senator Marta Suplicy (from the Partido dos Trabalhadores or Worker's Party), the current mayor of São Paulo, introduced a wide-ranging domestic-part-nership bill into the Brazilian Congress in 1996 that would law grant same-sex couples many of the rights and responsibilities of those united through matrimony. As of this writing, this bill is stalled in the Brazilian Congress, having encountered stiff opposition from the Catholic Church and evangelical Christians.

4. Brazilian women writers such as Lya Luft (*Reunião de família,* 1982; *As parceiras,* 1986); Márcia Denser (*Muito prazer: Contos eróticos femininos,* 1982); Leila Míccolis (*Sangue cenográfico: Poemas de 1965 a março de 1997,* 1997); Lygia Fagundes Telles (*A noite escura e mais eu,* 1995); Maria Regina Moura (*Exercício de um modo,* 1987; *Poemas do recolhimento e do frio,* 1996); and Miriam Alves (editor with Carolyn Richardson Durham of *Enfim nós: Escritoras negras brasileiras contemporâneas/ Finally Us: Contemporary Black Brazilian Women Writers,* 1994) have been exploring, at a variety of registers and degrees of intensity, issues regarding lesbian desire.

The following is a list of pioneering contemporary male Brazilian authors and literary texts (outside of Caio Fernando Abreu) that have overtly thematized homo-sexuality and bisexuality: Aguinaldo Silva (*Primeira carta aos andróginos,* 1975; *A república dos assassinos,* 1976; *No pais das sombras,* 1979; Gasparino Damata (*Os solteirões,* 1976); Darcy Penteado (*Nivaldo e Jerônimo,* 1981); Herbert Daniel (*Passagem para o próximo sonho,* 1982); Silviano Santiago (*Stella Manhattan,* 1985); João Silvério Trevisan (*Devassos no paraíso,* 1986 and 2000, translated as *Perverts in Paradise,* 1986). The last work is an account of a pioneering "archaeological" study conducted by João Silvério Trevisan on homosexuality and Brazilian culture since the arrival of the Portuguese in the sixteenth century.

5. Author Glauco Mattoso is the subject of a dissertation by Steve Butterman (University of Wisconsin).

6. There are very few critical studies that deal with Brazilian gay literature. Of those, one of the most exhaustive to date, also dealing with Portugal and Luso-phone Africa, is *Lusosex: Sexuality and Gender in the Portuguese-Speaking World,* edited by me and Susan Canty Quinlan (2002). David W. Foster has published two studies that deal with Brazilian gay fiction in conjunction with Spanish-speaking Latin America: *Gay and Lesbian Themes in Latin American Writing* (1991) and *Sexual Textualities: Essays in Queer/ing Latin American Writing* (1997). His edition (with Roberto Reis) *Bodies and Biases* (1996) deals mostly with Spanish-speaking Latin America but includes two essays on sexuality and literary/cultural discourses in Brazil.

7. As a result of increased civil resistance against the military junta on the part of workers and students in 1968, the infamous Ato Institucional n° 5 (Institutional Act no. 5) was put into effect. The ensuing result was a "declaration of war" by the

military against the opposition (either the armed opposition or its nonarmed expressions). This entailed numerous disappearances of political opponents; strict censorship of intellectuals, artists and students; university purges; and the flight into exile of important sectors of the Brazilian intelligentsia.

8. By 1986, statistics indicated that Brazil, alongside the United States, had among the highest number of AIDS cases reported outside of Africa. In 1998, Brazil ranked fourth on the United Nations' list of infected countries, with 580,000 adult carriers of HIV. According to Dr. Ruth Cardoso, wife of the president of Brazil, "AIDS is Brazil's second-leading cause of death in people ages 20 to 49" (Lawrence K. Altman, "At AIDS Conference, a Call to Arms against 'Runaway Epidemic'"). In the year 2000, however, there were approximately 34 million people with AIDS in the world, two-thirds of them in Africa. South Africa has 4.2 million people who have HIV/AIDS, more than any other nation ("AIDS in South Africa"). As of this writing, the AIDS epidemic in Brazil has stabilized, as the AIDS death rate nationally has been cut by half (Rosenberg, "Look at Brazil," 29). Brazil is considered to have the most successful AIDS treatment program in the developing world (Barbara Crossette, "U.S. Drops Case over AIDS Drugs in Brazil," 4). This major breakthrough has been possible due to the government's commitment in making AIDS a national priority, which is reflected in its liberal approach to drug patents in times of national emergency. Thus, Brazil now produces its own affordable anti-AIDS drugs, which would otherwise be sold by multinational pharmaceutical companies at exorbitant prices. Anti-AIDS drugs have become widely available in Brazil through a highly organized network of treatment and prevention programs. Brazil's success in curtailing the spread of the disease is also due to the history of AIDS activism among gays and the existence of 600 nongovernmental groups that work on AIDS around the country.

9. In December 1994, the Brazilian Supreme Court acquitted Fernando Collor de Mello, as it found the prosecution unable to prove its corruption charges against the former president.

10. "Liminal" here signifies the interstitial space or the space in between. "Liminal" was originally used by anthropologist Arnold Van Gennep, who studied the realm of ritual within culture. The term was used to describe threshold- or intermediate-stage rites in human societies. This particular term has since been adapted by contemporary literary and cultural criticism. For more details, see Irena R. Makaryk, ed., *Encyclopedia of Contemporary Literary Theory* (Toronto: University of Toronto Press, 1993), 578–79.

11. Arjun Appadurai, "Disjuncture and Difference in the Global Economy." Appadurai is discussed extensively in Michael J. Shapiro and Howard R. Alker, eds., *Challenging Boundaries: Global Flows, Territorial Identities*, 3–5.

12. I would like to acknowledge Marcelo Secron Bessa for bringing this insight to my attention.

13. I wish to thank Rodolfo A. Franconi and Susan C. Quinlan for bringing to my attention the fact that Caio Fernando received the most pleasure in the last few months of his life from receiving cards and postcards with pictures of the sun. The sun was his symbol for life.

14. The literal English translation of this title is "Beauty, a horrible story," which suggests a richer spectrum of meanings that simultaneously encompass feelings of love, solidarity, and abjection shared by mother and son as they unite in their

awareness of the increased decrepitude of their bodies but also the profound human ties that bind them.

15. Ana Cristina César (1952–83) was a prominent lesbian poet who took her own life.

16. For a full discussion of Abreu's novel *Onde andará Dulce Veiga?* please refer to my article "Writing after Paradise and before a Possible Dream: Brazil's Caio Fernando Abreu."

17. In an interview that appeared in *O Estado de São Paulo* ("Inventário irremediável: Caio Fernando (1949–1996) fala da vida antes da morte"), the author points out that the figure of Dulce Veiga was inspired by a character of the same name in the novel *A estrela sobe* (1949) by Marques Rebelo. This character was later portrayed by Odete Lara in film director Bruno Barreto's adaptation of Rebelo's novel.

18. As of the 1980s, Brazil had become a net world exporter of television programs and advertising (ranked seventh worldwide), and of popular music (ranked sixth). The dynamic at play is most evident in Portugal and in Lusophone Africa, and to a lesser degree in the rest of Latin America. Brazilian popular music is also widely available in North American and other European markets, while dubbed Brazilian soap operas can be seen on Italian, French, and Spanish television, among others. As Renato Ortiz asserts, Brazil has shifted from the "defense of the national-popular to the export of the international-popular" (*A moderna tradição brasileira*, 182–206).

19. In *Tentative Transgressions: AIDS and Homosexuality in the Contemporary Brazilian Theatre* (soon to be published by the University of Wisconsin Press), Severino Albuquerque provides the most exhaustive study to date of Brazilian theatrical representations of homosexuality as well as AIDS through history. Here Caio Fernando Abreu is featured as one of the most prominent contemporary playwrights in Brazil. In his study Albuquerque also provides a rigorous and in-depth analysis of several of Abreu's plays and of theatrical adaptations of short stories and novellas written by Abreu.

20. Renato Farias adapted the novella "Pela noite" for the stage with much success in Porto Alegre and Rio de Janeiro between 1994–96 with the enthusiastic support of Caio Fernando Abreu (for more details see Albuquerque, *Tentative Transgressions*).

21. The term "abjection" is being used here as that which is degraded or cast out of "sociality," as it relates to AIDS and the multiplicity of negative associations connected to the disease since the beginning of the epidemic. This term has two primary sources: Judith Butler, in the context of her analysis of sex-gender identities and (homo)erotic desire (*Bodies That Matter*, 243), and Julia Kristeva, who identifies a wide spectrum of psychoanalytical processes that underlie the production of the "abject" (*Powers of Horror: An Essay on Abjection*, 1–31). The two critics coincide in their definition of the "abject" as essentially that which is so other or so opposite to the I that it becomes the jettisoned object that defies meaning and is therefore radically excluded.

22. This dynamic gains added potency with the realization that since the late 1990s people with AIDS, particularly in industrialized societies, have been able to extend their lives indefinitely given the availability of protease inhibitors and various other combinations of drugs that suppress the advancement of the HIV virus. Unfortunately, this was not an option for Caio Fernando Abreu, nor is it yet an

affordable option for tens of millions of people living with AIDS throughout the world today, especially in Africa and Asia. Besides, not all the drugs available are effective for all people with HIV.

23. In *Bodies, Pleasures, and Passions* (1991), Richard Parker amply describes the coexistence of various paradigms within the Brazilian sexual culture whereby contemporary imported models would coexist with more traditional notions of sexuality and gender. The notion of a "gay community" modeled after what is found in North America, various parts of Europe, Australia, and other countries and coterminus with a political movement has found echo in elite segments of the larger urban areas of Brazil, while more traditional notions persist in rural and working-class segments of the population, where sexual acts do not translate into political consciousness and where sexual identity is structured around a vertical axis of active/passive and male/female. In the latter case, from a "gay perspective" the subject would be considered bisexual, but he would consider himself to be performing the "male" role regardless of the gender of the sexual object of choice. This is a model not exclusive to Brazil, as it is still widespread in Latin American and Mediterranean cultures (Tomás Almaguer, "Chicano Men: A Cartography of Homosexual Identity and Behavior," 257; Arno Schmitt, "Different Approaches to Male-Male Sexuality/Eroticism from Morocco to Uzbekistan," 6) and was also common in the United States earlier this century, particularly in rural areas and among the working classes (John D'Emilio, "Capitalism and Gay Identity," 471). Today the "imported models" from the metropoles have gained greater acceptance and legitimation, becoming more widespread in countries such as Brazil while coexisting with traditional models of sexual culture.

In *Beneath the Equator* (1999), Richard Parker updates and expands the arguments put forth in his previous book by situating his study of the Brazilian sexual culture in more concrete socioeconomic and geopolitical terms within the context of industrialization and urbanization in Brazil, together with the process of globalization. He states that local sexual cultures today are caught more than ever in the crosscurrents of global processes of change. The sexual culture in Brazil and elsewhere throughout the world, particularly with regard to same-sex desire, is more the result of the interaction of local practices, international meanings, and world consumer markets.

24. The English translation of "Sargento Garcia" is included in Leyland's *My Deep Dark Pain is Love* (1983).

25. For a detailed discussion of Abreu's short story anthology *Morangos mofados,* please refer to my article entitled "Estar entre o mofo e a esperança: *Morangos mofados* de Caio Fernando Abreu" (1992).

26. "Dama da noite" was adapted into a performance monologue by Brazilian stage actor Gilberto Gawronski with French, Portuguese, and English versions. It is said that the first rehearsals took place in the hospital room where Caio Fernando Abreu spent some of his last days. The performance piece has since become very successful, with shows in Lyon (France), Rio de Janeiro, São Paulo, and New York. In 1998, Mário Diamante made a short film version of the solo performance with Gawronski as the protagonist. For an in-depth analysis of the performance piece, see Albuquerque, *Tentative Transgressions,* pp. 59–65.

27. The English translation of Abreu's short story "Aquele dois" ("Those Two") is featured in Leyland's *My Deep Dark Pain Is Love* (1983).

28. For a more detailed discussion on the problematic of the "utopia of the other" as it informs the fiction of Caio Fernando Abreu and Clarice Lispector, as well as Portuguese authors Vergílio Ferreira, Maria Isabel Barreno, José Saramago, and Maria Gabriela Llansol, please refer to chapter 5 ("Worlds in Transition and Utopias of Otherness").

29. See Levinas's works *Le temps et l'autre* (1947, trans. 1987 as *Time and the Other*) and *Totalidade e infinito* (1961, trans. 1987 as *Totality and Infinity*) for a philosophical formulation of the concept of being and the other and of the ethical commitment toward the other.

4. Women's Difference in Contemporary Portuguese Fiction

1. Darlene Sadlier, *The Question of How,* xiii.

2. In the novel *O Inventário de Ana* (1982), Maria Isabel Barreno explored various issues that would be central to *Crónica do tempo* (The chronicle of time), which describes the effects of major historical changes in individual lives, more specifically in the lives of the three women protagonists. In contrast to *Crónica do tempo,* which remains within a "historical real" plane, *Inventário da Ana* takes us into a poetic-fantastic dimension where the female subject (in this case, Ana) searches for the mythical origins of women.

3. The term *deterritorialization* stems from Gilles Deleuze and Félix Guattari's innovative philosophical work *A Thousand Plateaus* (1987). Through a vastly interdisciplinary approach, the philosophers construct a series of conceptual matrices that originate in a multiplicity of fields such as geography, geology, botany, and architecture in order to reflect on sociocultural phenomena. The notion of "territoriality" and its shifting movements of deterritorialization and reterritorialization are central to *A Thousand Plateaus* and has been incorporated into a variety of contemporary critical and theoretical discourses. This dynamic refers to the spatial, material, emotional, and psychological elements that constitute or deconstitute a given society, group, or individual. Deleuze and Guattari describe the series of movements ("lines of intensity") that affect disparate micro or macro instances or realms, such as an object, a book, an apparatus, or a system (508). In the case of *Crónica do tempo,* I am using the notion of "deterritorialization" in order to describe the changes that the city of Lisbon has undergone over the decades. This novel thematizes the social and cultural changes within Portuguese society that are most vividly felt in the large urban center and that are a result of important political and economic shifts, both domestically and globally.

4. Even though the "ontological disorientation" alluded to in reference to Barreno's *Crónica do tempo,* which is seen as resulting from major historical and cultural changes since World War II, is shared equally by both men and women, it is the changes affecting gender relations, and in particular the role of women in Portuguese society, that greatly concern this novel, as well as other works by Barreno.

5. As Isabel Allegro de Magalhães reminds us in *O sexo dos textos,* in women's writing the house often functions metonymically and metaphorically as the space of writing, of coming into being, the space where the body is written. Specifically, in the case of Manuela in the early twentieth-century Lisbon of *Crónica do tempo,* as well as in that of Maria Josefa in colonial Capeverdean society of Barreno's novel *O*

senhor das ilhas (1994), the house is the space where one can realize oneself onto-logically, however imperfectly and in spite of the enormous social and material barriers imposed on one in one's own time and place.

6. Homi Bhabha, *The Location of Culture*, 148.

7. In her article "Home Bound: The Construct of Femininity in the Estado Novo" (1996), Ana Paula Ferreira argues that the national project under Salazar could not have been achieved without the "rhetorical involvement of womanhood and femininity as ideological signs, and of 'women,' as socio-political subjects" (134). Salazar's nationalist project, according to Ferreira, inevitably centered on the family unit, the "Portuguese home," and women—obviously conceived within a traditional and patriarchal mode—would be the pillar of this unit and home. Salazarism assigned women an educational as well as an economic task. They were ultimately deemed responsible for the economic welfare of the entire Portuguese nation-family, as well as for the behavior, if not the thoughts and desires, that were considered appropriate for its members. Ultimately, Ferreira points out, Portuguese fascism placed women in the paradoxical position of becoming willing accomplices, illustrating quite vividly the Foucaultian theorization of the dynamics of power and discourse within society.

8. For a full definition of *historical time* as it pertains to women and the nation, see Kristeva's "Women's Time," 187–213.

9. The ambiguity in my usage of the terms *myth, utopia,* and even *metanarrative* is deliberate. I wish to establish an analogy between the fundamentally teleo-logical terms myth as used by Vergílio Ferreira in *Invocação ao meu corpo* and *Pensar; métarecit* or *metanarrative* as used by Jean-François Lyotard in *The Postmodern Condition;* and *utopia* as it is used in *Crónica do tempo* by Maria Isabel Barreno. I believe all three terms incorporate the impulse of organizing collective imaginaries that project themselves into a future of redemption and progress. For a more elaborate discussion of my usage of these terms, refer to chapter 5.

10. This brings to mind echoes of novelist and philosopher Vergílio Ferreira and his ideas about the notion of myth. According to Ferreira, the precariousness of human existence is the measure of its own provisional status as myth. The weight attributed to a given myth or utopia can only reflect the weight and measure of its creators, that is, human beings: "Mas a grandeza do mito tem a grandeza que tivermos, que é a da vida em que nos reflectimos. É possível viver sem mitos? O impossível é sonhá-los hoje para uma grandeza que não há" (But the greatness of myths is the equivalent of our own greatness, which is the life in which we reflect ourselves. Is it possible to live without myths? What's impossible today is to dream of them for a greatness which does not exist) (*Pensar*, 249).

11. Bhabha, *The Location of Culture*, 148.

12. Sousa Santos has formulated an exhaustive critique of historically dominant Portuguese cultural discourses that have invariably adopted a negative point of view with regard to the nation. This is what Sousa Santos defined as the Portuguese "national jeremiad": a matrix of discourses that reached its height in the nineteenth century with the *Geração de 70* and that more often than not reveals a skeptical, frustrated, and resentful spirit toward the historic fate of Portugal within the modern world.

13. The relevance of Lídia Jorge's novel *O vale da paixão* to the discussion surrounding shifting definitions of nationhood and alternative ways of speaking of the

nation within Portuguese contemporary literature came up in conversations with Ana Paula Ferreira, always an engaging interlocutor, for which I remain grateful.

14. See Levinas's works *Le temps et l'autre* (1947) and *Totalidade e infinito* (1961) for a philosophical formulation of the concept of being and the other, and the ethical commitment toward the other.

15. In Graça's stories all female characters have names that start with *G* (Gracinda, Gabriela, and Gisela), and the male characters have names starting with *V* (Valentim, Vicente, etc.). Even if this detail may appear at first to be playfully banal—as the narrator herself points out—it inevitably signals a continuum between the characters' lives and the life of the narrator and her family, a continuum between fiction and the real that the author does not want the reader to forget.

16. In his dialogue with Christie McDonald, entitled "Choreographies," published in *The Ear of the Other* (1988), Jacques Derrida speculated on what he considers the skepticism of certain women vis-à-vis history, political dogmas, or utopias (be they Marxist or even feminist). The particular female subject (or "maverick feminist") that he posited is a subject of (an)other history: "a history of paradoxical laws and nondialectical discontinuities, a history of absolutely heterogeneous pockets, irreducible particularities, of unheard-of and incalculable sexual differences" (167).

17. The historical weight of the metaphor-synthesis that serves as the title of Barreno's novel *O chão salgado,* or "salted ground," is relativized as it undergoes a process of resignification. On the one hand, the "*chão salgado*" can be seen as the plot of land (during the Inquisition) where there was once a house, mansion, or monastery inhabited by those who were accused of terrible heresies. The compound was eventually destroyed and its inhabitants burned alive. The plot of land would have been "salted" so that nothing would grow for centuries and the physical space would remain a symbol of treason and punishment that would inspire fear and respect (23–24). On the other hand, this symbolic space is also portrayed in Barreno's novel as a benignly enchanted site that embodies a special kind of energy that was to be preserved for posterity as a sign for those who sought it. Both Valentim and Gracinda spend a night of peace and inspiration on this salted ground.

5. Worlds in Transition and Utopias of Otherness

1. The inclusion of Brazilian writer Clarice Lispector within a group of writers who have actively and persuasively engaged the question of utopias may surprise certain readers and critics of her work given that this question is not explicitly treated in her fictional production. However, since one of the primary arguments developed here is the emergence of the "utopia of the other" as an ultimate cultural and ontological frontier in contemporary times, and since Lispector devotes much attention to the subject's relationship with the other, in the form of a reader, for instance, where this relationship is intrinsic to acts of writing and reading, and since the act of writing acquired a vital importance to her in her final years related to questions of life and death, Clarice Lispector has indeed much to contribute to this discussion, and her inclusion within this heterogeneous group of writers is most pertinent and valuable.

2. See *The Utopia Reader* (1999).

3. Lyotard has been one of the thinkers most closely associated with postmodernism since the publication of *La Condition postmoderne* in 1979. Particularly from

this point on, his philosophy focused on critiques of totalizing forms of thought (embedded in the notion of "metanarratives") and attempts to develop an alternative epistemology based on the heterogeneity and plurality within language, which allows for multiple points of articulation in philosophical, political, historical, or religious discourses (to name a few), where none can claim to speak for all. Lyotard, on the other hand, has been amply criticized for the philosophical/political aporia of his critical move of advancing his own metanarrative of postmodernity, or for not carefully distinguishing between empowering and disabling narratives, or for rejecting normative political or philosophical positions while providing his own normative positions. For a critical account of Lyotardian thought, see Steven Best and Douglas Kellner, *Postmodern Theory* (1991).

4. Along with Fernando Pessoa and Maria Gabriela Llansol, Vergílio Ferreira (1916–1996) was the most philosophical writer in twentieth-century Portuguese culture. His fiction is deeply informed by ontological and phenomenological concerns at the level of content as well as form. In fact, throughout the last thirty years of Ferreira's career, his vast fictional production was accompanied by the production of a remarkable philosophical corpus in the form of essays and diaries in which the author reflected upon questions regarding the destiny of humanity and the meaning of existence, as well as subjectivity, death, myths, the body, God, art, and politics, among others. One of the most exhaustive studies of the philosophical basis for much of Ferreira's cultural production is Gavilanes Laso's *Vergílio Ferreira: Espaço simbólico e metafísico* (1989).

5. For a more detailed discussion of the status of myths and metanarratives in Vergílio Ferreira's cultural production, please refer to my article "Beauty 'At the Surface of Love's Face': Myth and Metanarratives in Vergílio Ferreira's Contemporary Fiction" (1997).

6. See Nietzsche's "On Truth and Lie" (1982).

7. Other paradigmatic definitions of myth were advanced by major twentieth-century thinkers such as Malinowski, Cassirer, Eliade, and Lévi-Strauss, but given the scope and limitations of the present study, these definitions are not incorporated into my general discussion of the overlapping conceptual field between utopias, metanarratives, and myths. The definitions of myth that have been alluded to so far in this study by Vergílio Ferreira, Roland Barthes, and Nietzsche reveal a greater kinship to the definitions of metanarratives or utopias that interest us here than do those advanced by Malinowski, Cassirer, Eliade, or Lévi-Strauss. For a comparative study of myth as defined by these four thinkers, please refer to Ivan Strenski's *Four Theories of Myth in Twentieth-Century History* (1987).

8. The horrors and despair brought by both world wars led Jewish Austrian intellectual Stefan Zweig to coin the notion of "Brazil, country of the future," which further reinforced and updated the utopian mythologies associated with Brazil since 1500. Zweig's notion was thoroughly embraced and appropriated by Brazilian elites in the middle of the twentieth century.

9. In *Visão do Paraíso* (1959).

10. See Chaui's "O mito fundador do Brasil."

11. In *Toward a New Common Sense* (1995), Boaventura de Sousa Santos presents a sociological analysis of what he views as the "exhaustion of the paradigm of modernity." Santos defines modernity as the emergence, from the sixteenth and seventeenth centuries on, of an ambitious and revolutionary sociocultural paradigm

based on a dynamic equilibrium between social regulation and emancipation. Social regulation is seen as constituted by the principles of the state, market, and community, while emancipation is seen as constituted by the three Weberian "logics of rationality": the aesthetic-expressive rationality of the arts and literature, the cognitive-instrumental rationality of science and technology, and the moral-practical rationality of ethics and the rule of law. This paradigm, dynamic and ambitious, has also engendered tensions, contradictions, unfulfilled promises, and irredeemable social deficits. Santos argues that since the nineteenth century, science and law have been entrusted as regulatory mechanisms of the social excesses and deficits of modernity, to the detriment of its emancipatory energies. Thus, Santos says there is a need for a new "map of emancipatory practices." (For more details of his theoretical paradigm, please refer to *Toward a New Common Sense,* pp. 1–55.)

12. Jurandir Freire Costa's essay "A ética democrática e seus inimigos" is part of a larger collection of timely essays written by renowned Brazilian intellectuals and social activists, among them Frei Betto, Cristovam Buarque, and Luís Fernando Veríssimo (*O desafio ético,* 2000), who call for a drastic rethinking of the dominant values of rampant individualism and alienation from the other that are partly the result of the most extreme forms of capitalism that prevail in Brazilian society today (as well as elsewhere throughout the world). Cristovam Buarque, Brazilian economist, politician, activist, and public intellectual, has focused his attention on the reinvention of utopias, thus calling for the need to subordinate the economy to social objectives and ethical values. Buarque's restless and socially committed thinking is dispersed in numerous articles, some of which have been republished together in the book *Os instrangeiros* (2002), which could be translated as "The Native Foreigners."

13. For details of Bakhtin's own definitions of ontology and alterity and their relevance to the fiction of Caio Fernando Abreu, see chapter 3.

14. The "Vergilian subject" described here is clearly masculine, as are the subjects (in the form of narrators or protagonists) of the novels being considered here. The masculine "his" is intended as such.

15. Vergílio Ferreira's passionate impulse to subvert totalizing discourses was a constant in his fifty years of cultural production. This impulse derived from his rejection of ideologies that organize themselves institutionally into universal truths and that preclude the subject from finding his or her own measure of truth independently. Yet Ferreira never ceased to criticize the oppressive power structures in Portugal in his novels published between the 1950s and the early 1970s, even in implicit, veiled, or allegorical fashions, as for example in *Manhã submersa, Aparição, Cântico final, Apelo da noite,* and *Nítido nulo.* At the same time, Ferreira openly distanced himself from Portuguese neorealism (in *Aparição, Cântico final,* and *Apelo da noite*), as he contested their prevailing views regarding the status of art and literature in society. Ferreira rejected the view that they should be subservient to ideological programs (Marxism, in this case). The novel *Apelo da noite* (1954) best illustrates Ferreira's difficult third position, in which he rejected the oppressive Salazar regime at the same time as he rejected its staunchest source of opposition, the Portuguese Communist Party (which was outlawed at the time but to which many neorealists still adhered). The protagonist of *Apelo da noite* is caught in the dilemma of being an intellectual who opposes the authoritarian right-wing regime of the time, but who cannot submit himself to Communist Party dogma. In this way, Vergílio Ferreira anticipated his own struggle with the April Revolution of 1974, in particu-

lar, wanting to maintain intellectual and political independence at a historical moment at which political dogmas were dominant. This situation created great strife between Ferreira and the Portuguese leftist intelligentsia.

16. Marxism (as posited by the Portuguese Communist Party, a loyal follower of pre-Perestroika communism), together with Christianity, remained for years the major ideological spaces criticized by Vergílio Ferreira, as can be seen in his later novels *Nítido nulo, Signo sinal, Para sempre, Até ao fim,* and *Em nome da terra.* Ferreira's interest in Marxism greatly subsided after the fall of the Berlin Wall. Christianity, on the other hand, continued to be an object of his critical interest in his novel *Na tua face,* published shortly before his death.

In *Na tua face* Ferreira offered his familiar strategy of intermeshing philosophical fiction and fictionalized poetry at the edge of life and at the crossroads of history, but this time the author opened new thematic paths as he problematized the aesthetic and moral dimensions of beauty. Assuming that beauty is a totalizing narrative construct in Western culture, Vergílio Ferreira desired to underline its constructedness, as well as its inherent contingency and its exclusivist implications. In addition, he set out to undermine the workings of beauty (and its counterpart, ugliness) as key elements of a coherent and unified cultural discourse. In *Na tua face* Ferreira relativized the categories of beauty and ugliness. He stripped them of their weight as distinct and hierarchized cultural measures. In the novel, what is beautiful and what is ugly become matters of value judgment. In fact, *Na tua face* presents itself as a space where what traditionally has been regarded as aesthetically or physically abject, unseemly, incomplete, deformed, or even horrendous acquires a new ontological meaning. The ugly and the horrible are posited as human inventions, while nature continues on its course regardless, making no judgment one way or another. The narrator invokes a time beyond "lymphatic delicate pinderic beauty." He calls forth his own time of horror, of darkness ("trago em mim o meu tempo de horror"), 158.

17. See Maria Alzira Seixo, "Vergílio Ferreira, os modernos, os pós-modernos e a questão das dominantes," 121.

18. See Fernanda Irene Fonseca, *Vergílio Ferreira: A celebração da palavra* (1992).

19. The nostalgia for the "whole" that is so palpable throughout Vergílio Ferreira's fictional and nonfictional *démarche* is the underlying theme of Helder Godinho's *O universo imaginário de Vergílio Ferreira* (1985), the first major critical work on Ferreira. In spite of Godinho's exhaustive as well as rigorous analysis of the symbolic universe within Ferreira's fiction up until the early 1980s and its relation to the notions of the "whole" or a "universal order," his analytical framework suffers from a tendency to locate Vergílio Ferreira within a constellation of absolute or essentialist philosophical categories. This critical tendency precludes a fuller account of the ideological, narratological—all in all, the discursive paradoxes and contradictions— that are also at the heart of Ferreira's literary and philosophical being, which reveal an author and a thinker caught between totalizing and nontotalizing thought currents. These paradoxes and contradictions become clearer through an analysis of the status of utopias, myths, or metanarratives in Ferreira's work.

20. For a detailed comparative study on Clarice Lispector and Vergílio Ferreira regarding the question of the phenomenological, please refer to my "Being Here with Vergílio Ferreira and Clarice Lispector: At the Limits of Language and Subjectivity."

21. Lúcia Helena, in "A literatura segundo Lispector" (1991) and "A problematização da narrativa em Clarice Lispector" (1992), makes two important critical

moves. First of all, she reinserts Clarice Lispector's fictional enterprise within the context of the historical development of Brazilian literature, something that had been lost in Hélène Cixous's readings of her work. Secondly, she locates Lispector's works in a more politically contestatory place—a place that has been generally denied her in the past, from Antonio Candido to Hélène Cixous, since Lispector's works can be and have often been read as ahistorical, or at times the criticism itself has been ahistorical (for instance, in the case of Cixous).

Lúcia Helena divides the critical reception of Lispector's fiction into two phases: an existentialist phase represented by the work of Benedito Nunes and a feminist phase represented by Hélène Cixous. Here I would like to add additional categories that may give a fuller sense of the various Lispectorian critical approaches at work today: historically grounded feminist approaches (seen in the work of Lúcia Helena and Marta Peixoto), poststructuralist approaches (seen in the work of Earl Fitz, and João Camillo Penna), and Jewish cultural hermeneutics approaches (seen in the work of Nelson Vieira).

22. In her essay "A literatura segundo Lispector" Lúcia Helena highlights the narrative and ideological devices utilized by Lispector in order to critique the dominant sex-gender system in Brazil, at the same time as the author relativizes fixed or "universal" categories such as "male" or "female," pointing to their intrinsic instability. Furthermore, Helena points to the fact that even if the patriarchal vicious circle has not been destroyed in Lispector's fictional world, it has undergone a process of constant corrosion and dialogization.

23. This is a reading that subscribes to Cixous's lyrical gesture in interpreting the character of Macabea ("How does one desire wealth or poverty?" in *Reading with Clarice Lispector*). It was in fact after Hélène Cixous's theorization of *écriture féminine* in the early 1980s—based to a large extent on Lispector's work—that feminist readings were catapulted onto center stage in the critical reception of Lispector's fiction. It was also the moment at which Lispector was discovered outside the Portuguese-speaking world, to such an extent that between the late 1980s and the 1990s her works were canonized at a number of academic institutions (outside of Brazil and Portugal, Lispector was first discovered in Francophone areas, and then through the translations of Cixous's works into English she became known in Anglophone countries, particularly in the U.S. academy). In spite of the valid critiques of Cixous's appropriative gestures vis-à-vis Clarice Lispector's work advanced by Marta Peixoto (in *Passionate Fictions*), Cixous's critical focus on Lispector has been crucial in providing Lispector the visibility she deserves.

24. In 1994 Marta Peixoto published *Passionate Fictions*, the first critical book on Lispector written in English by a Brazilianist. The main objective Peixoto wished to accomplish with her book was to rescue Lispector from readings that limited her to the ontological or to the maternal, the nurturing, or the always giving (as exemplified by Cixous). While she accepts these readings, Peixoto desires to offer yet another entryway into Lispector that incorporates an inscription of the feminine that is not sentimentally withdrawn from struggles of power. She retains the term "violence" as descriptive of Lispector's fictional trajectory: according to Peixoto, Lispector thematizes the violence stemming from patriarchal power from the beginning of her writing career. Later on, violence from other sources is incorporated—the violence of the class structure, of the political system, and, most important, of the act of narrating itself. For instance, Peixoto states that in *A hora da estrela* (The

hour of the star) Lispector's elaborate (meta)fictional web ultimately stresses how writer, narrator, and reader are all implicated in the oppression of the subaltern (in this case, Macabéa). Peixoto demonstrates how this novel inscribes the violence that victimizes Macabéa: *A hora da estrela* is not only critical of the violence inflicted by society on its main character, but it is self-critical of the motivations of literature and of the author herself.

Peixoto provides a powerful argument for reading Lispector under a more socially committed light, especially if we consider works such as *A hora da estrela, Laços de família* (*Family ties,* 1960), and *A via crucis do corpo* (The stations of the body, 1974, translated in 1989 and included in the collection *Soulstorm*). However, it would be more accurate to state that Lispector's fictional production as a whole offers a tense oscillation between existential/ontological concerns and social/feminist concerns that ultimately cannot be dissociated from one another. Yet Peixoto's overemphasis of the social in Clarice Lispector's writing emerges as a valid reaction to criticism that presents Lispector as removed from social concerns. In fact, this interpretive differend hints at the constitutive ambiguity of the Lispectorian literary text as well as its profound semantic ambiguity (as Earl Fitz points out in "The Passion of Logo(centrism), or, the Deconstructionist Universe of Clarice Lispector"), whereby it can hardly be contained within any one interpretive approach or critical school.

25. As can be observed in earlier Lispector novels such as *A paixão segundo G. H.* (The passion according to G. H., 1964) and *Água viva* (The stream of life, 1973), the structural logic that prevails is reflective of the flow of the author/narrator's feelings. This type of structure (or lack thereof), especially in *Água viva* and *Um sopro de vida,* results in free-flowing and extremely fragmented narratives that defy the very notion of the novel itself. We clearly see the irrational, the nonlinear, the emotional superseding a Cartesian notion of being, which in turn has a profound impact on the constitution of the novel as a genre and what writing meant to Clarice Lispector.

26. In his efforts to situate Clarice Lispector on the literary and philosophical map of Western contemporary cultural debates, Earl Fitz, in his article "The Passion of Logo(centrism)," focuses on the coinciding impulses between Lispector and poststructuralist thinkers. Clarice Lispector's preoccupation with the question of meaning—how it is produced, processed, and reconstituted into literary representation—and its bearing upon the human condition is akin to that of the work of critics such as Derrida, Barthes (in his later work), Kristeva, and Irigaray, among others. According to Fitz, various Lispectorian texts "generate precisely the sense of linguistic destabilization and unreliability that Derrida expresses in the term *différance*" (37). This last term refers to "meaning" as the result of a constant slippage between signifiers and signified, a relationship that is arbitrary and imperfect. Furthermore, Fitz points out that Lispector's writing practice, in which the production of language is a flowing mental process rather than a stable conclusion and texts are created an open, fluid, poetically rendered process, is closely related to Derrida's notion of *écriture* (and, of course, to Cixous's theorization of *écriture féminine*).

27. This conflation of thinking-feeling at the crux of being, which became such a vital force in novels such as *A paixão segundo G. H.* and *Água viva,* has already been explored in Debra Castillo's essay "Negation." For Castillo, this epistemological move in *A paixão segundo G. H.* represents "an expansion of the Cartesian formula

that moves from the realm of thought to that of feeling: I think, therefore I exist, becomes I am therefore I adore" (203). *A paixão segundo G. H.* is in fact constructed around the axis "I am" (in a temporary state, since in Portuguese it is *estou*) and "I adore" *(adoro)*. Later on in her essay, Castillo points out that both "I" (subject) and "am" (state of being) are in fact severely problematized in Lispector's work. Subjectivity cannot be contained in the verb "to be," so instead the author begs us "to read between the lines of what can be said for the essential unsayable that is beyond speech" (214).

28.   In no other work by Clarice Lispector is the presence of music as strong as in *Um sopro de vida.* This presence is so strong that it transpires in the linguistic constructions. Furthermore, the intense excitement of the Lispectorean narrator over the power of music has to do with what it reveals of the self. Through music more than through words is it possible to come near the most intimate depths of our beings and the world we inhabit: "Estou ouvindo música. Debussy usa as espumas do mar morrendo na areia, refluindo e fluindo. Bach é matemático. Mozart é o divino impessoal. Chopin conta a sua vida mais íntima, Schoenberg, através do seu eu, atinge o clássico eu de todo o mundo. Beethoven é a emulsão humana em tempestade procurando o divino e só o alcançando na morte. Quanto a mim, que não peço música, só chego ao limiar da palavra nova" (20). (I'm listening to music. Debussy uses the foam of the sea dying in the sand, flowing back and forth. Bach is the mathematician. Mozart is the divine impersonal. Chopin tells us his most intimate life story. Schoenberg, through his I, touches the classical I in everyone. Beethoven is the stormy human emulsion, searching for the divine but only reaching it at the hour of his death. As for me, I do not ask for music, I only reach the threshold of the new word.)

29.   Both Maria José Somerlate Barbosa and Teresa Cristina Montero Ferreira point out, based on conversations they have had with individuals who knew Clarice Lispector, that she became aware of having cancer only a few months before her death. The unawareness of her life-threatening disease gives even more poignancy to her near-obsession with death in her later works *A hora da estrela* and *Um sopro de vida,* which were both presumably written before she found out about her condition. I thank both authors for this important piece of information.

30.   In Vergílio Ferreira's diary of 1989 *(Conta corrente—Nova série 1),* there is an entry that describes a gathering with Lygia Fagundes Telles and Nélida Piñón in which Clarice Lispector's literary works were discussed. Vergílio Ferreira points out what he believes to be philosophical affinities between his novel *Aparição,* published in 1959, and some of Clarice Lispector's novels. After foreclosing any possibility of "influence" in any one direction, all three writers agree that there has indeed been a "coming together" of both writers. A literary/philosophical identification between the two authors was reiterated to me in conversations with Vergílio himself in 1992.

The first comparative study of Lispector and Ferreira was published by Ivo Lucchesi (*Crise e escritura: Uma leitura de Clarice Lispector e Vergílio Ferreira,* 1987). This work stresses differences and similarities between Ferreira's earlier works *(Aparição, Estrela polar,* and *Alegria breve)* and Lispector's later works *(Água viva, A hora da estrela,* and *Um sopro de vida).* According to Lucchesi, both were writers who fictionalized the human condition through literary works in which they problematized the act of writing as they problematized being. Lucchesi's analysis is an important first step in establishing a critical dialogue between Ferreira and Lispector that, at the same time, opens the door for more expansive and updated studies.

31. The importance of the phenomenological in the fiction of Clarice Lispector has already been pointed out by various critics, among them Marta Peixoto and Benedito Nunes. Both of these critics, however, emphasize particular aspects that differ from the ones highlighted here. Peixoto, for instance, focuses on the importance of the epiphany, which provides the female subject a crucial moment of self-awareness of her place in patriarchal society. The epiphany may open the possibility of the transgression of conventional roles for women, even if only temporarily, in "*Family Ties:* Female Development in Clarice Lispector." Nunes, on the other hand, provides a very close reading of the novel *A paixão segundo G. H.* and describes the phenomenological experience lived by the protagonist after having consumed the cockroach. According to Nunes, this experience is of a mystical nature in which there is a complete transubstantiation of subject and object at the same time as there is a complete loss of identity on the part of the subject. This "loss of identity" would signify experiencing a "plenitude of being" that cannot be conveyed in language (*O drama da linguagem: Uma leitura de Clarice Lispector,* 73–75).

32. Maria Gabriela Llansol has been prolific as a writer since 1962 and slowly but surely has gathered significant critical attention and some literary awards, even if she still has only a small yet devoted readership, not only in Portugal, but also in Brazil. The critical reception of Llansol's work has gained momentum since the late 1980s and has focused largely on establishing various hermeneutical paths to the understanding of one of the most complex and rewarding intellectual projects in the Portuguese language today. Some of the most important critical readings of Llansol's work have been produced by Fernando Pinto do Amaral, Lúcia Castello Branco, Eduardo Prado Coelho, António Guerreiro, Lúcia Helena, Augusto Joaquim, Silvina Rodrigues Lopes, Eduardo Lourenço, and Jorge Fernandes da Silveira.

33. Llansol's writing has been described as "nomadic" (António Guerreiro, "O texto nómada de Maria Gabriela Llansol"), as a traveling text in constant movement between writing/reading communities and phenomenological moments/spaces. Lúcia Helena describes it as an example of "laboratory writing" that is highly metafictional and intertextual, following a medieval tradition of interpreting the text at the same time as it is being written. In fact, within Llansol's writing practice there is a collapse between the activities of writing, reading, and interpreting, which all seem to take place simultaneously as the text develops.

34. The character Aossê, for instance, is based on the figure of Fernando Pessoa and takes on androgynous qualities, becoming simultaneously male and female, or becoming one or the other at different times. Infausta, on the other hand, is the female heteronym of Aossê, or the female heteronym that Pessoa may have never created, echoing Virginia Woolf's creation of Shakespeare's hypothetical female sister in *A Room of One's Own.* (Recent archival discoveries made by Richard Zenith on the unpublished manuscripts by Fernando Pessoa reveal one poem written by a presumed female heteronym. For more information, see Richard Zenith, "Fernando Pessoa's Gay Heteronym?" [2002].) Here Llansol subverts and transfigures Portuguese cultural myths such as Fernando Pessoa to serve her own cultural/ethical project. Figures such as Camões, Copernicus, Pessoa, Bach, and Spinoza are evoked as concrete historical figures of a European cultural saga, but they become subordinate to Llansol's own specific preoccupation with Portugal's relationship to western Euro-

pean culture or with the transhistorical destiny of Western culture (in the sixteenth or seventeenth centuries, as well as today). For example, the staged encounter between Camões and Copernicus never took place historically, but in Llansol's text it becomes the opportunity to conjecture how each would have influenced and enriched the other in terms of his world-view and gift to the world. Both figures are seen as protagonists of sweeping cultural changes in the context of sixteenth-century Europe: in the case of Copernicus, the confluence of astronomical discoveries and the secularization of thought, in the case of Camões, the confluence of epic and lyric poetry and the maritime discoveries.

35. The Beguines were members of protofeminist Christian communities that developed in Belgium around the late twelfth century and later spread to the Low Countries, Germany, and northern France. They assumed lives outside the socially endorsed alternatives of wife or cloistered nun. The beguines were not bound by vows and were not subject to papal enclosure, nor did they renounce the possibility of marriage. Some communities cultivated intense forms of mysticism that led many to suspect them of heresy. "Beguinage" could be described as spontaneous women's movements where each community was autonomous, with no rules or constitution, and members could pursue lives of freedom and simplicity with a minimal amount of bureaucratic complications. Some communities, in fact, still exist today in Belgium (see Elizabeth T. Knuth, "Women Writers of the Middle Ages," and the *New Encyclopaedia Britannica*, 1998). Hadewijch of Brabant, a thirteenth-century poet, was one of the greatest exponents of Beguine spirituality as well as one of the key mystics of her time, and she established a new genre of mystic love poetry. Within the writing of Maria Gabriela Llansol, as Lúcia Helena points out in her article "Estratégias Narrativas na Obra de Maria Gabriela Llansol" (1991), Hadewijch plays a pivotal role in many "luminous scenes" *(cenas fulgor)*.

36. I wish to thank Jorge Fernandes da Silveira for originally pointing out this connection to me.

37. When José Saramago won the Nobel Prize for literature in 1998, the award was interpreted in Portugal, as well as in Brazil and throughout Portuguese-speaking Africa, as a belated recognition of the force and vitality of the Portuguese language, and in particular of all of its national literary expressions. Thus, Saramago's Nobel Prize automatically acquired a pan-Lusophone status, with various countries to differing degrees claiming it as their own. The author has now become the most visible and outspoken Portuguese-speaking intellectual in the world today.

38. Since the 1980s a plethora of critical articles and books have accompanied Saramago's remarkable fictional production, focusing primarily on the historiographical, narratological, and mythical aspects that are crucial for understanding his work. See, among others, Maria Alzira Seixo, Teresa Cristina Cerdeira da Silva, Giovanni Pontiero, Horácio Costa, Beatriz Berrini, and Conceição Madruga.

39. Saramago's novel, *Todos os nomes* (All the names, 1997) dramatizes the universal solitude and precariousness of everyday contemporary life, as well as the contingent nature of the "name" as a defining trait that would identify a human life in an otherwise highly anonymous and bureaucratized world. As in previous novels, such as *Levantado do chão* and *Baltasar and Blimunda,* Saramago wished to privilege the anonymous and "common" lives of those whom the grand narratives of history, politics, and the arts have not recorded.

40. José Saramago and Vergílio Ferreira coincide in their preoccupation with the ideological hegemony of Christianity in the history of the Western world. This preoccupation is at the center of Saramago's *O evangelho segundo Jesus Cristo* (The gospel according to Jesus Christ, 1991), where the figure of Jesus is confronted with a series of moral dilemmas between being human and being "the son of God." This novel becomes a meditation on the questions of power, free will, freedom of consciousness, and the role of religious faith in human society. Vergílio Ferreira, for his part, considers Marxism (at least until the fall of the Berlin Wall) and Christianity two of the most dominant myths of the twentieth century. Ferreira's own critique of Christianity (as well as Marxism) derived from his rejection of ideologies that organize themselves institutionally into universal truths and preclude the individual's finding his or her own measure of truth independently.

Bibliography

Abreu, Caio Fernando. *Morangos mofados.* São Paulo: Editora Brasiliense, 1982.

———. *Triângulo das águas.* Rio de Janeiro: Nova Fronteira, 1983.

———. *Os dragões não conhecem o paraíso.* São Paulo: Companhia das Letras, 1988.

———. *Dragons.* Trans. David Treece. London: Boulevard Books, 1990.

———. *Onde andará Dulce Veiga?* São Paulo: Companhia das Letras, 1990.

———. *Ovelhas negras.* Porto Alegre, Brazil: Editora Sulina, 1995.

———. *Estranhos estrangeiros.* São Paulo: Companhia das Letras, 1996.

———. *Pequenas epifanias.* Porto Alegre: Editora Sulina, 1996.

———. *Teatro completo.* Porto Alegre: Editora Sulina, 1997.

———. *Whatever Happened to Dulce Veiga?* Trans. Adria Frizzi. Austin: University of Texas Press, 2000.

Agamben, Giorgio. *The Coming Community.* Trans. Michael Hardt. Minneapolis: University of Minnesota Press, 1993.

"AIDS in South Africa." *New York Times,* 12 July 2000, natl. ed., A26.

Albuquerque, Luís de, ed. *Dicionário da História dos descobrimentos portugueses.* Lisboa: Editorial Caminho, 1994.

Albuquerque, Severino J. *Tentative Transgressions: AIDS and Homosexuality in the Contemporary Brazilian Theatre.* Madison: University of Wisconsin Press, forthcoming.

Alexandre, Valentim. "The Colonial Empire." In *Modern Portugal,* ed. António Costa Pinto, 41–59. Palo Alto, Calif.: Society for the Promotion of Science and Scholarship, 1998.

Almaguer, Tomás. "Chicano Men: A Cartography of Homosexual Identity and Behavior." In *The Lesbian and Gay Studies Reader,* ed. Henry Abelove, Michèle Aina Barale and David M. Halperin, 255–73. New York and London: Routledge, 1993.

Almino, João. "O diálogo interrompido." *Rumos* 1 (1999): 26–35.

Altman, Lawrence K. "At AIDS Conference, a Call to Arms against 'Runaway Epidemic.'" *New York Times,* 29 June 1998, natl. ed., A13.

Alves, Miriam, and Carolyn Richardson Durham, eds. *Enfim nós: Escritoras negras brasileiras contemporâneas/Finally Us: Contemporary Black Brazilian Women Writers.* Colorado Springs: Three Continents Press, 1994.

Amaral, Fernando Pinto do Amaral. "A Escrita Fulgurante de Maria Gabriela Llansol." *Colóquio/Letras* 132–33 (1994): 196–200.

Anderson, Benedict. *Imagined Communities.* Rev. ed. London and New York: Verso, 1991.

Anderson, James M. *The History of Portugal.* Westport, Conn.: Greenwood Press, 2000.

Andrade, Oswald de. "Manifesto antropofágico." In *Do Pau-Brasil à antropofagia e às utopias.* Rio de Janeiro: Civilização Brasileira, 1972.

Antonil, André João. *Cultura e opulência do Brasil.* São Paulo: Companhia Editora Nacional, 1967.

Antunes, António Lobo. *O manual dos inquisidores.* Lisboa: Publicações D. Quixote, 1996.

———. *O esplendor de Portugal.* Lisboa: Publicações D. Quixote, 1997.

———. *Exortação aos crocodilos.* Lisboa: Publicações D. Quixote, 1999.

Anzaldúa, Gloria. *Borderlands/La Frontera.* San Francisco: Spinsters/Aunt Lute, 1987.

Appadurai, Arjun. "Disjuncture and Difference in the Global Cultural Economy." *Public Culture* 2 (1990): 1–23.

Arenas, Fernando. "Intertextos 'Onde o Mar Acaba': *O ano da morte de Ricardo de Ricardo Reis* de José Saramago." *Lucero* 1 (1990): 33–47.

———. "Estar Entre o Lixo e a Esperança: *Morangos mofados* de Caio Fernando Abreu." *Brasil/Brazil* 8 (1992): 53–67.

———. "Beauty 'at the Surface of Love's Face': Myth and Metanarratives in Vergílio Ferreira's Contemporary Writing." *Santa Barbara Portuguese Studies* 4 (1999): 157–69.

———. "Being Here with Vergílio Ferreira and Clarice Lispector: At the Limits of Language and Subjectivity." *Portuguese Studies* 14 (1999): 1–14.

———. "Writing after Paradise and before a Possible Dream: Brazil's Caio Fernando Abreu." *Luso-Brazilian Review* 36 (1999): 13–21.

Arenas, Fernando, and Susan Canty Quinlan, eds. *Lusosex: Gender and Sexuality in the Portuguese-Speaking World.* Minneapolis: University of Minnesota Press, 2002.

Arendt, Hannah. *The Human Condition.* Chicago: Chicago University Press, 1958.

Attridge, Derek. "Innovation, Literature, Ethics: Relating to the Other." *PMLA* 114 (1999): 20–31.

Azevedo, Aluísio. *O cortiço.* São Paulo: Editora Ática, 1984.

———. *The Slum: A Novel.* Trans. David H. Rosenthal. New York: Oxford University Press, 2000.

Baganha, Maria Ioannis B. "Portuguese Emigration after World War II." In *Modern Portugal,* ed. António Costa Pinto, 189–205. Palo Alto, Calif.: Society for the Promotion of Science and Scholarship, 1998.

Barreno, Maria Isabel. *O inventário de Ana.* Lisboa: Edições Rolim, 1982.

———. *A morte da mãe.* Lisboa: Editorial Caminho, 1989.

———. *Crónica do tempo.* Lisboa: Editorial Caminho, 1990.

———. *O chão salgado.* Lisboa: Editorial Caminho, 1992.

———. *Os sensos incomuns.* Lisboa: Editorial Caminho, 1993.

———. *O senhor das ilhas.* Lisboa: Editorial Caminho, 1994.

———. *O mundo sobre o outro desbotado.* Lisboa: Editorial Caminho, 1995.

Barreno, Maria Isabel, Maria Velho da Costa, and Maria Teresa Horta. *Novas cartas portuguesas.* Lisboa: Editorial Futura, 1974.

————. *New Portuguese Letters.* London: Readers International, 1994.

Barthes, Roland. *Mythologies.* Paris: Éditions du Seuil, 1957.

Bary, Leslie. "Oswald de Andrade's 'Cannibalist Manifesto.'" *Latin American Literary Review* 38 (1991): 35–47.

Bastos, Baptista. *José Saramago: Aproximação a um retrato.* Lisboa: Publicações D. Quixote, 1996.

Berrini, Beatriz. *José Saramago: O romance.* Lisboa: Editorial Caminho, 1998.

Bessa, Marcelo Secron. *Histórias positivas.* Rio de Janeiro and São Paulo: Editora Record, 1997.

Best, Steven, and Douglas Kellner. *Postmodern Theory.* New York: Guilford Press, 1991.

Bhabha, Homi K. "DissemiNation: Time, Narrative and the Margins of the Modern Nation." In *The Location of Culture,* 139–170. London and New York: Routledge, 1994.

Birmingham, David. *A Concise History of Portugal.* Cambridge, U.K.: Cambridge University Press, 1993.

Block, Ernst. *The Principle of Hope.* Trans. Neville Plaice, Stephen Plaice, and Paul Knight. Cambridge, Mass.: MIT Press, 1986.

Bosi, Alfredo. *Dialética da colonização.* São Paulo: Companhia das Letras, 1992.

————. *História concisa da literatura brasileira.* 32nd ed. São Paulo: Editora Cultrix, 1994.

Boxer, C. R. *Portuguese Seaborne Empire, 1415–1825.* New York: A. A. Knopf, 1969.

Branco, Camilo Castello. *A brasileira de Prazins.* Mem Martins, Portugal: Edições Europa-América, n.d.

————. *Eusébio Macário.* Mem Martins, Portugal: Edições Europa-América.

Brito, Bernardo Gomes de, ed. *História Trágico-Marítima.* Mem Martins, Portugal: Edições Europa-América, n.d.

————. *The Tragic History of the Sea.* Ed. and trans. C. R. Boxer. Cambridge, U.K.: The Halyut Society, 1959. Reprint, with a new translation and a foreword by Josiah Blackmore, Minneapolis: University of Minnesota Press, 2001.

Buarque, Chico. *Estorvo.* São Paulo: Companhia das Letras, 1991.

————. *Turbulence.* New York: Pantheon, 1992.

Buarque, Cristovam. *Os instrangeiros.* Rio de Janeiro: Garamond, 2002.

Butler, Judith. *Bodies That Matter.* New York and London: Routledge, 1993.

Butterman, Steve. "Brazilian Literature of Transgression and Postmodern Anti-Aesthetics in Glauco Mattoso." Ph.D. diss. Univ. of Wisconsin, Madison, 2000.

Caminha, Adolfo. *Bom-Crioulo* [1895]. São Paulo: Editora Ática, 1983.

————. *Bom-Crioulo: The Black Man and the Cabin Boy.* Trans. E. A. Lacey. San Francisco: Gay Sunshine Press, 1982.

Caminha, Pêro Vaz de. *Carta de Pêro Vaz de Caminha a El-Rei D: Manuel sobre o achamento do Brasil.* Mem Martins, Portugal: Publicações Europa-América, 1987.

Candido, Antonio. *Literatura e sociedade.* São Paulo: Companhia Editora Nacional, 1967.

————. "O Significado de *Raízes do Brasil.*" Introduction to *Raízes do Brasil,* by Sérgio Buarque de Holanda. São Paulo: Companhia das Letras, 1995.

————. *On Literature and Society.* Trans. Howard S. Becker. Princeton, N.J.: Princeton University Press, 1995.

Capistrano de Abreu, João. *Capítulos de história colonial, 1500–1800.* Rio de Janeiro: Livraria Briquiet, 1954.

Carey, John, ed. *The Faber Book of Utopias*. London: Faber and Faber Ltd., 1999.

Carvalho, Bernardo. *Aberração*. São Paulo: Companhia das Letras, 1993.

———. *Os bêbados e os sonâmbulos*. São Paulo: Companhia das Letras, 1996.

Castelo, Cláudia. *O modo português de estar no mundo: O luso-tropicalismo e a ideologia colonial portuguesa*. Porto, Portugal: Edições Afrontamento, 1998.

Castello, José. "Inventário irremediável: Caio Fernando (1949–1996) fala da vida antes da morte." *O Estado de São Paulo*, 9 Dec. 1995.

Castello Branco, Lúcia. "Escrever, amar, morrer talvez. . . ." *Viva voz* (1997): 25–31.

Castillo, Debra. "Negation." In *Talking Back*, 185–215. Ithaca, N.Y.: Cornell University Press, 1992.

Cervo, Amado, and José Calvet de Magalhães. *Depois das caravelas: As relações entre Portugal e Brasil, 1808–2000*. Brasília: Editora Universidade de Brasília, 2000.

Chanady, Amaryll, ed. *Latin American Identity and Constructions of Difference*. Hispanic Issues 10. Minneapolis: University of Minnesota Press, 1994.

Chase-Dunn, C., and T. D. Hall. "Comparing World Systems: Concepts and Working Hypotheses." *Social Forces* 71 (1993): 851–86.

Chaui, Marilena. *Seminário*. São Paulo: Editora Brasiliense, 1983.

———. *Conformismo e resistência*. São Paulo: Editora Brasiliense, 1986.

———. "O mito fundador do Brasil." *Folha de São Paulo Online*, 26 Mar. 2000. http://www.uol.com.br/fsp/.

Cixous, Hélène. Foreword to *The Stream of Life*, by Clarice Lispector. Minneapolis: University of Minnesota Press, 1989.

———. *L'heure de Clarice Lispector*. Paris: Des femmes, 1989.

———. *Reading with Clarice Lispector*. Minneapolis: University of Minnesota Press, 1990.

Claeys, Gregory, and Lyman Tower Sargent, eds. *The Utopia Reader*. New York: New York University Press, 1999.

Coelho, Eduardo Prado. *A noite do mundo*. Lisboa: Imprensa Nacional/Casa da Moeda, 1984.

Costa, Jurandir Freire. "A ética democrática e seus inimigos." In *O desafio ético*, ed. Ari Roitman, 77–89. Rio de Janeiro: Garamond, 2000.

Crossette, Barbara. "U.S. Drops Case over AIDS Drugs in Brazil." *The New York Times*, 26 June 2001, natl. ed., A4.

DaCosta-Holton, Kimberly. "Dressing for Success: Lisbon as European Cultural Capital." *Journal of American Folklore* 111 (1998): 173–96.

Damata, Gasparino. *Os solteirões*. Rio de Janeiro: Pallas S.A., 1976.

DaMatta, Roberto. *Carnavais, malandros, e heróis*. 3rd ed. Rio de Janeiro: Zahar Editores, 1981.

Daniel, Herbert. *Passagem para o próximo sonho*. Rio de Janeiro: Editora Codecri, Ltda., 1982.

Daniel, Herbert, and Richard Parker. *AIDS: A terceira epidemia*. São Paulo: Iglu Editora, 1991.

Davis, J. C. "The History of Utopia: The Chronology of Nowhere." In *Utopias*, ed. Alexander, Peter, and Roger Gill, 1–18. London: Duckworth and Co., 1984.

De Abreu, Capistrano. *Capítulos da história colonial do Brasil*. Ed. José Honório Rodrigues. 6th ed. Rio de Janeiro: Civilização Brasileira, 1976.

———. *Chapters of Brazil's Colonial History*. Trans. Arthur Brakel. New York and Oxford: Oxford University Press, 1997.

Deleuze, Gilles, and Félix Guattari. *A Thousand Plateaus.* Trans. Brian Massumi. Minneapolis: University of Minnesota Press, 1987.

D'Emilio, John. "Capitalism and Gay Identity." In *The Lesbian and Gay Studies Reader,* ed. Henry Abelove, Michèle Aina Barale, and David M. Halperin, 467–76. New York and London: Routledge, 1993.

Denser, Márcia. *Muito prazer: Contos eróticos femininos.* Rio de Janeiro: Record, 1982.

Derrida, Jacques. *Of Grammatology.* Trans Gayatri Chakravorty Spivak. Baltimore and London: Johns Hopkins University Press, 1976.

———. *The Ear of the Other.* Ed. Christie McDonald. Trans. Peggy Kamuq and Avital Ronell. Lincoln and London: University of Nebraska Press, 1988.

———. *Acts of Literature.* Ed. Derek Attridge. New York and London: Routledge, 1992.

———. *The Gift of Death.* Trans. David Wills. Chicago: University of Chicago Press, 1995.

Diffie, Bailey W., and George D. Winius. *Foundations of the Portuguese Empire, 1415–1580.* Minneapolis: University of Minnesota Press, 1977.

Dussel, Enrique. "Beyond Eurocentrism: The World-System and the Limits of Modernity." In *The Cultures of Globalization,* ed. Fredric Jameson and Masao Miyoshi. Durham, N.C., and London: Duke University Press, 1998.

Enders, Armelle. *História da África lusófona.* Mem Martins, Portugal: Editorial Inquérito, 1997.

Featherstone, Mike, ed. *Global Culture.* London: SAGE Publications, 1990.

Featherstone, Mike, Scott Lash, and Roland Robertson, eds. *Global Modernities.* London: SAGE Publications, 1995.

Ferreira, Ana Paula. "Home Bound: The Construct of Femininity in the Estado Novo." *Portuguese Studies* 12 (1996): 133–44.

Ferreira, M. Ema Tarracha, ed. *Literatura dos descobrimentos e da expansão portuguesa.* Lisboa: Biblioteca Ulisseia de Autores Portugueses, 1993.

Ferreira, Vergílio. *Manhã submersa.* Lisboa: Bertrand Editora, 1953.

———. *Aparição.* Lisboa: Bertrand Editora, 1958.

———. *Cântico final.* Lisboa: Bertrand Editora, 1960.

———. *Estrela polar.* Lisboa: Bertrand Editora, 1962.

———. *Apelo da noite.* Lisboa: Bertrand Editora, 1963.

———. *Alegria breve.* Lisboa: Bertrand Editora, 1965.

———. *Invocação ao meu corpo.* Lisboa: Bertrand Editora, 1969.

———. *Nítido nulo.* Lisboa: Bertrand Editora, 1971.

———. *Signo sinal.* Lisboa: Bertand Editora, 1979.

———. *Para sempre.* Lisboa: Bertrand Editora, 1983.

———. *Até ao fim.* Lisboa: Bertrand Editora, 1987.

———. *Em nome da terra.* Lisboa: Bertrand Editora, 1990.

———. *Pensar.* Lisboa: Bertrand Editora, 1992.

———. *Contra-corrente: Nova série 1.* Lisboa: Bertrand Editora, 1993.

———. *Na tua face.* Lisboa: Bertrand Editora, 1993.

"FHC pede tolerância com divergências." *Folha de São Paulo Online,* 23 Apr. 2000. http://www.uol.com.br/fsp/.

Fitz, Earl E. "The Passion of Logo(centrism), or, the Deconstructionist Universe of Clarice Lispector." *Luso-Brazilian Review* 25 (1988): 33–43.

Fonseca, Fernanda Irene. *Vergílio Ferreira: A celebração da palavra*. Coimbra: Almedina, 1992.

Foster, David William. *Gay and Lesbian Themes in Latin American Writing*. Austin: University of Texas Press, 1991.

———. *Sexual Textualities: Essays on Queer/ing Latin American Writing*. Austin: University of Texas Press, 1997.

Foster, David William, and Roberto Reis. *Bodies and Biases: Sexualities in Hispanic Cultures and Literatures*. Hispanic Issues 13. Minneapolis: University of Minnesota Press, 1996.

Freyre, Gilberto. *Casa-grande e senzala* [1933]. 30th ed. Rio de Janeiro: Editora Record, 1992.

———. *The Masters and the Slaves*. Trans. Samuel Putnam. New York: Knopf, 1946.

———. *Um brasileiro em terras portuguesas*. Lisboa: Edições Livros do Brasil, 1954.

———. *Integração portuguesa nos trópicos*. Lisboa: Col. ECPS, 1958.

———. *O luso e o trópico*. Lisboa: Comissão Executiva das Comemorações do V Centenário da Morte do Infante D. Henrique, 1961.

———. *Ordem e progresso*. 3rd ed. Rio de Janeiro: Editora José Olympio, 1974.

———. *Sobrados e mucambos*. 5th ed. Rio de Janeiro: Editora José Olympio, 1977.

Gândavo, Pêro de Magalhães. *Tratado da terra do Brasil: História da província de Santa Cruz a que vulgarmente chamamos Brasil*. Belo Horizonte: Editora Itatiaia, 1980.

García Canclini, Néstor. *Consumidores y ciudadanos: Conflictos multiculturales de la Globalización*. México D.F.: Grijalbo, 1995.

Godinho, Helder. *O universo imaginário de Vergílio Ferreira*. Lisboa: Instituto de Investigação Científica, 1985.

Government of Macao. August 1998. http://www.macau.gov.mo.

Green, James N. *Beyond Carnival: Homosexuality in Twentieth-Century Brazil*. Chicago: Chicago University Press, 1999.

Guerreiro, António. "O texto nómada de Maria Gabriela Llansol." *Colóquio/Letras* 91 (1986): 66–69.

Hall, Stuart, ed. *Modernity: An Introduction to Modern Societies*. Cambridge, Mass.: Blackwell, 1997.

Hand, Sean, ed. *The Levinas Reader*. Oxford: Blackwell, 1989.

Hardt, Michael, and Antonio Negri. *Empire*. Cambridge, Mass.: Harvard University Press, 2000.

Helena, Lúcia. "A literatura segundo Lispector." *Tempo Brasileiro* 104 (1991): 25–42.

———. "Estratégias narrativas na obra de Maria Gabriela Llansol." *Luso-Brazilian Review* 2 (1991): 37–48.

———. "A problematização da narrativa em Clarice Lispector." *Hispania* 75 (1992): 1164–73.

———. *Nem musa, nem medusa*. Niterói, R.J.: Editora da Universidade Federal Fluminense, 1997.

Herr, Richard, ed. *The New Portugal*. Berkeley, Calif.: Research Series/International and Area Studies, 1992.

Hess, David J., and Roberto DaMatta, eds. *The Brazilian Puzzle*. New York: Columbia University Press, 1995.

Hobsbawm, Eric. *Nations and Nationalisms*. Cambridge, U.K.: Cambridge University Press, 1990.

Holanda, Sérgio Buarque de. *Visão do Paraíso.* 5th ed. São Paulo: Editora Brasiliense, 1992.

———. *Raízes do Brasil.* 26th ed. São Paulo: Companhia das Letras, 1995.

Holloway, Mark. "The Necessity of Utopia." In *Utopius,* ed. Alexander, Peter, and Roger Gill, 179–88. London: Duckworth and Co., 1984.

Hutcheon, Linda. *Poetics of Postmodernism.* New York: Routledge, 1988.

Jameson, Fredric. *Postmodernism, or, The Cultural Logic of Late Capitalism.* Durham, N.C.: Duke University Press, 1991.

Joaquim, Augusto. "Posfácio" to *Interrogação ao destino, Malraux,* by Vergílio Ferreira. Lisboa: Bertrand Editora, 1998.

———. "Posfácio" to *Um falcão no punho,* by Maria Gabriela Llansol. Lisboa: Relógio D'Água Editores, 1998.

Johnson, Randal. "The Dynamics of the Brazilian Literary Field." *Luso-Brazilian Review* 31 (1994): 5–22.

Jorge, Lídia. *O vale da paixão.* Lisboa: Publicações Dom Quixote, 1998.

———. *La couverture du soldat.* Trans. Geneviève Leibrich. Paris: Métaillié, 1999.

Kaufman, Helena, and Ana Klobucka, eds. *After the Revolution.* Lewisburg, Pa./London: Bucknell University Press/Associated University Presses, 1997.

Knuth, Elizabeth T. "Women Writers of the Middle Ages." May 1997. http://www.millersv.edu/~english/homepage/duncan/medfem/medfem.html.

Kristeva, Julia. *Powers of Horror: An Essay on Abjection.* New York: Columbia University Press, 1982.

———. "Women's Time." In *The Kristeva Reader,* ed. Toril Moi, 187–213. New York: Columbia University Press, 1986.

Kumar, Krishan. *Utopianism.* Minneapolis: University of Minnesota Press, 1991.

Kushner, Tony. *Angels in America, Part One: Millennium Approaches.* New York: Theatre Communications Group, 1992.

———. *Angels in America, Part Two: Perestroika.* New York: Theatre Communications Group, 1992.

La renaissance de l'utopie. Magazine Littéraire 387 (spec. issue, 2000): 18–66.

Larsen, Neil. *Reading North by South.* Minneapolis and London: University of Minnesota Press, 1995.

Laso, José Luis Gavilanes. *Vergílio Ferreira: Espaço simbólico e metafísico.* Lisboa: Publicações Dom Quixote, 1989.

Lesser, Jeffrey. *Welcoming the Undesirables: Brazil and the Jewish Question.* Berkeley, Calif.: University of California Press, 1995.

Levinas, Emmanuel. *Time and the Other.* Trans. Alphonso Lignis. Pittsburg, Pa.: Duquesne University Press, 1968.

———. *Totality and Infinity.* Trans. João Pinto Ribeiro. 1987.

———. *Entre Nous.* Paris: Éditions Grasset et Fasquelle, 1991.

Levine, Robert W., and John J. Crocitti, eds. *The Brazil Reader: History, Culture, Politics.* Durham, N.C.: Duke University Press, 1999.

Leyland, Winston, ed. *My Dark Deep Pain Is Love: A Collection of Latin American Gay Fiction.* San Francisco: Gay Sunshine Press, 1983.

Linhares, Maria Yedda, ed. *História general do Brasil.* Rio de Janeiro: Editora Campus, 1990.

Lispector, Clarice. *Laços de família.* Rio de Janeiro: Francisco Alves Editora, 1960.

———. *A paixão segundo G. H.* Rio de Janeiro: Francisco Alves Editora, 1964.

————. *Family Ties.* Trans. Giovanni Pontiero. Austin: University of Texas Press, 1972.

————. *Água viva.* Rio de Janeiro: Editora Nova Fronteira, 1973.

————. *A via crucis do corpo.* Rio de Janeiro: Francisco Alves Editora, 1974.

————. *A hora da estrela.* Rio de Janeiro: Francisco Alves Editora, 1977.

————. *Um sopro de vida.* Rio de Janeiro: Francisco Alves Editora, 1978.

————. *The Passion According to G. H.* Trans. Ronald W. Sousa. Minneapolis: University of Minnesota, 1988.

————. *Soulstorm.* Trans. Alexis Levitin. New York: New Directions, 1989.

————. *The Stream of Life.* Trans. Elizabeth Lowe and Earl Fitz. Minneapolis: University of Minnesota Press, 1989.

————. *The Hour of the Star.* Trans. Giovanni Pontiero. New York: New Directions, 1992.

Llansol, Maria Gabriela. *Contos do mal errante.* Lisboa: Edições Rolim, 1986.

————. *Um beijo dado mais tarde.* Lisboa: Edições Rolim, 1991.

————. *Lisboaleipzig 1: O encontro inesperado do diverso.* Lisboa: Edições Rolim, 1994.

————. *Lisboaleipzig 2: O ensaio de música.* Lisboa: Edições Rolim, 1994.

————. *Inquérito às quatro confidências.* Lisboa: Relógio D'Água Editores, 1996.

————. *Ardente texto Joshua.* Lisboa: Relógio D'Água Editores, 1998.

————. *Um falcão no punho.* 2nd ed. Lisboa: Relógio D'Água Editores, 1998.

————. *O livro das comunidades.* Lisboa: Relógio D'Água Editores, 1999.

Lopes, Cristina Rodrigues. *Teoria da des-possessão.* Lisboa: Blackson, 1988.

Lourenço, Eduardo. *Nós e a Europa.* Lisboa: Imprensa Nacional/Casa da Moeda, 1988.

————. *O labirinto da saudade.* 5th ed. Lisboa: Publicações Dom Quixote, 1992.

————. *We the Future.* Lisbon: Assirio e Alvim, 1997.

————. *Nós como futuro.* Lisboa: Assírio e Alvim/Pavilhão de Portugal/Expo '98, 1998.

————. *O esplendor do caos.* Lisboa: Gradiva, 1998.

————. *A nau de Ícaro seguido de Imagem e miragem da lusofonia.* Lisboa: Gradiva, 1999.

————. "Espírito de Timor invade o Rio." *Jornal de letras, artes e ideias,* 1999.

Lucchesi, Ivo. *Crise e escritura: Uma leitura de Clarice Lispector e Vergílio Ferreira.* Rio de Janeiro: Forense Universitária, 1987.

Luft, Lya. *Reunião de família.* Rio de Janeiro: Nova Fronteira, 1982.

————. *As parceiras.* Rio de Janeiro: Nova Fronteira, 1986.

Lund, Joshua. "Barbarian Theorizing and the Limits of Latin American Exceptionalism." *Cultural Critique* 47 (2001): 54–90.

Lyotard, Jean-François. *The Postmodern Condition: A Report on Knowledge.* Trans. Geoff Bennington and Brian Massumi. Minneapolis: University of Minnesota Press, 1984.

————. *The Differend.* Trans. George Van Den Abbeele. Minneapolis: University of Minnesota Press, 1988.

————. *The Postmodern Explained.* Trans. Don Barry, Bernadette Maher, Julian Pefanis, Virginia Spate, and Morgan Thomas. Minneapolis: University of Minnesota Press, 1993.

Madureira, Luís. "Tropical Sex Fantasies and the Ambassador's Other Death: The Difference in Portuguese Colonialism." *Cultural Critique* 28 (1994): 149–73.

Magalhães, Isabel Allegro de. *O sexo dos textos*. Lisboa: Editorial Caminho, 1995.

Manuel, Frank E., and Fritzie P. Manuel. *Utopian Thought in the Western World*. Oxford, U.K.: Basil Blackwell, 1979.

Maranhão, Haroldo. *O tetraneto d'El Rei*. Rio de Janeiro: Francisco Alves, 1982.

Marin, Louis. *Utopiques: Jeux d'espaces*. Paris: Les Éditions de Minuit, 1973.

Marques, A. H. de Oliveira. *Breve história de Portugal*. Lisboa: Editorial Presença, 1995.

Martins, Wilson. *História da inteligência brasileira*. 6 vols. São Paulo: Editora Cultrix, 1978.

Mattelart, Armand. *Histoire de l'utopie planétaire*. Paris: La Découverte, 1999.

Mattoso, José. *A identidade nacional*. Cadernos Democráticos 1. Lisboa: Fundação Mário Soares/Gradiva, 1998.

McHale, Brian. *Constructing Postmodernism*. New York and London: Routledge, 1992.

McNee, Malcolm. "The Arts in Movement: Cultural Politics and Production in Brazil's Landless Rural Workers Movement (MST)." Ph.D. diss. Univ. of Minnesota, Twin Cities, 2003.

Medeiros, Paulo de. "Introdução: Em nome de Portugal." *Literatura, nacionalismos, identidade*. *Discursos* 13:10 (spec. issue, 1996): 13–29.

Míccolis, Leila. *Sangue cenográfico: Poemas de 1965 a março de 1997*. Rio de Janeiro: Editora Blocos, 1997.

Miranda, Ana. *Boca do inferno*. Lisboa: D. Quixote, 1990.

Mitchell, Mark, ed. *The Penguin Book of International Gay Writing*. New York: Penguin Books, 1995.

More, Thomas. *Utopia*. Ware, Hertfordshire, U.K.: Woodsworth Edition, 1997.

Morse, Richard M. "Balancing Myth and Evidence: Freyre and Sérgio Buarque." *Luso-Brazilian Review* 32 (1995): 47–57.

Mota, Carlos Guilherme. *Ideologia da cultura brasileira (1933–1974)*. São Paulo: Editora Ática, 1977.

Mota, Carlos Guilherme, ed. *Viagem incompleta: A experiência brasileira*. Vols. 1 and 2. São Paulo: Editora SENAC, 2000

Mota, Carlos Guilherme, and Fernando Novais. *O processo político da independência do Brasil*. São Paulo: Editora Moderna, 1982.

Mota, Lourenço Dantas, ed. *Introdução ao Brasil: Um banquete nos trópicos*. São Paulo: Editora SENAC, 1999.

Moura, Maria Regina. *Exercício de um modo*. Rio de Janeiro: Rotograf, 1987.

———. *Poemas do recolhimento e do frio*. Niterói, Brazil: Eduff, 1996.

Nietzsche, Friedrich. "On Truth and Lie." In *The Portable Nietzsche*, trans. Walter Kaufmann, 42–47. New York: Viking Penguin, 1982.

Noll, João Gilberto. *Rastros do verão*. Porto Alegre: L&PM Editores, 1986.

———. *Harmada*. São Paulo: Companhia das Letras, 1993.

Novais, Fernando, ed. *História da Vida Privada no Brasil*. São Paulo: Companhia das Letras, 1997.

Nunes, Benedito. *O drama da linguagem: Uma leitura de Clarice Lispector*. São Paulo: Editora Ática, 1989.

Ortiz, Renato. *A moderna tradição brasileira*. São Paulo: Editora Brasiliense, 1988.

Parker, Richard. *Bodies, Pleasures, and Passions*. Boston: Beacon Press, 1991.

———. *Beneath the Equator*. New York and London: Routledge, 1999.

Pascoaes, Teixeira de. *Arte de ser português*. Lisboa: Editores Delraux, 1978.

Pease, Donald E. "National Identities, Postmodern Artifacts, and Postnational Narratives." In *National Identities and Post-Americanist Narratives,* ed. Pease, Donald E., 1–13. Durham and London: Duke University Press, 1994.

Peixoto, Marta. "*Family Ties:* Female Development in Clarice Lispector." In *The Voyage In: Fictions of Female Development,* ed. Elizabeth Abel, Marianne Hirsch, and Elizabeth Langland, 287–303. Hanover, N.H.: University Press of New England for Dartmouth College, 1983.

———. *Passionate Fictions: Gender, Narrative, and Violence in Clarice Lispector.* Minneapolis: University of Minnesota, 1994.

Penna, João Camillo. "Clarice Lispector and the 'Thing': The Question of Difference." Ph.D. diss. Univ. of California, Berkeley, 1994.

Penteado, Darcy. *Nivaldo e Jerônimo.* Rio de Janeiro: Codecri, 1981.

Peperzak, Adriaan T., Simon Critchley, and Robert Bernasconi, eds. *Emmanuel Levinas: Basic Philosophical Writings.* Bloomington and Indianapolis: Indiana University Press, 1996.

Pessoa, Fernando. *Mensagem.* Mem Martins, Portugal: Europa-América, 1988.

Pieterse, Jan Nederveen. "Globalization as Hybridization." In *Global Modernities,* ed. Mike Featherstone, Scott Lash, and Roland Robertson, 45–68. London: SAGE Publications, 1995.

Pinto, António Costa, ed. *Modern Portugal.* Palo Alto, Calif.: Society for the Promotion of Science and Scholarship, 1998.

Pinto, Fernão Mendes. *Peregrinação.* Mem Martins, Portugal: Publicações Europa-América, 1988.

———. *Peregrination.* Trans. Rebecca D. Catz. Chicago: University of Chicago Press, 1989.

———. *Peregrination.* Trans. Michael Lowery. Manchester, U.K.: Carcanet, 1992.

Portella, Eduardo. "Gilberto Freyre, além do apenas moderno." *Rumos* 1 (1998–99): 36–43.

Prado, Caio, Jr. *Formação do Brasil contemporâneo.* 1st re-ed. São Paulo: Editora Brasiliense, 1945.

———. *The Colonial Background of Modern Brazil.* Trans. Suzette Macedo. Berkeley: University of California Press, 1967.

Prado, Paulo. *Retrato do Brasil.* 6th ed. Rio de Janeiro: J. Olympio, 1962.

Priore, Mary del, ed. *História das Mulheres no Brasil.* São Paulo: Editora Contexto, 1997.

Quadros, António. *A ideia de Portugal na literatura portuguesa dos últimos 100 anos.* Lisboa: Fundação Lusíada, 1989.

———. *Portugal: Razão e mistério.* Lisboa: Guimarães Editores, 1986.

Quental, Antero de. *Causas da decadência dos povos peninsulares.* Lisboa: Ulmeiro, 1970.

Quinlan, Susan Canty, and Fernando Arenas, eds. *Lusosex: Gender and Sexuality in the Portuguese-Speaking World.* Minneapolis: University of Minnesota Press, 2002.

Real, Miguel. *Portugal: Ser e representação.* Algés, Portugal: Difel, 1998.

Reis, Carlos. *Diálogos com José Saramago.* Lisboa: Editorial Caminho, 1998.

Reis, José Carlos, ed. *As identidades do Brasil.* São Paulo: Editora FGV, 1999.

Reis, Roberto. *The Pearl Necklace: Toward an Archaeology of Brazilian Transition Discourse.* Gainesville: University Press of Florida, 1992.

———. *Por sobre os ombros*. Rio de Janeiro: Editora Universitária da Universidade Estadoal do Rio de Janeiro, 1995.

Ribeiro, Darcy. *O povo brasileiro*. São Paulo: Companhia das Letras, 1995.

Ribeiro, Joao Ubaldo. *Viva o povo brasileiro*. Rio de Janeiro: Nova Fronteira, 1984.

Riccordi, Paulo de Tarso, ed. *Caio de amores*. Porto Alegre: Mercado Aberto, 1997.

Ricoeur, Paul. *L'Idéologie et L'Utopie*. Paris: Éditions du Seuil, 1997.

Roitman, Ari, ed. *O desafio ético*. Rio de Janeiro: Garamond, 2000.

Rosenberg, Tina. "Look at Brazil." *New York Times Magazine*. 28 Jan. 2001, natl. ed.: 26.

Rotello, Gabriel. *Sexual Ecology*. New York: Dutton, 1997.

Rothstein, Edward. "Paradise Lost: Can Mankind Live without Its Utopias?" *New York Times*, 5 Feb. 2000, natl. ed., A17.

Sadlier, Darlene. *The Question of How*. New York: Greenwood Press, 1989.

Salvador, Frei Vicente do. *História do Brasil*. Belo Horizonte: Editora Itatiaia, 1982.

Santiago, Silviano. "O entre-lugar do discurso latino-americano." In *Uma literatura nos trópicos*, 11–29. Rio de Janeiro: Editora Perspectiva, 1978.

———. *Stella Manhattan*. Rio de Janeiro: Editora Rocco, 1985.

———. *Keith Jarrett no Blue Note*. Rio de Janeiro: Editora Rocco, 1996.

———. *The Space In-Between: Essays on Latin American Culture*. Durham, N.C.: Duke University Press, 2001.

Santiago, Silviano, ed. *Intérpretes do Brasil*. Vols. 1, 2, and 3. Rio de Janeiro: Editora Nova Aguilar, 2000.

Santos, Boaventura de Sousa. "Onze teses por ocasião de mais una descobeta de Portugal." *Luso-Brazilian Review* 29 (1992): 97–113.

———. *Pela mão de Alice*. Porto, Portugal: Edições Afrontamento, 1994.

———. *Toward a New Common Sense*. New York and London: Routledge, 1995.

Santos, Gilda, ed. *Brasil e Portugal: 500 anos de enlaces e desenlaces, 1 e 2*. Rio de Janeiro: Real Gabinete Português de Lectura, 2001.

Saraiva, António José. *A cultura em Portugal: Livro III*. Lisboa: Gradiva, 1991.

Saraiva, Arnaldo. *O modernismo brasileiro e o modernismo português*. Porto, 1986.

Saraiva, José Hermano. *História de Portugal*. Mem Martins, Portugal: Publicações Europa-América, 1993.

———. *Portugal: A Companion History*. Manchester, U.K.: Carcanet, 1997.

Saramago, José. *Levantado do chão*. Lisboa: Editorial Caminho, 1980.

———. *Memorial do convento*. Lisboa: Editorial Caminho, 1982.

———. *O ano da morte de Ricardo Reis*. Lisboa: Editorial Caminho, 1984.

———. *A jangada de pedra*. Lisboa: Editorial Caminho, 1986.

———. *Baltasar and Blimunda*. Trans. Giovanni Pontiero. New York: Harcourt Brace and Co., 1987.

———. *O evangelho segundo Jesus Cristo*. Lisboa: Editorial Caminho, 1991

———. *The Year of the Death of Ricardo Reis*. Trans. Giovanni Pontiero. Orlando: Harcourt Brace Jovanovich, 1991.

———. *In Nomine Dei*. São Paulo: Companhia das Letras, 1993.

———. *The Gospel According to Jesus Christ*. Trans. Giovanni Pontiero. New York: Harcourt Brace and Co., 1994.

———. *Ensaio sobre a cegueira*. Lisboa: Editorial Caminho, 1995.

———. *The Stone Raft*. Trans. Giovanni Pontiero. New York: Harcourt Brace and Co., 1995.

————. *Cadernos de Lanzarote: Diário 4.* Lisboa: Editorial Caminho, 1997.

————. *Todos os nomes.* Lisboa: Editorial Caminho, 1997.

————. *Blindness.* Trans. Giovanni Pontiero. New York: Harcourt Brace and Co., 1999.

————. *All the Names.* Trans. Margaret Jull Costa. New York: Harcourt Brace and Co., 2000.

Schmitt, Arno. "Different Approaches to Male-Male Sexuality/Eroticism from Morocco to Uzbekistan." In *Sexuality and Eroticism among Males in Moslem Societies,* ed. Arno Schmitt and Jehoeda Sofer, 1–23. New York, London, and Norwood, Australia: Haworth Press, 1992.

Schwarz, Roberto. "As ideias fora de lugar." In *Ao vencedor as batatas.* Rio de Janeiro: Livraria Duas Cidades, 1977.

————. "Misplaced Ideas: Literature and Society in Nineteenth Century Brazil." In *Misplaced Ideas: Essays on Brazilian Culture,* trans. John Gledson. London and New York: Verso, 1992.

Seixo, Maria Alzira. "Vergílio Ferreira, os modernos, os pós-modernos e a questão das dominantes." *Colóquio/Letras* 134 (1994): 121–26.

Sekles, Flávia. "Distribuição de renda piora." *Jornal do Brasil Online,* 17 Nov. 1998. http://www.jb.com.br.

Shapiro, Michael J., and Hayward R. Alker, eds. *Challenging Boundaries: Global Flows, Territorial Identities.* Minneapolis: University of Minnesota Press, 1996.

Siebers, Tobin. "Introduction: What Does Postmodernism Want? Utopia." In *Heterotopia: Postmodern Utopia and the Body Politic,* ed. Tobin Siebers, 1–38. Ann Arbor: University of Michigan Press, 1994.

Silva, Agostinho da. *Um Fernando Pessoa.* Lisboa: Guimarães Editores, 1959.

————. *Dispersos.* Ed. Paulo Borges. Lisboa: Instituto de Cultura e Língua Portuguesa, 1988.

————. *Reflexão.* Lisboa: Guimarães Editores, 1990.

Silva, Aguinaldo. *Primeira carta aos andróginos.* Rio de Janeiro: Pallas S.A., 1975.

————. *A república dos assassinos.* Rio de Janeiro: Civilização Brasileira, 1976.

————. *No país das sombras.* Rio de Janeiro: Civilização Brasileira, 1979.

Silva, Rodrigues da. "Visionar o futuro, já." *Jornal de letras, artes e ideias* 770 (2000): 18–20.

Silveira, Jorge Fernandes da. "A Crise dos Gêneros e a Ficção Lírica de Maria Gabriela Llansol." *Revista Letra* 4 (1993): 96–101.

Simecka, Milan. "A World with Utopias or without Them?" In *Utopias,* ed. Alexander, Peter, and Roger Gill, 169–77. London: Duckworth and Co., 1984.

Skidmore, Thomas K. *Black into White: Race and Nationality in Brazilian Thought.* Durham, N.C.: Duke University Press, 1995.

Snodgrass, Mary Ellen, ed. *Encyclopedia of Utopian Literature.* Santa Barbara, Calif.: ABC-CLIO, 1995.

Soares, Mário. "Portugal depois do 'fim do império': Balanços e perspectivas para o Próximo Milénio." In *Portugal na viragem do século: Os portugueses e os desafios do milénio,* ed. Fernando Rosas and Maria Fernanda Rollo, 155–79. Lisboa: Assírio e Alvim/Pavilhão de Portugal/Expo '98, 1998.

Sontag, Susan. *AIDS and Its Metaphors.* New York: Farrar, Straus and Giroux, 1988.

Sousa, Gabriel Soares de. *Tratado descriptivo do Brasil em 1587.* Rio de Janeiro: Companhia Editora Nacional, 1879.

Spix, Johann Baptist von, and Karl Friedrich Philip von Martius. *Travels in Brazil in the Years 1817–1820 Undertaken by Command of His Majesty the King of Bavaria.* London: Longmans, 1824.

Stam, Robert. *Tropical Multiculturalism.* Durham, N.C., and London: Duke University Press, 1997.

Station, Elizabeth. "Activists Take on AIDS." In *Fighting for the Soul of Brazil,* ed. Kevin Danaher and Michael Shellenberger, 197–203. New York: Monthly Review Press, 1995.

Strenski, Ivan. *Four Theories of Myth in Twentieth-Century History.* Iowa City: University of Iowa Press, 1987.

Teixeira, Francisco M. P. *História concisa do Brasil.* São Paulo: Global Editora, 1993.

Telles, Lygia Fagundes. *A noite escura e mais eu.* Rio de Janeiro: Editora Nova Fronteira, 1995.

Todorov, Tzvetan. *Mikhail Bakhtin: The Dialogical Principle.* Minneapolis: University of Minnesota Press, 1984.

Trevisan, João Silvério. *Devassos no paraíso.* São Paulo: Editora Max Limonad, 1986; Rio de Janeiro and São Paulo: Editora Record, 2000.

———. *Perverts in Paradise.* Trans. Martin Foreman. London: GMP Publishers, 1986.

Varnhagen, Francisco Adolpho de. *História geral do Brasil.* São Paulo: Melhoramentos, 1975.

Veloso, Caetano. *Verdade tropical.* São Paulo: Companhia das Letras, 1997.

Vieira, Nelson. *Brasil e Portugal: A imagem recíproca.* Lisboa: Instituto de Cultura e Língua Portuguesa, 1991.

Wallerstein, Emmanuel. *Geopolitics and Geoculture.* Cambridge, U.K.: Cambridge University Press, 1991.

Wallis, Brian. "Selling Nations: International Exhibitions and Cultural Diplomacy." In *Museum Culture: Histories, Discourses, Spectacles,* eds., Daniel J. Sherman and Iris Rogoff. 1994.

Waugh, Patricia. *Practising Postmodernism, Reading Modernism.* London and New York: Edward Arnold, 1992.

Wheeler, Douglas. *Historical Dictionary of Portugal.* Metuchen, N.J.: Scarecrow Press, 1993.

Yúdice, George. "Postmodernity and Transnational Capitalism in Latin America." In *On Edge: The Crisis of Contemporary Latin American Culture,* ed. George Yúdice, Jean Franco, and Juan Flores, 1–28. Minneapolis: University of Minnesota Press, 1992.

Zenith, Richard. "Fernando Pessoa's Gay Heteronym?" In *Lusosex: Gender and Sexuality in the Portuguese-Speaking World,* ed. Susan C. Quinlan and Fernando Arenas. Minneapolis: University of Minnesota Press, 2002.

Index

Fernando Arenas is associate professor of Portuguese, Brazilian, and Lusophone African literary and cultural studies in the Department of Spanish and Portuguese Studies at the University of Minnesota. He is the coeditor (with Susan Canty Quinlan) of *Lusosex: Gender and Sexuality in the Portuguese-Speaking World* (Minnesota, 2002). His current research includes Lusophone African literature, film, popular music, and media, as well as homoerotic desire throughout Brazilian and Portuguese literatures and cultures.